Security, Strategy,
and Critical Theory

CRITICAL SECURITY STUDIES

Ken Booth, SERIES EDITOR
UNIVERSITY OF WALES, ABERYSTWYTH

Security, Strategy, and Critical Theory

Richard Wyn Jones

LYNNE
RIENNER
PUBLISHERS

BOULDER
LONDON

Published in the United States of America in 1999 by
Lynne Rienner Publishers, Inc.
1800 30th Street, Boulder, Colorado 80301
www.rienner.com

and in the United Kingdom by
Lynne Rienner Publishers, Inc.
3 Henrietta Street, Covent Garden, London WC2E 8LU

Library of Congress Cataloging-in-Publication Data
Wyn Jones, Richard Ll.
    Security, strategy, and critical theory   /   Richard Wyn Jones.
        p.   cm.—(Critical security studies)
    Includes bibliographical references.
    ISBN 1-55587-335-9 (hc.   :   alk. paper)
    1. Security, International—Philosophy.   2. International
relations—Philosophy.   3. Critical theory.   I. Title.   II. Series.
JZ5595.W96   1999
327.1'7'01—DC21   99-21482
                                                              CIP

British Cataloguing in Publication Data
A Cataloguing in Publication record for this book
is available from the British Library.

Printed and bound in the United States of America

The paper used in this publication meets the requirements
⊗ of the American National Standard for Permanence of
Paper for Printed Library Materials Z39.48-1984.

5 4 3 2 1

My grandfather Emyr Wyn Jones
followed the writing of this book with enormous interest—
an interest occasioned in part by our familial bonds,
but also by his passionate, Quaker-inspired support
for the worldwide struggle for peace and justice.
Sadly, he died just as the final draft was being completed.
I dedicate the book to his memory.

Contents

vii

PART 2
TRADITIONAL AND CRITICAL SECURITY STUDIES

Preface

Despite its recent origins (discussed in the Introduction), the term "critical security studies" (CSS) has become relatively familiar to those interested in the study of international relations and, in particular, security. It has been the subject of books, journal articles, and numerous conference papers. Unsurprisingly, however, given the status of international relations as a divided discipline, there has been little agreement as to what "it" is.

For some, critical security studies is little more than a typological device—a useful label to apply to all those approaches to the study of security that are not based on the narrow metatheoretical assumptions that underpin so much of security studies, especially in the United States (Krause 1998). According to this view, CSS does not constitute a distinct approach in itself, but is rather a collection of disparate approaches whose central presumptions and concerns may well be mutually contradictory. In other words, critical security studies is defined by what it is not.

For others, however, critical security studies is a distinctive project in its own right: an ambitious attempt to combine the insights of previous alternative work in the field with a particular set of metatheoretical principles and precepts to develop a new, emancipation-oriented paradigm for the theory and practice of security (Bilgin, Booth, and Wyn Jones 1998). This work falls squarely into the latter camp. In the book I outline and argue for an approach to security studies based on the work of the Frankfurt School—the originators of critical theory as that term is usually understood. Put another way, I argue that the prenomial "critical" in critical security studies should be taken seriously; that critical security studies should be developed in the shadow—or, better perhaps, in the light—of Frankfurt School critical theory.

The arguments of the book are developed through a two-part structure. In Part 1, I explore the origins of the "critical" in critical security studies by discussing the ways in which the key writings of the Frankfurt School treat

ix

the themes of theory, technology, and emancipation. This discussion then informs Part 2, in which I argue for critical theory–based understandings of security, strategy, and the relationship between theory and practice in the field of security, thus laying the conceptual foundations for critical security studies.

Acknowledgments

One of the many joys afforded by the completion of this book is that it finally allows me the opportunity to acknowledge the support that I have received during its extended gestation.

First, I would like to thank my colleagues in the Department of International Politics at the University of Wales, Aberystwyth. I have benefited enormously from being part of such an intellectually stimulating environment. Steve Smith, head of the department, not only has been largely responsible for fostering a renaissance in this venerable department's fortunes but has also been very supportive on a personal level. He has my grateful thanks on both counts. I am also indebted to Mick Cox and Michael Williams, who have both been the source of constant, good-humored encouragement.

A number of discussion group organizers, panel conveners, and journal editors have allowed me to try out many of the arguments contained within the book in various public forums. In particular I would like to thank participants in the Cambrian Discussion Group in Aberystwyth, the organizers of various critical security studies panels at BISA and ISA annual conferences to which I have contributed papers, Alex Danchev at Keele, and Adran Athroniaeth, Urdd Graddedigion Prifysgol Cymru. In addition, those students who have taken the critical security studies master's option at Aberystwyth in recent years have made a major contribution, by both forcing me to clarify my own thinking and continually pushing CSS in new directions.

Some of the arguments in the book were first set out in previous articles and chapters. I am grateful for permission to draw upon material from "The Nuclear Revolution" in Alex Danchev (ed.), *Fin de Siècle: The Meaning of the Twentieth Century* (London: Tauris Academic Studies, 1995); "'Message in a Bottle'? Theory and Praxis in Critical Security Studies," *Contemporary Security Policy* Vol. 16, No. 3 (December 1995);

"Gwleidyddiaeth Ryddfreiniol ar ôl Auschwitz: Athroniaeth Wleidyddol Theodor Wiesengrund Adorno," *Efrydiau Athronyddol* Vol. 59 (1996); and "'Travel Without Maps': Thinking About Security After the Cold War," in Jane Davis (ed.), *Security Issues in the Post–Cold War World* (Brookfield, Vt.: Edward Elgar, 1996).

Previous drafts of the book were read by Chris Brown and Mike Sheehan. Their detailed, perceptive, and encouraging comments have proven to be invaluable. Although family and other friends may have escaped reading the text, their influence has helped shape it. In particular, I wish to thank Ella and Gareth Wyn Jones, Jerry Hunter, and Rhys Jones. Eli Stamnes deserves a special mention for having both read and commented on the manuscript and put up with its author. My thanks also to Paul Williams for his assistance in preparing the index.

I want to pay special tribute to Ken Booth, who has contributed to this book in so many ways. It was he who first suggested that I combine my dual interests in critical theory and security. He may well have lived to rue that day given that he has now read and carefully commented upon more drafts of both the parts and the whole than he may care to remember. Most important, as the following pages will reveal, many of my own ideas have developed through engagement with his. He, of course, should bear no responsibility for my interpretations or elaborations.

—*R. W. J.*

Introduction

The relevance of critical theory to the academic study of international relations was first announced in 1981 when Robert W. Cox published his seminal essay "Social Forces, States and World Orders: Beyond International Relations Theory." This essay, along with its companion, "Gramsci, Hegemony and International Relations: An Essay in Method" (1983), set out the bare bones of an alternative approach to the study of world politics whose principles and precepts stood in stark contrast to those underpinning the various approaches that had been dominant until that point. Since then, a number of scholars have attempted to flesh out these bones by applying the central ideas to some of the concrete issues that animate international relations. This book represents a milestone in my own attempts to understand and apply the basic ideas of critical theory to some of the conceptual issues at the heart of one of the discipline's most important subfields, namely, security studies. At its broadest and most ambitious, it may be viewed as an attempt to vindicate Mark Hoffman's bold claim that critical theory should provide the basis for "the next stage in the development of International Relations Theory" (M. Hoffman 1987: 244). For if it can be demonstrated that a critical theory–based approach can generate a distinctive and superior understanding of security, then this may be seen as evidence of a broader utility.

In retrospect, the decision to attempt to think "critically" about security and strategy has proven to be a particularly fortuitous one. The collapse of the Soviet bloc was accompanied by the shattering of the Cold War verities that had ensured that, for forty years, most discussion of national security (in the United Kingdom and the United States as well as in Eastern Europe) approximated more a recitation of supposed timeless wisdom than genuine intellectual contention and debate. With the removal of these fetters, analysts of differing theoretical persuasions have entered the fray and subjected notions of security (in particular) to unprecedented scrutiny. The ensuing debates have been among the most interesting, illuminating, and stimulating discussions in the field of international relations in recent times. Some of the major theoretical and metatheoretical disputes in the discipline have been played out in these debates—in a relatively confined intellectual space and around a concrete set of issues. Various realists, neorealists, neoliberal institutionalists, feminists, poststructuralists, and critical theorists have locked horns on the terrain of security. As a result, a consideration of these debates provides fascinating insights into the concrete analytical implications that arise from the different ontological, epistemological, and methodological assumptions embraced by these approaches.

I do not claim to provide a comprehensive account of these debates as such. Although the work of other authors is of course discussed—some in depth—this is done as a means to an end rather than an end in itself. The aim of this book is rather to develop the conceptual foundations of a critical theory approach to the study of security—what I call critical security studies. This term originates from a conference held in Toronto in May 1994 (Booth 1997a: 108). Since then, panels have been held under the banner of "critical security studies" at various other international conferences, and the term has gained widespread currency in the discipline at large. In their preface to a book of contributions to the Toronto conference, the organizers, Keith Krause and Michael C. Williams, specifically invoke Cox's conceptualization of critical theory in order to explain the "appending of the term *critical* to *security studies*" (Krause and Williams 1997: x–xi; see also Klein 1997: 364). However, as Krause and Williams are aware, not all of those who contributed to their volume are committed to critical theory as understood by Cox (Krause and Williams 1997: x–xx). This book, however, seeks to take seriously the origins of the prenomial "critical" in critical security studies by outlining an understanding based firmly on the assumptions of critical theory.

Part 1 of the book is essentially an exploration and exposition of critical theory and, in particular, of those themes developed in the literature that are particularly pertinent to the study of security. This broad-ranging survey is rendered necessary by the fact that none of the excellent general discussions of critical theory (for example, Jay 1973; Held 1980; Dubiel 1985; Benhabib 1986; Kellner 1989; Hohendahl 1991; Bronner 1994; Wiggershaus 1994; Calhoun 1995) focus systematically on those theoretical issues that are—or should be—of central concern to security studies. Moreover, the literature that specifically attempts to apply the ideas of critical theory to the study of international relations—an approach I call critical international theory—offers little by way of guidance. Although excellent material has emerged from these efforts (notably, R. Cox 1981, 1983, 1996; Linklater 1990a, 1990b, 1992, 1996a, 1996b, 1998a, 1998b; M. Hoffman 1987, 1991; Neufeld 1995), the authors would not claim to provide more than a partial treatment of some aspects of the critical theory literature relevant to their interests, and none are specifically concerned with security (M. Hoffman 1993 is a partial exception).

Indeed, one of the striking features of critical international theory is its rather curious, at times even tenuous, connection with what is usually regarded (in social theory circles at least) as critical theory, namely, the work of the Frankfurt School. Take, for example, the work of Robert Cox himself. Although his essays in the early 1980s heralded the arrival of critical theory in international relations, he has never cited the work of Frankfurt School critical theorists. Significantly, neither does he mention their work in a semiautobiographical essay in which he discusses the intellectual influences and personal experiences that have helped shape his work (R. Cox 1996: 19–31). Rather, the main influence on his thought seems to have been a form of Hegelian Marxism as refracted through the work of Antonio Gramsci. Though this intellectual heritage provides many interesting linkages to and parallels with Frankfurt School critical theory—indeed, as I argue later, it may provide a valuable corrective in some respects—there are clearly significant differences.

A similar pattern can be observed in the work of other prominent critical international theorists. Andrew Linklater, for example, utilizes the writings of Jürgen Habermas extensively but also draws heavily on the English School (for example, Linklater 1996a). Mark Neufeld also has certainly been influenced by the work of the Frankfurt School, and yet he may well be as indebted to the work of Charles Taylor as he is to that of Max Horkheimer or Habermas. Similarly, Mark Hoffman, also prominent in applying Habermas to international relations, makes use of the ideas of other thinkers who have emerged from quite different intellectual traditions: in his case, John Burton (M. Hoffman 1992). Although this eclecticism is not necessarily problematic in terms of the work of these particular theorists, it does mean that critical theory has been appropriated by international relations in a fairly unsystematic, even haphazard, manner (a point developed in more detail by Haacke 1996). All of this means that a discussion of some of the most relevant parts of the critical theory literature is a necessary foundation for the subsequent discussion of security and strategy.

Frankfurt School critical theory is not a unified body of thought. There is hardly a single issue beyond the most general in which can be identified *the* critical theory position. Rather, it is a tradition characterized by major differences both between various proponents and across time; in the latter case, significant differences have emerged even within the work of individual thinkers. This means that concepts cannot be simply appropriated from the critical theory literature and applied to issues in the security realm without reference to their origins. To do so would fly in the face of the critical method, which stresses the situatedness of knowledge. It would also ignore the insights that may be derived from understanding the evolution of concepts across time as a result of various material and ideational developments. Thus, Part 1, "Traditional and Critical Theory," is structured to provide an overview of the development of three key conceptual issues across three distinct historical stages in the development of critical theory. These key issues are all centrally relevant to the study of security.

- Theory: the understanding(s) of the social role of theory and theorists
- Technology: the understanding(s) of the social role and the impact of technology
- Emancipation: the understanding(s) of the prospects for and possible contours of a more emancipated order

Specifically, in Chapter 1, "Promise: Toward a Critical Theory of Society," I outline how the three key concepts were understood as part of the earliest formulation of critical theory developed by members of the Frankfurt School in the 1930s, and in particular by the then dominant figure Max Horkheimer. I do so largely through an examination and evaluation of the arguments propounded by Horkheimer in his famous programmatic essay, "Traditional and Critical Theory."

In Chapter 2, "Impasse: Emancipatory Politics After Auschwitz," I discuss the alternative, extremely bleak version of critical theory subsequently developed by key members of the Frankfurt School in response to the rise of fascism in central and southern Europe and the Stalinization of the Bolshevik experiment in the East. I also consider some of the main lines of argument in the now classic study *Dialectic of Enlightenment,* written by Horkheimer and his colleague Theodor Adorno and first published in 1947.

In Chapter 3, "Redemption: Renewing the Critical Project," I examine the routes by which the succeeding generations of critical theorists have sought to redeem the promise of early critical theory from the impasse represented by *Dialectic of Enlightenment.* In contrast to the preceding chapters, my argument is not developed through a focus on a specific text but is advanced through a broader consideration of how certain key thinkers—namely, Jürgen Habermas, Axel Honneth, Ulrich Beck, and Andrew Feenberg—have conceptualized the three key concepts central to the development of critical security studies.

In Part 2, "Traditional and Critical Security Studies," I apply insights gleaned from the discussion of critical theory in Part 1 to some of the central conceptual questions underpinning security studies. Detailed consideration is given to

- Security: the conceptualization of security
- Strategy: the conceptualization of strategy
- Practice: the referent(s) of and for security specialists

My aim is not only to criticize the prevailing orthodoxy in security studies—what I term traditional security studies—but also to outline an alternative approach for a critical security studies.

Specifically, in Chapter 4, "Theory: Reconceptualizing Security," I intervene in the contemporary debates around the conceptualization of security and in particular those centered on the broadening, deepening, and extending of the concept. In this chapter I criticize well-established positions in these debates as well as some alternative positions developed by writers influenced by poststructuralist ideas. I also argue that a more theoretically and practically helpful conceptualization of security is one that

- Eschews statism
- Recognizes that military threats are far from the only phenomena with major security implications and, therefore, that other issues have a place on the security agenda
- Anchors the theory and practice of security in a broader concern with human emancipation

Such an understanding of security forms the basis for an alternative critical security studies.

In Chapter 5, "Technology: Reconceptualizing Strategy," I reconceptualize strategy in a way that is consistent with assumptions and precepts of critical security studies. I argue that, despite its own professed intentions, the traditional approach to the study of the military dimension in world politics—that is, strategy—tends to ignore ends and to concentrate almost exclusively on means. I also charge that although the traditional approach to strategy has tended to fetishize military hardware, it has actually revealed a naive understanding of technology and particularly the relationship between military technology and strategic culture. In place of the traditional approach I argue for an alternative conceptualization of strategy that embraces ends, regarding normative issues as intrinsic to the study, and is based on a dialectical understanding of technology.

In the sixth and final chapter, "Emancipation: Reconceptualizing Practice," I focus on the possible audiences for and purposes of critical security studies. I reject the ways in which traditional security studies has conceptualized the relationship between the theory and practice of security. But because of the deficiencies in the Frankfurt School's account of the theory-practice nexus, which are identified in Part 1, I develop an alternative understanding based instead on the ideas of Gramsci. I argue that proponents of critical security studies should eschew the temptations of seeking the ears of soldiers and statesmen and should instead seek to aid in the development of counterhegemonic positions linked to the struggles of emancipatory social movements.

In the Epilogue I summarize the main lines of arguments developed in Part 2.

I do not claim to reveal new knowledge as such in this book; instead, I aim to make a contribution in terms of method and critical evaluation. This book is an attempt to rethink, reevaluate, and reorient. The result is the elaboration and clarification of what may be best considered as a kind of conceptual tool kit. Ultimately, the validity of this tool kit—indeed, of the whole critical security studies enterprise—depends on its ability to shed new light on real-world problems. In particular, as I argue at length, critical theory stands or falls by its ability to illuminate the possibilities for emancipatory transformation—however faint—extant in a given situation. And although the development of the tool kit has certainly been informed by practice, the challenge remains to apply it far more systematically: It is on this application that I intend to focus in the future.

The process of applying the tool kit is, of course, a process that will inevitably lead to the dialectical transformation of the concepts themselves. To think critically is to embark on an open-ended journey in which ideas are continually challenged, refined, rejected, and renewed in the light of changing perceptions and changing practices. Inevitably, therefore, even if the ideas contained in this book are deeply felt and strongly expressed, they remain, in this all-important sense, preliminary and tentative. It is in this spirit that I now enter them into the public sphere.

PART 1

Traditional and Critical Theory

1

Promise: Toward a Critical Theory of Society

All social theories and political philosophies reflect, to a greater or lesser extent, the preoccupations of the historical epoch in which they were conceived and formulated. Intellectuals are not, to use Karl Mannheim's expression, "free-floating." Whatever they may desire to do—indeed, whatever they think they are doing—they cannot withdraw from the world and simply ponder and reflect dispassionately upon it. That said, thought cannot simply be reduced to its historical and social context; to view thought solely as a reflection of its context is to ignore the possibility of reflexivity and creativity, of human agency. William Connolly captures the complex relationship between thinkers, thoughts, and their contexts well.

> Thought can be inspired, influenced, restrained by its circumstances, but not determined by them. . . . Thought has a moment of autonomy that makes it irreducible to the social and personal circumstances in which it arises, even if it cannot be understood well without taking its context of creation into account. Contexts inspire thought; great thinkers are inspired to reconstitute contexts. (Connolly 1988: 17)

The question for intellectuals, therefore, is not whether they can be perfectly detached and objective, but whether they can reflect upon their own relationship to the social world and attain a certain critical distance from it.

The founding fathers of critical theory were acutely aware that theoretical works of all kinds—including their own—are situated in a particular and mutable milieu. This is underlined by Max Horkheimer's comments in the preface to the 1979 reissue of the original German version of *Dialectic of Enlightenment,* where he writes:

> We [referring to both Theodor Adorno and himself] would not now maintain without qualification every statement in the book: that would be irreconcilable with a theory that holds that the core of truth is historical, rather

9

> than an unchanging constant to be set against the movement of history. The work was written when the end of the Nazi terror was within sight; nevertheless, in not a few places the reality of our times is formulated in a way no longer appropriate to contemporary experience. (Adorno and Horkheimer 1979: ix)

All intellectual work is rooted in a particular social and historical context, and as that context is gradually transformed, some elements of the work will lose their resonance and relevance, whereas others may come to appear more important than was initially the case.

Given the importance of the interrelationship between ideas and their epoch, it is apposite that I should begin this discussion of critical theory by noting some of the contexts in which these ideas were developed. Indeed, the failure to do so would be particularly inappropriate given that Horkheimer and his colleagues were reacting quite self-consciously to a period of almost unparalleled turmoil. The social and institutional context within which critical theory was developed will be examined first. This will be followed by an exposition, analysis, and evaluation of what is undoubtedly the seminal text of early critical theory, Max Horkheimer's programmatic essay "Traditional and Critical Theory."

THE FRANKFURT SCHOOL IN CONTEXT

From the perspective of the radical left in central Europe, the interwar years can be characterized as a roller-coaster ride from wild optimism following the Bolsheviks' seizure of power in Russia, to bleak pessimism in the face of the seemingly inexorable rise of fascism, to an almost blank incomprehension in the wake of the signing of the Nazi-Soviet pact. Nowhere was this reversal of fortunes more pronounced and more dramatic than in Germany.

From the days of Karl Marx and Friedrich Engels, Germany had been the "great hope" of the international communist movement. Its working class was large, well organized, and, relatively speaking, militant. The German Social Democrat Party (SPD) was the mainstay of the Second International, and it was widely assumed on the left that the German proletariat would act as the catalyst for world revolution. Even when the SPD's leadership distanced itself from the legacy of Marxism, the revolutionary left remained strong. The German Communist Party (KPD) was second only to the Bolsheviks in size and influence when the Third International was founded in March 1919.

But by the late 1920s, from the perspective of the nondogmatic revolutionary left, Germany no longer presented a major source of hope and inspiration. Rather, it was the prime exemplar of the growing weakness of left-wing political practice and the aridity of socialist theory. On the one hand, the SPD appeared hopelessly quiescent and reformist; on the other, in line with more general trends in the international communist movement, the KPD had become a sectarian body whose policies reflected Soviet concerns and interests rather than its own domestic realities (see Claudin 1975).

Superficially, these were not the most propitious of times for socialist theorists, particularly those working in Germany. For the pragmatist SPD, theory was regarded with suspicion; for the Stalinist KPD, theory had become merely a means for the post facto justification of (Soviet) policy. Furthermore, the working class—the proletariat that had provided both the subject and the addressee for Marxist-inspired socialist theory—was proving to be a receptive audience for Nazi propaganda. However it is remarkable that many—if not most—great theoretical works are the products of times of turmoil. Figures as disparate as Saint Augustine, Thomas Hobbes, John Locke, and Carl von Clausewitz were all inspired by strife and upheaval. In contrast, periods of calm seem to foster a certain intellectual quiescence and lassitude: "Happiness writes in white ink." So it should come as no surprise that it was precisely in this difficult, turbulent period that the members of the Frankfurt School began their attempt to revivify Marxian thought.

With the benefit of hindsight, it is apparent that the Frankfurt School was only one of several groups and individuals that were attempting at this time—in a wholly uncoordinated fashion—to revive and reorient Marxian theory. Indeed, compared with many of their contemporaries, the members of the Frankfurt School were attempting to do so in circumstances that were, relatively speaking, more favorable. Although Gramsci suffered appallingly under a prison regime personally overseen by Benito Mussolini, and Leon Trotsky and his comrades were under constant threat from Stalinist assassins, the members of the Frankfurt School were supported by the resources of their institutional home, the Institut für Sozialforschung (Institute for Social Research).

The Institut für Sozialforschung (IfS) was founded in 1923 after Felix Weil, the left-wing son of a wealthy German émigré grain merchant in Argentina, persuaded his father to endow a research institute (the two classic studies of the IfS are Wiggershaus 1994 and Jay 1973; Dubiel 1985 provides valuable insights into its modus operandi). Although affiliated with Frankfurt University, the IfS was almost completely autonomous. Not only was it financially independent, but it had its own facilities and its director enjoyed almost complete control over its affairs—a fact that was not only important in terms of protecting the institute's independence but also, as we shall see, very significant in terms of the intellectual orientation of its work.

Under its first director, the eminent Austro-Marxist Carl Grünberg, the IfS became an important center for contemporary Marxist thought. However, even though Georg Lukács and Karl Korsch were among the contributors to the institute's journal, on the whole the IfS's Marxism was of a fairly orthodox variety. It was only after Grünberg's retirement in 1929 and his replacement by Max Horkheimer that the institute became the focus for the novel, innovative, and distinctively unorthodox thought that later became associated with the Frankfurt School.

Horkheimer was born in 1895, the son of wealthy assimilated German Jews. Rejecting pressure to enter the family textile business, he instead pursued his academic predilections. His initial interest was in psychology, but he switched the main focus of his energies to philosophy. He also became increasingly attracted to Marxism, although his engagement with it was of a rather different nature from that of the previous generation of Marxist thinkers. For figures such as Vladimir Lenin, Karl Kautsky, Franz Mehring, Georgy Plekhanov, and Horkheimer's close contemporary Gramsci, theorizing was a nonacademic pursuit carried out more often than not in the context of concrete political struggles.

Under Horkheimer's directorship, the IfS formed the vanguard of Marxism's retreat from the streets and shop floors into academia. Although this development was no doubt occasioned—in the 1930s at least—by the rise of fascism, it was also accompanied by a significant shift in the focus of Marxian theory. For the previous generation of activist-theorists, it was the political economy of contemporary society that demanded attention and analysis. For Horkheimer's IfS, as well as subsequent generations of Western Marxists, the focus of theoretical activity alighted almost exclusively on cultural, superstructural phenomena and philosophical issues (Anderson 1976).

Horkheimer used the power accorded him by the institute's founding statutes to collect around him an outstanding group of young intellectuals who were specialists across a broad range of disciplines. Of these, Friedrich Pollock, Herbert Marcuse, Leo Lowenthal, Erich Fromm, and, subsequently, Theodor Adorno formed the core group of Horkheimer's IfS. Surrounding this inner circle was a wider group of equally able figures working within or in association with the institute. These included Otto Kirchheimer, Franz Neumann, and Adorno's close friend and collaborator, Walter Benjamin (Wiggershaus 1994 provides a biographical panorama of leading members of the IfS). One of the most noteworthy features of the group that Horkheimer gathered around him was its relative homogeneity in terms of background and intellectual outlook.

They were all sons of relatively wealthy families and, despite their radicalization and espousal of egalitarian ideals, maintained a bourgeois lifestyle. As one can imagine, their detractors, both Marxist and non-

Marxist, eagerly seized upon this apparent contradiction. Perhaps the most famous denunciation came from a person whose early work had a profound influence on the development of critical theory, the Hungarian Marxist Georg Lukács. He wrote that the members of the Frankfurt School had taken up residence in the "Grand Hotel Abyss" from which they surveyed the barbarity around them fortified by "excellent meals and artistic entertainments" (Lukács 1971: 22). Against this, as Martin Jay dryly comments: "It seems unlikely that the rejuvenation of Marxist theory to which they heavily contributed would have been materially advanced by a decision to wear cloth caps" (Jay 1973: 36).

Lukács is nevertheless surely right to suggest that the founders of critical theory did distance themselves from the political struggles of ordinary people. Like Horkheimer, they all seem to have been drawn to Marxism intellectually as opposed to having come to it via participation in practical politics. Indeed apart from Marcuse, who was briefly active in the revolutionary Soldiers' Council established in Berlin after World War I, none had any direct experience of the political practice. Certainly none were at any time closely associated with either the SPD or the KPD. This noninvolvement had its positive side in that the founders of critical theory were not drawn into the slavish justification of particular political programs that characterized the work of so many theorists affiliated with particular parties or movements—of which Lukács himself was a prime exemplar. Nevertheless, their detachment came at a price. Even such a vigorous defender of the Frankfurt School's legacy as Jay is moved to speculate whether its notoriously obstruse theorizing would have been more concrete had those involved in its genesis had a closer connection to "real life" politics (Jay 1973: 36).

Another common feature of the group that formed the core of Horkheimer's institute was that they were all Jewish, though as Wiggershaus notes, many "had largely been forced back into affiliation with Judaism by the Nazis" (Wiggershaus 1994: 4). Wiggershaus suggests that this common religious identity may have relevance to understanding why young men of such solidly bourgeois backgrounds aligned themselves so firmly with the left. To be Jewish was to be marginalized, and among some Jews at least, this generated solidarity with others marginalized by the prevailing order.

Yet another common characteristic of Horkheimer's group was the catholic nature of its intellectual interests. Even in the inner core, there was a remarkable range of expertise. Marcuse, for example, studied with Martin Heidegger and Edmund Husserl (Kellner 1984). Adorno, quite apart from his detailed knowledge of European philosophical thought in general and aesthetic theory in particular, was a renowned musicologist who had studied with Alban Berg and was a member of Arnold Schönberg's circle.

Fromm is perhaps best known for his engagement with Freudian psychoanalysis but was also deeply interested in Judaic theology (Thomas 1984). In his time, Pollock was a well-known radical political economist.

This breadth of expertise was no coincidence. Rather, it was the result of a conscious attempt on the part of Horkheimer to gather together experts in the various fields of "bourgeois science" who were willing—because of their radical sensibilities—to cooperate in a research enterprise dedicated to integrating their various specializations within an interdisciplinary framework guided by a version of Marxian social theory. By integrating Marxism and the most up-to-date work in a myriad of academic disciplines, the aim was to generate a hybrid vigor or synergy through which Marxist thought could be rescued from its ossification and in which the artificial boundaries separating academic disciplines could be broken down and the work of scientists given new direction and purpose. This approach was initially described in Horkheimer's inaugural lecture as "interdisciplinary materialism" but was later refined and renamed "critical theory" (Horkheimer 1993: 1–14; 1972: 188–253). Horkheimer's own role in the program was central; it was he who provided the metatheoretical framework with which the specialists were to operate. Moreover, through his editorship of the institute's journal, Horkheimer also had detailed input into the specialists' individual efforts (Dubiel 1985: 119–188).

Horkheimer's achievement in giving intellectual direction to the work of his coterie of collaborators is rendered all the more remarkable by the fact that much of his energies and organizational talents were engaged in ensuring that the IfS and its members were able to continue working—and living—despite the Nazis' coming to power in Germany as part of the seemingly inexorable rise of fascism in Europe. Quick to realize that developments in Germany were likely to mean that the group of left-wing, Jewish intellectuals working in the institute would be exiled from their homeland, Horkheimer laid plans to ensure that when this occurred, they could continue to enjoy much of the financial and intellectual infrastructure that had been built up in Frankfurt. Thus, by the time police occupied the IfS building in March 1933, most of the institute's members had already regrouped beyond the grasp of the Nazis. (The only tragic exception to this was Walter Benjamin, a loose affiliate of the IfS who took his own life in 1940 [see Broderson 1996]).

Following initial attempts to reestablish the institute in Geneva, it was soon decided that Europe would not provide the security and stability necessary for the successful development of interdisciplinary materialism. Thus, in 1934, the IfS moved to Columbia University in New York, where it remained until the U.S. entry into World War II.

During this period, the sense of isolation that had already been apparent in the pre-exile writings of the institute's members became ever more palpable and poignant. Horkheimer, for example, wrote of how "truth has sought refuge in among small groups of admirable men. But these have been decimated by terrorism and have little time for refining the theory" (Horkheimer 1972: 237–238). This sense of alienation reflected both the displacement and longing that tend to afflict exiles in general and was also a specific reaction to the institute's U.S. sanctuary.

It was almost inevitable that the institute's members, as Jewish Marxists, would feel estranged in a country in which both Judaism and Marxism generated much hostility and prejudice—at both official and popular levels. Furthermore, the speculative and theoretical nature of much of their work sat uneasily in an intellectual culture that prized empiricism and pragmatism above all else. To compound matters, some of the mandarin sensibilities of the institute's members—a disdain toward popular culture that has historically characterized the central European intelligentsia—were undoubtedly offended by that relentlessly commercial and populist energy that animates so much of U.S. culture (see, for example, the essays collected in Adorno 1994).

The isolation of the IfS was further reinforced by its decision to continue publishing the bulk of its work in German in an effort to resist the Nazis' debasement of that language. The consequence of this wholly laudable stand was that its work was largely ignored in its new home and its intellectual and practical political possibilities left largely unexplored. Despite this, the institute's period of isolation was, without doubt, enormously productive. It was in New York, following the publication of Horkheimer's essay "Traditional and Critical Theory" in 1937, that the outlines of the Frankfurt School's critical theory of society were sketched out.

TRADITIONAL AND CRITICAL THEORY

The publication of "Traditional and Critical Theory" (Horkheimer 1972: 188–252) was a significant event in the development of the Frankfurt School's thought for a number of reasons. Not least of these was that it was the first time that the term "critical theory" had been adopted by a member of the institute to describe its thinking.

As I have already noted, the intellectual project that Horkheimer attempted to develop at the IfS had previously been known as "interdisciplinary materialism." Although some may well regard the renaming as a mere cosmetic exercise undertaken by a cautious director eager to hide his institute's Marxist roots by adopting an even vaguer label for its work, the members of the IfS were adamant, as its later historians have been, that the new label signified an intellectual development of real import. According to the members, it symbolized an increased self-awareness of the nature of the project on which they were engaged. Thus Adorno was to argue that "the Horkheimerian formulation 'critical theory' . . . [was] not an attempt to make materialism acceptable, but to bring it to theoretical self-consciousness" (Therborn 1970: 71; see also Dubiel 1985: 61). The importance of the symbolic significance of this act of rebaptism is borne out by the fact that the essay in which it occurred did indeed provide the first relatively systematic exposition of the institute's metatheoretical position. Although many of the ideas discussed in "Traditional and Critical Theory" are scattered throughout previous essays in the *Zeitschrift,* it was in this essay that the strands were woven together for the first time to form a coherent whole (Horkheimer's other *Zeitschrift* essays are collected in Horkheimer 1972, 1993).

The main lines of these arguments will now be reconstructed. I will consider Horkheimer's conception of theory before proceeding to a discussion of his notion of emancipation and his understanding of the social role of technology.

Theory

The essay's opening sentence sets out its agenda: It is an attempt to answer the question "What is 'Theory'?" (Horkheimer 1972: 188). Horkheimer proceeds by outlining the hegemonic, traditional understanding of the term. He does so through a discussion of a generalized, even idealized, model of scientific theory:

> Theory for most researchers is the sum total of propositions being so linked with each other that a few are basic and the rest derive from these. The smaller the number of primary principles in comparison with the derivations, the more perfect the theory. The real validity of the theory depends on the derived propositions being consonant with the actual facts. If experience and theory contradict each other, one of the two must be reexamined. Either the scientist has failed to observe correctly or something is wrong with the principles of the theory. (Horkheimer 1972: 188)

Horkheimer associates this conception of theory with René Descartes's understanding of scientific method in which deductively conceived and logically consistent assumptions are tested against empirically observable reality; those assumptions are proven correct to the extent that they are confirmed by experimental observation. But I must emphasize that Horkheimer is unconcerned about the sources of those assumptions—whether they be via deduction, induction, rationalism, phenomenology, or by some other route (Horkheimer 1972: 189–190). Rather, what he wants to highlight is how this traditional understanding of theory conceives of the relationship between thought and reality, between subject and object. This relationship is, of course, one in which a strict dividing line is drawn between thought/ subject and reality/object.

Horkheimer's main aim is to show that this understanding of theory, developed initially in the natural sciences, has since been applied in most attempts to understand the social world. Indeed, the understanding of theory developed by the natural sciences has become ubiquitous as it has been universalized to all fields of knowledge and embraced by the various contending schools of thought within those fields, even those that, superficially at least, differ on fundamental theoretical issues. Horkheimer illustrates his argument by referring to an example from the field of sociology. He seeks to demonstrate that despite their vehement disagreements, both the Spencerian empirical tradition in the "Anglo-Saxon world" and the more abstract "Germanic" tradition of Ferdinand Tönnies, Emile Durkheim, and Max Weber share the same understanding of theory (Horkheimer 1972: 190–191).

In the present context, however, Horkheimer's critique is perhaps better demonstrated by applying it to one of the main theoretical debates in contemporary U.S. international relations. Kenneth Waltz may be viewed as a latter-day Teutonic deductivist. In his seminal study *Theory of International Politics,* he criticizes the inductive approach to theory building:

> If we gather more and more data and establish more and more associations . . . we will not finally find that we know something. We will simply end up having more and more data and larger sets of correlations. Data never speak for themselves. (Waltz 1979: 4)

Waltz instead champions a conception of theory building in which the theorist has a central—almost heroic—role: "The longest process of painful trial and error will not lead to the construction of a theory unless at some point a brilliant intuition flashes, a creative idea emerges" (Waltz 1979: 9). His opponents in the inductivist camp—now suitably computer literate, of course—include, most prominently, Bruce Russett and Karl Deutsch (the latter being Waltz's particular target in *Theory of International Politics*). Not for them the frivolous luxury of speculation but rather the solid but necessary task of data collection and collation. Only once this task is completed—or, at the very least, the sample size expanded to the point where results become significant—can theoretical knowledge be developed.

Following from Horkheimer's analysis however, whatever the disputes in the pages of *International Studies Quarterly* and whatever the exchanges at academic conferences, the differences between both positions are more apparent than real. Both attempt to build theory on the same natural science model; both regard theory as a set of logically consistent propositions that explain a particular empirical phenomenon, be it a natural process or a historical event. Thus, both are "not so much polarised as settled at different points on a continuum of modes of enquiry" (Maclean 1981a: 51). Both have similar epistemological positions on the nature of the relationship between thought and reality, subject and object; both are variations on a theme—that of traditional theory.

Horkheimer's assessment of traditional theory is carefully nuanced. On the one hand he is well aware of the many achievements of those disciplines that have been built on its foundations. Indeed, as becomes clear in "Traditional and Critical Theory," he believes that the kind of factual, instrumental knowledge generated by traditional theory will be necessary in any developed society, present or future. However, Horkheimer does object strenuously to the way that this "conception of theory was absolutised, as though it were grounded in the inner nature of knowledge as such or justified in some other ahistorical way, and thus . . . became a reified, ideological category" (Horkheimer 1972: 194). This reification blinds traditional theorists to the ways in which their theories are produced, to the social role of their work, and indeed to themselves. Horkheimer lists a number of illusions that are shared by traditional theorists, illusions he believes arise from this lack of reflexivity.

Traditional theorists imagine that they work in isolation from brute societal pressures and that their theorizing, despite possibly having socially useful applications, is propelled by the immanent logic of the research itself—a logic enforced by the research materials themselves and the methodology employed, even if leavened, perhaps, by some insight or intuition on the part of the individual researcher. Traditional theorists would refute any suggestion that the way in which they work is determined in any way by extrascientific factors. However this is exactly the charge laid at their door by Horkheimer, who argues that not only the decisions about what to study but also the way in which the results are interpreted is very much a social process rather than a purely scientific one. The former point might well be conceded by more sophisticated traditional theorists given the ways in which governments and their agencies target research resources into certain key areas into which researchers then tend to congregate. However, the latter point is a deeply controversial one.

Horkheimer illustrates his argument by referring to radical theoretical changes, or what are now known as, to use Thomas Kuhn's terminology, "paradigm shifts." (Brunkhorst [1993: 75] notes similarities between Horkheimer's arguments on theory change and those subsequently developed by Kuhn.) Horkheimer argues that the main impulse for major theory change is extrinsic to the theory itself and is related instead to "concrete historical circumstance." After all, if immanent logical considerations "were the only real issue, one could always think up further hypotheses by which one could avoid changing the theory as a whole" (Horkheimer 1972: 196). Far from being the independent and detached figures of their self-image, traditional theorists are inescapably a part of society in general and subject to the pressures existent within it. But how are these societal pressures transmitted to the theorists? Horkheimer compares the traditional theorist with the individual in capitalist society:

> The seeming self-sufficiency enjoyed by work processes whose course is supposedly determined by the very nature of the object [i.e., research in its traditional guise] corresponds to the seeming freedom of the economic subject in bourgeois society. The latter believe that they are acting according to personal determinations, whereas in fact even in their most complicated calculations they exemplify the working of an incalculable social mechanism. (Horkheimer 1972: 197)

Whether or not they are aware of it, agents cannot avoid being affected by the surrounding structures.

Yet one should not think that the influence is simply one way; Horkheimer was certainly no determinist. The interrelationship between society and scientists (or theorists) that he posits is subtle and complex. On the one hand, although Horkheimer argues that theorists are decisively shaped and influenced by society, he also argues that they are crucial "moments in the social process of production" within that society (Horkheimer 1972: 197). Although such fields as quantum physics or, indeed, international relations theory may appear to have little or nothing to do with the specific processes of production and manufacturing, they are in fact important parts of the social mechanism whereby the prevailing relations of production are maintained. Horkheimer notes that

> even the emptiness of certain areas of university activity . . . have their social significance. . . . An activity which in its existing forms contributes to the being of society need not be productive at all, that is be a money-making enterprise. Nevertheless it can belong to the existing order and help make it possible, as is certainly the case with specialized science. (Horkheimer 1972: 206)

Thus, whatever the pretensions and protestations of traditional theorists about their scholarly detachment and objectivity, Horkheimer is convinced that theorists and their theories play a vital role in the production and reproduction of the prevailing structures.

But how can traditional theories play a role in the production and reproduction of the status quo? In some cases the links are obvious. Much traditionally based theoretical work is engaged in an attempt to gain knowledge of various processes—be they physical or social—that will allow those processes to be controlled, manipulated, and utilized. Even apparently highly abstract work in theoretical physics, econometrics, or psychology may well have a practical payoff. But what about even more esoteric theoretical work in fields that appear to be even further removed from practice? There are two points that seem to arise from Horkheimer's discussion. First, just because links between theory and practice are not immediately apparent, they may still be extant—either in a very mediated form or across time. Second, traditional theories in all fields have the effect of normalizing and privileging one particular understanding of what constitutes knowledge. As we have seen, this form of knowledge entails a radical separation between subject and object and is ultimately concerned with the control and exploitation of the latter by the former. The privileging of this epistemology has the effect of undermining the truth-claims of those who wish to challenge the provenance of the prevailing order. It makes other ways of knowing—and other ways of being—illegitimate.

Thus, for Horkheimer it is clear that there is no theory of society "that does not contain political motivations," even if those motivations are often unconscious, "and the truth of these must be decided not in supposedly neutral reflection but in personal thought and action, in concrete activity" (Horkheimer 1972: 222). If traditional theory is implicated in the "conservation and continuous renewal" of the existing order, it is beholden to those that produce it to reflect on the nature of this order. For Horkheimer at least, there is no doubt that the political and economic structures that traditional theory helps support are utterly objectionable. Although "Traditional and Critical Theory" does not contain the lengthy and impassioned condemnations of capitalism that exemplify much Marxist and Marxist-inspired writing, the reader is left in no doubt whatsoever as to Horkheimer's position. He abhors an economic system that he regards as creating a "paralysing barrenness" in which "men by their own toil keep in existence a reality which enslaves them in ever greater degree" (Horkheimer 1972: 213).

Given the role of traditional theories in upholding a social order that he considers to be fundamentally unjust, Horkheimer suggests the adoption of an alternative, critical conception of theory. Critical theory is premised on the rejection of the prevailing order and aims at a root-and-branch reorganization of the way in which society is organized. As Horkheimer notes: "This theory is not concerned only with goals already posed by existent ways of life, but with men and all their potentialities" (Horkheimer 1972: 245). (His grounds for arguing for the existence of unfulfilled human potential will be considered later.) According to Horkheimer's formulation, critical theory is a reversion to an earlier, pre-Cartesian conception of social theory, when the study of society was conceived as part of the realm of ethics and concerned with the pursuit of the good life. As Horkheimer acknowledges, critical theory's goal is "man's emancipation from slavery.

In this it resembles Greek philosophy, not so much in the Hellenistic age of resignation as in the golden age of Plato and Aristotle" (Horkheimer 1972: 246). This reversion to an earlier conception of the role of theory, however, does not imply that critical theory completely rejects the legacy of traditional theory. Rather, traditional theory is viewed as a potentially important element in a "more just, more differentiated, more harmoniously organized" society (Horkheimer 1972: 205).

The problem is, of course, that as presently conceptualized and organized, traditional theory does not have the capability for bringing this "more differentiated, more harmoniously organized" society into existence. Indeed, it acts as a support mechanism for the status quo. This situation can change only if traditional theories are incorporated into a new critical framework. Such a framework involves two crucial revisions to traditional understandings of theory, the first epistemological and the second organizational.

Epistemologically, critical theory involves "a radical reconsideration, not of the scientist alone, but of the knowing individual as such" (Horkheimer 1972: 199). In contradistinction to the traditional view of reality as a given on which the theorist must focus, Horkheimer argues that the relationship between the subject and the object is far more complex and interdependent. He observes:

> The objects we perceive in our surroundings—cities, villages, fields, and woods—bear the mark of having been worked on by man. It is not only in the clothing and appearance, in outward form and emotional make-up that men are the product of history. Even the way they see and hear is inseparable from the social life-process as it has evolved over the millennia. The facts which our senses present to us are socially performed in two ways: through the historical character of the object perceived and through the historical character of the perceiving organ. Both are not simply natural, they are shaped by human activity. (Horkheimer 1972: 200)

Indeed, Horkheimer argues that the degree of interaction has increased in the modern age: "In the higher stages of civilization conscious human action unconsciously determines not only the subjective side of perception but in larger degree the object as well" (Horkheimer 1972: 201).

Awareness of the dialectical interdependence of the perceiving subject and the perceived object is crucial to the critical conception of theory. This realization implies that both the subject and the object—in this instance, the individual human being and society, respectively—are, in principle at least, susceptible to intentional, progressive change. (Given the current vogue for various forms of social constructivism, it is worthy to note that although Horkheimer argues that both subject and object are socially constituted, he does so within the context of a materialist framework. Thus, unlike many contemporary postmodernists—and old-fashioned idealists—Horkheimer does not dismiss biology and the natural world. Rather, his interest is in the nexus between the natural and the social.)

Thus critical theorists refuse to accept the present structures of society, both its concrete organizational forms and its more general cultural framework, as immutable givens. Of course, they are under no illusions as to the reality of these structures—their painstaking dissection and study is one of the main features of the critical theorist's work. Nevertheless, this willingness to face up to reality simultaneously includes a commitment to its transformation and a belief that such a transformation is feasible. Following Marx, critical theorists seek to understand the world in order to change it.

The implications of this epistemological stance are far-reaching. As Horkheimer makes clear, critical theory rejects the traditional "separation of value and research, knowledge and action, and other polarities" (Horkheimer 1972: 208). According to critical theory, such dichotomies are epistemological fallacies created by the hegemonic, Cartesian model of theory: They are as philosophically unjustified as they are politically debilitating. Indeed, according to the critical conception of theory, the way in which traditional theorists have tended to compartmentalize their activities by dividing their scholarly work from other aspects of their lives—for example, political activity—is basically inhuman. For Horkheimer, truly rational thought must entail the struggle for a rational society.

In addition to this epistemological shift, critical theory entails major organizational changes to the process of theory building that characterizes traditional theory. Such a reorganization is necessary to counter the way in which traditionally based disciplines have become overspecialized.

By making a series of cetirus paribus assumptions, these disciplines have generated detailed understandings of particular processes. However, they fail to understand the place and the role of the processes that have been isolated in the social totality. The traditional disciplines generate knowledge that is reified and static; knowledge that ignores the whole in favor of a fetishization of the parts. As Wolfgang Bonß notes, there is an ambiguous dynamic within the traditional approach to research:

> On the one hand, reified structures, independent of the subject, can be articulated in great detail; on the other hand, the fiction of a "presuppositionless" analysis of social reality leads to an uncritical reproduction of the dominant principles of utilization, exploitation, and administration. (Bonß 1993: 103–104)

The very process by which knowledge is generated through the traditional conception of science (such as increased differentiation and specialization) creates an ever greater blindness among theorists about the dynamics for change that exist within the totality.

A critical theory approach would, in contrast, overcome the narrowness and myopia of the specialized sciences by reintegrating their perspectives within a framework organized by progressive social theory. In his inaugural lecture as director of the IfS, Horkheimer outlined a vision of an interdisciplinary research project involving an "ongoing dialectical interpenetration" of philosophy and empirical research, aimed toward "philosophically oriented social inquiry" (Horkheimer 1993: 9). The model for such an approach was provided by Marx's critique of political economy. In *Capital,* Marx integrated the central concepts of classical political economy into a theoretical framework that grasped the totality of economic and social relations (Marx 1976a). It was this ability to integrate study of the particular with consideration of the general that Horkheimer and his colleagues sought to emulate.

From the preceding argument it is clear that Horkheimer believed that traditional theories, if given a suitably radical epistemological overhaul and if thoroughly reorganized within a critical framework, could indeed be an element in the creation and maintenance of "a more just, more differentiated, more harmoniously organised" society (Horkheimer 1972: 205). But what was the basis for Horkheimer's claim that such a society—even if desirable—was possible? And through which mechanisms did he envisage that such a society could be brought about? These questions will form the focus of the next section.

Emancipation

The first point to note is that the ultimate referent object in all of Horkheimer's discussion of emancipation is individual human beings. He regards emancipation as the liberation of individual human beings from suffering and the promotion of their happiness. Horkheimer writes contemptuously of the tendency of traditional theorists to "concern themselves with 'man as such' [rather] than human beings in particular" (Schmidt 1993: 30). Critical theory is concerned with the corporeal, material existence and experiences of human beings. Accordingly, the emancipation of a particular class or group is not an end in itself but rather a means to an end. That end is to bring society "under the control of its elements, namely, the human beings who live in it" (Brunkhorst 1993: 80).

But what does this mean in terms of real—and potential—social processes and relationships? Without doubt, the main thrust of Horkheimer's arguments is resolutely Marxist in character. He equates emancipation with the increased domination of nature: Human beings are freer when they are less subject to the vicissitudes of nature. Furthermore, the possibilities for a better life are already present in the existing forces of production. The problem is that their potential is squandered because of the way in which they are utilized for the benefit of capital rather than that of humanity. This view is clear in the following passage from "Traditional and Critical Theory":

> The idea of a reasonable organisation of society that will meet the needs of the whole community, are immanent in human work but are not correctly grasped by individuals or by the common mind. . . . Unemployment, economic crises, militarization, terrorist regimes—in a word, the whole condition of the masses—are not due, for example, to limited technological possibilities, as might have been the case in earlier periods, but to the circumstances of production which are no longer suitable to our time. The application of all intellectual means for the mastery of nature is hindered because in the prevailing circumstances these means are entrusted to special, mutually opposed interests. Production is not geared to the life of the whole community while heeding also the claims of individuals, it is geared to the power-backed claims of individuals while being concerned hardly at all with the life of the community. (Horkheimer 1972: 213)

As long as the forces of production are utilized within a capitalist framework, their emancipatory potential will remain unfulfilled.

Quite clearly, the type of alternative society that Horkheimer regards as preferable to the prevailing order is based on some form of socialist planning, even if a number of comments suggest that members of the Frankfurt School had few illusions about Soviet-style planning (see Dubiel 1985: 15–20, 41–44, 73–76). Horkheimer regularly refers to the possibility of developing a "rational society," "the right kind of society," one that is "self-determined," regulated according to "planful decision," and inhabited by a new "self-aware mankind" (Horkheimer 1972: 229, 241).

The particular understanding of emancipation underlying the arguments presented in "Traditional and Critical Theory" play a vital role in critical theory. As Moishe Postone and Barbara Brick point out: "Social production, reason, and human emancipation are intertwined and provide the standpoint of a historical critique" (Postone and Brick 1993: 234). Rather than criticizing the prevailing order in terms of some blueprint for an ideal society, Horkheimer criticizes that order on the basis of the unfulfilled potential that already exists within it. This is a form of immanent critique. Immanent critique arises from critical theory's rejection of the epistemological validity of both scientism's strict differentiation between subject and object and idealist notions of some all-knowing suprahistorical subject. Postone and Brick provide a neat summary:

> An immanent critique does not critically judge what "is" from a conceptu-
> al position outside of its object—such as a transcendental "ought". Instead
> it must be able to locate that "ought" . . . as a possibility that is immanent
> to the unfolding of the existent society. (Postone and Brick 1993: 230)

The grounds for immanent critique must be sought within the object of that
critique.

As will become apparent in the next chapter, the existence of immanent, unrealized, or unfulfilled possibilities within the reality of any given
order is vital in order to allow this approach critical purchase on its object
of study. Take, for example, an analysis of society. If critical theory cannot
locate emancipatory potential immanently within the real world, then it
must either succumb to a paralyzing pure negation or appeal to some extrasocietal basis for critique—thus transposing itself into a metaphysics or
even theology. But in 1937 at least, Horkheimer was still relatively sanguine about the existence of emancipatory possibilities within the prevailing order. He was also convinced, again in traditional Marxist fashion, that
a class existed within society that had the potential to realize those possibilities: the proletariat. Horkheimer writes:

> Because of its situation in modern society the proletariat experiences the
> connection between work which puts ever more powerful instruments into
> men's hands in their struggle with nature, and the continuous renewal of
> outmoded social organisation. (Horkheimer 1972: 213)

The proletariat experienced the disjuncture between humanity's potential to
control nature (that is, the emancipatory possibilities) provided by the ever
more powerful forces of production at its disposal and the use to which that
potential is actually put under capitalist relations of production

However, Horkheimer was less sanguine about the possibility of the
proletariat actually exercising the power that, "objectively considered," it
enjoys in order to "change society" (Horkheimer 1972: 214). Two sets of
reasons are advanced to explain this pessimism: The first sits full square
within the Marxist tradition; the second heralds the genesis of the argument
that, when fully developed in the book *Dialectic of Enlightenment* (see
Chapter 2), will eventually entail a thorough revision of critical theory's
relationship to that tradition.

The main argument advanced in "Traditional and Critical Theory" to
explain the proletariat's quiescence is a familiar one. Horkheimer refers to
the divisions within the working class between the skilled and unskilled
and the employed and unemployed. He also notes the failure of the working
class to recognize its real position and its real interests: "Even to the proletariat the world superficially seems quite different than it really is"

(Horkheimer 1972: 214). The lessons he draws are that critical theorists must avoid "canonising" the proletariat or attaching themselves uncritically to "some more advanced sector of the proletariat, for example a party or its leadership" (Horkheimer 1972: 215). Rather, they must retain their independence and integrity and act as a "critical promotive factor in the development of the masses" and exercise "an aggressive critique not only against the conscious defenders of the *status quo* but also against distracting, conformist, or utopian tendencies within his own household" (Horkheimer 1972: 216).

According to Horkheimer, the aim of a critical theorist is to form "a dynamic unity with the oppressed class, so that his presentation of societal contradictions is not merely an expression of the concrete historical situation but also a force within it to stimulate change" (Horkheimer 1972: 215). The result he hopes to secure is "a process of interactions in which awareness comes to flower along with its liberating but also its aggressive forces which incite while also requiring discipline" (Horkheimer 1972: 215).

Apart perhaps from the implied criticism of contemporary Communist parties, this position—part explanation, part exhortation—was not an unfamiliar one in many intellectual, left-wing circles in the 1930s. However, later in "Traditional and Critical Theory," Horkheimer begins to develop another, far bleaker line of argument. According to Horkheimer, the proletariat's submission in the face of the prevailing order is not a "false consciousness," which even if stubborn, is potentially erasable. Rather, he attributes the working class's quiescence to a far more serious and intractable malaise. Modern capitalism, Horkheimer argues, has extinguished the individual's potential for autonomous activity. In the age of monopoly capitalism,

> the individual no longer has any ideas of his own. The content of mass belief, in which no one really believes, is an immediate product of the ruling economic and political bureaucracies, and its disciplines secretly follow their own atomistic and therefore untrue interests: they act as mere functions of the economic machine. (Horkheimer 1972: 237)

Faced by what he perceives as the overwhelming power of the state's bureaucratic apparatus and the mass media, Horkheimer seems to suggest that his hope—expressed, of course, in the same essay—that critical theory could act "as a promotive factor in the development of the masses" is destined to remain unfulfilled. However, at this stage at least, the deeply pessimistic implications of this line of argument are not pursued. Domination and submission are not yet regarded as the inevitable and inescapable results of society's development. Rather, the overall thrust is that progressive change is possible, even if it is unlikely to occur in the short run. Although "truth has sought refuge in small groups of admirable men,"

Horkheimer still maintains that this truth can, in principle, be articulated and communicated to a class within society that, "objectively speaking," has the power to emancipate humanity and its "elements." Thus emancipation remains a possibility, and critical theory remains both valid and necessary. Without it, "the ground is taken from under the hope of radically improving human existence" (Horkheimer 1972: 233).

Technology

Horkheimer's attitude toward technology is implicit rather than explicit in "Traditional and Critical Theory." It can be reconstructed from his standpoint on the possibility and possible contours of emancipation. This standpoint, outlined in the previous section, may well be open to charges of vagueness, although Horkheimer does comment:

> In regard to the essential kind of change at which the critical theory aims, there can be no . . . concrete perception of it until it actually comes about. If the proof of the pudding is in the eating, the eating here is in the future. (Horkheimer 1972: 220–221)

Nevertheless, although Horkheimer makes no concrete suggestions about the type of institutions that would exist in a more emancipated society, it is clear that he conceives such a society as being characterized by the following: a further lessening of humankind's vulnerability to the vagaries of nature; a planned, rational utilization of the forces of production; an increasing self-awareness among humankind of its place in the natural world (including, inter alia, a realization of the falsity of the subject/object dichotomy); and the susceptibility of human relations to conscious determination. It is through these developments that individual suffering may be alleviated and happiness pursued.

Much of this viewpoint is predicated on a benign view of technology. Technological developments—or development of the forces of production—are seen as creating ever greater possibilities for the domination of nature and, hence, emancipation. If this potential is not utilized, then, the argument goes, it can hardly be blamed on technology per se. Rather, it reflects a failing in the human organization of the forces of production— that is, failings in the relations of production. Should those relations of production be revised or revolutionized so that technology is deployed in a planned, rational manner, then human freedom will be greatly enhanced.

THE PROMISE OF A CRITICAL THEORY OF SOCIETY

Horkheimer proposed that critical theory of society is based on the following elements.

• Epistemologically, critical theory rejects the subject-object dichotomy—and the consequent sharp differentiation between fact and value—that underlies traditional theory. It argues for its replacement by an acceptance of the dialectical interrelatedness of knower and known and a recognition of the inevitably political nature of all social theory.

• In terms of research organization, critical theory rejects traditional theory's tendency to break down the study of the social world into the study of a series of discrete, unintegrated fields or disciplines, regarding such an approach as reifying and, ultimately, conservative. Critical theory proposes instead the reintegration of the various subfields of traditional theory into a framework organized by a progressive social theory and committed to developing an understanding of the dynamics of the whole rather than merely the characteristics of the parts.

• Recognizing the inherently political nature of all social theory, critical theory is committed to understanding these dynamics in order to play a role in the process of changing and improving society. Indeed, it is critical theory's commitment to emancipation—understood as the development of possibilities for a better life already immanent within the present—that provides its point of critique of the prevailing order.

• It understands emancipation as the more rational and purposeful utilization of already existing forces of production in order to bring nature under rational human control. This understanding itself presupposes a benign view of technology.

Thus the promise of critical theory was the development of an epistemologically sophisticated understanding of the social totality, an understanding that could play a part in the realization of the progressive potential inherent within it. Horkheimer held to the belief that progressive social change was a possibility even during the rise of fascism in the 1930s. But gradually, in the shadow of Auschwitz, that hope was almost wholly extinguished. The next chapter will examine this transformation in outlook and the consequent failure of the critical theory of the 1940s to redeem its earlier promise.

2

Impasse:
Emancipatory Politics
After Auschwitz

Although Theodor Adorno had been affiliated with the IfS since the late 1920s, it was not until 1938 that he became one of its core members. It was then that he left Europe, after spending four miserable years of exile trying to establish himself at Oxford, in order to join Horkheimer and his colleagues in the United States. There he soon began to play an increasingly prominent role in the development of critical theory, a process given impetus by two parallel developments, namely, the U.S. entry into World War II and Horkheimer's decision to move to California.

The U.S. entry into World War II led to the fragmentation of the institute as most of its members became involved in the Allied war effort. The centrifugal pressures were further intensified when Horkheimer left New York for California so that he might expend less time and energy on administrative tasks and more on his own research work. There he joined the brilliant German émigré community that included such luminaries as Arnold Schönberg, Bertolt Brecht, Thomas Mann, and Hanns Eisler. Both developments meant an end to the close-knit, collegiate atmosphere that had characterized the life and work of the IfS immediately after its exile; they also heralded a radical departure in the institute's intellectual direction.

In 1941 Adorno traveled west to join his compatriot and immediately started work with Horkheimer on a manuscript that would eventually be published in 1947 under the title *Dialectic of Enlightenment*. This was a work that fundamentally changed the trajectory of critical theory; it was also a work that announced Adorno's emergence as its main protagonist. It effectively heralded the abandonment of the version of critical theory outlined by Horkheimer in "Traditional and Critical Theory" and its replacement with another that Adorno would eventually fully develop in *Negative Dialectics* (1973) and *Aesthetic Theory* (1997).

Given its historical significance, the arguments developed in *Dialectic of Enlightenment* will be outlined and assessed in this chapter. Particular attention will be given to the ways in which the key notions of theory, technology, and emancipation are treated. I will follow this discussion with a critique charging that the despairing worldview underlying the work is based on an overly pessimistic assessment of the progressive possibilities extant in the modern world. Furthermore, and crucially, I will argue that any understanding of the shift from the position advanced in "Traditional and Critical Theory" to that exhibited in *Dialectic of Enlightenment* cannot simply be reduced to an account of the changing historical context. Although the barbarity symbolized above all else by Auschwitz had a profound impact on both authors, there were problems with the original theoretical model outlined in "Traditional and Critical Theory" that were in themselves quite capable of producing a profound impasse in critical theory.

DIALECTIC OF ENLIGHTENMENT

The research project that culminated in the publication of *Dialectic of Enlightenment* was conceived in October 1941, soon after the Nazi regime banned Jewish emigration and decreed that all Jews within its jurisdiction would henceforth be required to wear the Star of David. Rumors that Jews were being murdered by the regime were already filtering out of Germany, yet the U.S. government was still reluctant to soften its immigration policy toward them (Rubenstein 1997 offers a spirited defense of the immigration policies of the Western liberal democracies). Another European war had begun, and world war was imminent; a catastrophic fate awaited European Jewry.

In these circumstances, Adorno and Horkheimer aimed at "nothing less than the discovery of why mankind, instead of entering into a truly human condition, is sinking into a new level of barbarism" (Adorno and Horkheimer 1979: xi). The starting point for this quest is stated clearly in the work's introduction:

> We are wholly convinced . . . that social freedom is inseparable from enlightened thought. Nevertheless, we believe that we have just as clearly recognised that the notion of this very way of thinking . . . already contains the seed of the reversal universally apparent today. If enlightenment does not accommodate reflection on this recidivist element, then it seals its own fate. (Adorno and Horkheimer 1979: xiii)

However, as will become clear, in their effort to reflect on this "recidivist element" within enlightenment while remaining true to its ideal of human freedom, Adorno and Horkheimer reach an understanding of the trajectory of human history so bleak as to undermine any hope that the promise of enlightenment might ever be realized.

The first move the authors take on this fateful path is to recast the whole conception of enlightenment itself. Enlightenment is no longer understood as the school of thought first developed in Scotland and France in the late eighteenth century, dedicated to the triumph of human reason over such atavistic tendencies as myth, magic, superstition, and religion. Rather, the concept is extended to include the whole of human history far back into mythic prehistory and is used to describe humankind's growing domination over nature. Their understanding of this process leads to three, further related arguments. First, Adorno and Horkheimer argue that rather than opposing myth, enlightenment actually reverts to myth. Second, they argue that far from presaging the development of an ethical, rational society, enlightenment is deeply implicated in the irrationality and immorality so painfully apparent in contemporary society. Finally, and most strikingly given the epoch in which *Dialectic of Enlightenment* was written, they claim that "enlightenment is totalitarian" (Adorno and Horkheimer 1979: 134).

Thus, to state the argument at its starkest, the barbarism that Adorno and Horkheimer were committed to understanding was not a negation of enlightenment but rather its culmination; Auschwitz was not the opposite of enlightenment but its result. But how could two participants in the Marxist tradition, a tradition that regards itself as the true heir of enlightenment thought, find themselves in a position in which they argue that enlightenment is implicated in the worst atrocities of the modern world? The answer lies in the role of instrumental reason in the human domination of nature.

"Instrumental reason" is the name given to the ways of thinking (and being) involved in the gradual domestication of nature, ways of thinking oriented toward technical control and manipulation. Adorno and Horkheimer argue that in the course of bringing nature (what they call "outer nature") under human control, instrumental reason ultimately leads to the effacement of those aesthetic and instinctual elements in the human character (what they call "inner nature") that are not reducible to the instrumental domination of nature. Humanity becomes solely concerned with means in themselves—the most effective ways to bring nature under its dominion—and does not reflect on the ends to which those means might contribute. Thus, far from establishing the sovereignty of humankind, the process of dominating nature that *Dialectic of Enlightenment* identifies with enlightenment leads to a tragic atrophic process in human history. In their drive for self-preservation, humans utilize instrumental reason whose continued development leads to what Albrecht Wellmer has aptly described as the "progressive reification of consciousness" (Wellmer 1983: 92).

As reason becomes more and more functionally oriented, and as the ends of human activity are subject to an ever-decreasing amount of self-reflexive consideration and mediation, human beings are increasingly alienated. One aspect of the resulting "new barbarianism" is the general population's increasing susceptibility to various forms of irrationality (Adorno and Horkheimer 1979: 32). As people lose all sense of belonging and meaning in a world where all aspects of life are increasingly commodified and everything has a price but little has value, they are easy prey for myths of all kinds, be it the myth of the "volk" or that of astrology (on the latter see Adorno 1994: 34–127).

Closely related to this "mutual implication of enlightenment and myth" is the tendency of enlightenment to slip into immorality. As enlightenment is reduced to what might be called, in stark contrast to Kant's formulation, a "kingdom of means," truth becomes equated with scientific systematization. At this point, according to Adorno and Horkheimer, enlightenment "seals its own nullity," as thought is thus proscribed from "reflective consideration of its own goals" (Adorno and Horkheimer 1979: 85). The logical outcome of such thinking is that ultimate symbol of amoral depravity, the Marquis de Sade's Juliette. In the kingdom of means

> enlightenment possesses no argument against . . . [any] perversion of its proper nature, for the plain truth had no advantage over distortion, and rationalization none over the *ratio,* if they could prove no practical benefit in themselves. . . . Once it is harnessed to the dominant mode of production, the Enlightenment—which strives to undermine any order which has become repressive—abrogates itself. (Adorno and Horkheimer 1979: 93)

Against all its stated intentions, enlightenment cannot supply a defense or justification for moral behavior undertaken for its own sake.

Yet a further hardening of the case against enlightenment is provided in Adorno and Horkheimer's charge that "enlightenment is totalitarian" (Adorno and Horkheimer 1979: 134). This charge does not simply mean that enlightenment creates a society populated by damaged, alienated, non-thinking individuals who are susceptible to the blandishments of various totalitarian ideologies. Rather, as should already be clear, this in itself is a sign of a deeper malaise. "Enlightenment is totalitarian" in the sense that it, or more specifically its deification of instrumental reason, pervades every aspect of society, from its institutions to the very psyches of the individuals who populate it. Furthermore, Adorno and Horkheimer suggest that it is increasingly unlikely that humankind will be able to escape the atrophy of thought and being brought about by the all-pervasive impact of instrumental reason. This increasing unlikelihood is due to the crucial role they accord to what they term the "culture industry." Drawing on their experience of both Nazi propaganda and the media industry in the United States,

Adorno and Horkheimer suggest that the (then largely) nascent culture industry was quickly undermining human subjectivity itself. By transforming every aspect of human life—including its cultural forms—into a commodity, the industry was rapidly ensuring that every human need and every human emotion was programmed and attuned to the needs of monopoly capital. In such a society, "the individual is an illusion" (Adorno and Horkheimer 1979: 154).

Fifty years later, in an age of global media penetration, global media empires, global soap operas, an age in which local cultural production values ape ever more closely those of the global media players and the media generally has an ever greater impact on the lives of those exposed to it, their words appear prophetic indeed. It is thus disturbing to note that they believe that it is ever more unlikely that humankind will escape the shackles of this second-rate, superficial society:

> It is idle to hope that this self-contradictory, disintegrating "person" will not last for generations, that the system must collapse because of such a psychological split, or that the deceitful substitution of the stereotype for the individual will of itself become unbearable for mankind. . . . For centuries society has been preparing for Victor Mature and Mickey Rooney. (Adorno and Horkheimer 1979: 155)

Thus *Dialectic of Enlightenment* points to the development of what Helmut Dubiel has dubbed a "hermetic society": a society from which there is not only no political escape route but also no "private, individual escape, indeed not even an escape within one's own imagination" (Dubiel 1985: 122). It is little wonder, therefore, that enlightenment is seen as a form of "mass deception" (Adorno and Horkheimer 1979: 120–167).

Adorno and Horkheimer go on to claim that the anti-Semitism disfiguring the world as they wrote *Dialectic of Enlightenment* was itself the result of the malignancy they had identified as lying at the heart of the enlightenment project. Rejecting the notion that anti-Semitism is an aberration, a throwback to more primitive times, they argue that it is the most extreme manifestation of the rise of instrumental reason. Further, they argue that "the rational domination of nature [that] comes increasingly to win the day . . . and integrates all human characteristics" has disastrous implications for humankind (Adorno and Horkheimer 1979: 233). "In situations where blinded men robbed of their subjectivity are set loose as subjects," the result is anti-Semitism (Adorno and Horkheimer 1979: 233).

But why should the blinded men turn on Jews in particular? It is precisely because the Jews are stubbornly determined to be different and not to assimilate and conform wholly to the mores of the host population. In a world where individuals have surrendered their subjectivity, Jewish difference becomes an unbearable affront. Thus, for Adorno and Horkheimer, anti-Semitism is not a negation of enlightenment but arises out of it. Here the "dialectic of enlightenment" stands fully revealed: On the one hand, enlightenment has created the material basis for an emancipated society, but the very mode of thinking that makes this possible condemns humanity to ever greater barbarism. Not only is this tragic duality exhibited in the Nazi death camps, where some of the era's most modern technology was utilized in order to commit some of the most heinous crimes in human history, it permeates all aspects of life. So, for example, "the serum which a doctor gives a sick child is obtained by attacking defenceless animals" (Adorno and Horkheimer 1979: 223): Reason and domination are revealed as inextricably entwined.

The arguments advanced in *Dialectic of Enlightenment* are almost unremittingly bleak—so bleak as to imply that the original aim of the book—to recover the emancipatory impulses of enlightenment—is doomed to failure. The grip of instrumental reason is so tight and all-embracing that nothing can ever hope to escape it. Occasionally, the text seems to resist this logic. At one point Adorno and Horkheimer suggest a route to redemption that appears even more unlikely when one considers the time of writing:

> If thought is liberated from domination and if violence is abolished, the long absent idea is liable to develop that Jews are human beings. This development would represent the step out of an anti-Semitic society . . . and into human society. This step would also fulfil the Fascist lie, but in contradicting it: the Jewish question would prove in fact to be the turning point of history. . . . Mankind would develop from a set of opposing races to the species which, even as nature, is more than nature. (Adorno and Horkheimer 1979: 199–200)

However, they hint at no possible means by which this liberation may be attained, and indeed, if society is as hermetic as they suggest, no escape is possible. Adorno and Horkheimer are aware of this predicament:

> All work and pleasure are protected by the hangman. To contradict this is to deny all science and logic. It is impossible to abolish the terror and retain civilization. . . . Various conclusions can be drawn from this—from the grovelling respect for Fascist barbarity to refuge in the circles of Hell. But there is another conclusion: to laugh at logic if it runs counter to the interests of men. (Adorno and Horkheimer 1979: 217–218)

Although laughing at logic may be an entirely laudable reaction under their circumstances, it hardly represents a coherent plan for political action. Indeed, *Dialectic of Enlightenment* represents the moment when critical theory—or at least the strand represented by Adorno and Horkheimer— abdicated the political battlefield. If, as the authors suggest, "under the

given conditions, the mere continuation of an existence maintaining individual skills of a technical or intellectual nature leads to cretinism even in
the prime of life," then all resistance is useless (Adorno and Horkheimer
1979: 240–241).

Theory

The critique of instrumental reason advanced in *Dialectic of Enlightenment*
effectively heralds the end of the vision of critical theory that animated the
Frankfurt School's work in the 1930s. As detailed in Chapter 1,
Horkheimer's original vision was of a theoretical orientation that attempted
to integrate the insights of the specialized, "bourgeois" sciences within a
framework organized intellectually by Marxian social theory and committed to developing an understanding of society in order to aid in the task of
its transformation. The extent of the rupture from this position represented
by *Dialectic of Enlightenment* is made explicit in the book's introduction:

> Even though we had noticed for some time that in the modern scientific
> enterprise great discoveries are paid for with the growing decay of theo-
> retical culture, we still thought that we might join in to the extent that we
> would restrict ourselves largely to criticizing or developing specialized
> knowledge. Thematically, at any rate, we were to keep to the traditional
> disciplines of sociology, psychology and the theory of knowledge. The
> fragments collected in this volume show, however, that we had to abandon
> that confidence. (translation from Habermas 1984: 454; Adorno and
> Horkheimer 1979: xi)

In *Dialectic of Enlightenment* the specialized sciences are regarded as
irredeemably tainted by instrumental reason: They have no critical purchase on their objects; nor is there any possibility that it could ever be
acquired. According to this analysis, the familiar disciplines of the social
sciences are configured to gain a form of instrumental knowledge about
society that will aid its further manipulation, and it is useless to hope that
this could ever change.

In response to this situation, Adorno and Horkheimer "philosophized"
critical theory (see Dubiel 1985: 94–95). Instead of attempting to integrate
the insights of philosophy and the specialized sciences, they effectively
truncated the project of critical theory. Rather than standing "between
philosophy and social science," to recall the title of a collection of
Horkheimer's early essays, critical theory was repositioned to become a
purely philosophical enterprise (Horkheimer 1993). According to this
wholly philosophical conceptualization, critical theory was regarded as "a
mental preserve, a critical island, an encapsulation resistant to the instru-
mentalistic *Zeitgeist*" (Dubiel 1985: 95). Critical theory did not attempt to

engage theoretically with the real world; it became an effort to escape from that world's clutches and a denial that the world contained any truth. One important result of this effort was that the possibility of immanent critique, a critical tool Horkheimer had championed in "Traditional and Critical Theory," was abandoned.

As discussed in Chapter 1, immanent critique was a technique adopted by the Frankfurt School in the 1930s in order to criticize any prevailing order without appealing to an external, ahistorical Archimedean point in order to ground that critique. Immanent critique depends on comparing an object (a particular institution or situation) with the unrealized possibilities existent within it. But of course if it is true that enlightenment and domination are thoroughly entwined, as the "black writers of the bourgeoisie" argue (Adorno and Horkheimer 1979: 117), if the baleful effects of instrumental reason have insinuated themselves into every aspect of human existence, if Adorno is correct to argue that "nothing complicitous with this world can have any truth" (Jameson 1990: 177–178), then immanent critique becomes impossible. In the hermetic society dissected in *Dialectic of Enlightenment,* there is no immanent "ought" or "might be" according to which the "is" might be measured.

The abandonment of immanent critique left Adorno and Horkheimer with two choices. They could either succumb to a thoroughgoing relativism or attempt to identify a source of truth and grounding for critique external to society. Given their hostility toward relativism, which they regarded, to quote Adorno, as making "common cause with untruth" (Bronner 1994: 206), it is hardly surprising that they chose the latter path even if it left them open to many of the same charges that Horkheimer had made against traditional theory in "Traditional and Critical Theory." As will be briefly discussed in the concluding remarks to this chapter, Adorno sought for truth in aesthetics, whereas Horkheimer adopted a godless theology. What is important to note here is that both men effectively abandoned all hope that progressive change was possible in the social realm.

A further theoretical corollary of the critique of instrumental reason advanced in *Dialectic of Enlightenment* was the ending of critical theory's orientation toward political practice. The Horkheimer of "Traditional and Critical Theory" remained fully committed to Marx's famous dictum in the "Thesis on Feuerbach": "Philosophers have thus far only sought to understand the world; the point is to change it" (Marx 1976b: 5). Although he was less than sanguine that revolutionary change could be affected and certainly entertained no illusions about contemporary Communist parties, he still argued that the aim of the critical theorist should be to form "a dynamic unity with the oppressed class, so that his presentation of societal contradictions is not merely an expression of the concrete historical situation but also a force within it to stimulate change" (Horkheimer 1972: 215). But in the hermetic society depicted in *Dialectic of Enlightenment*, the proletariat has lost its emancipatory vocation. In a society wholly controlled by the iron logic of instrumental reason, Adorno and Horkheimer argue, human subjectivity has become an empty shell. Human beings have become mere pawns of instrumental rationality and in particular its most powerful modern manifestation, the culture industry. People cannot think for themselves let alone work for a better world.

The philosophized critical theory of *Dialectic of Enlightenment* does not hope to change this situation. Indeed, Adorno and Horkheimer argue that any attempt to do so would inevitably implicate the theory in the logic of instrumental rationality. The tragedy of the position in which the critical theorists found themselves is overwhelming. If their analysis is correct, then silence in the face of the prevailing order is tantamount to acquiescence with it. However, any attempt to intervene practically to change that order is doomed to succumb to and even strengthen the very instrumental rationality that they are attempting to resist:

> It is characteristic of the sickness [of contemporary society] that even the best intentioned reformer who uses an impoverished and debased language to recommend renewal, by his adoption of the insidious mode of categorization and the bad philosophy it conceals, strengthens the very power of the established order he is trying to break. (Adorno and Horkheimer 1979: xiv)

Caught between the Scylla of mute acceptance and the Charybdis of self-defeating efforts at political relevance, the only possible course open to Adorno and Horkheimer is that of pure negation.

In a hermetic society all critical theory can do is criticize the false totality in which it finds itself. It cannot hope to propose alternatives or exhort people to action; rather, critical theory must consist solely of the steadfast rejection of any notion that the world contains anything remotely resembling justice, liberty, and beauty—"nothing complicitous with this world can have any truth." And of course, given the totalitarian and totalizing impact of instrumental rationality on society, Adorno and Horkheimer are aware that it is highly unlikely that there can ever be an audience for their work. In response, they came to regard critical theory as a message in a bottle to be thrown at the mercy of history, its destination unknown. Even if the message should one day be taken up, then, in the words of Horkheimer, "we can hope for no more than that, would day ever break, our writings will be recognized as a very little star that had shown, though barely perceptible, in the horrible light of the present" (Dubiel 1985: 84). But of course the whole point of the analysis advanced in *Dialectic of Enlightenment* is that day will never break, and critical theory is thus condemned to perpetual practical irrelevance.

Emancipation

Emancipation is central to the version of critical theory developed by Horkheimer in "Traditional and Critical Theory." Immanent critique depends on the possibility of emancipatory social change, and critical theory's view of its own place in society—its ultimate aspiration to be involved in political praxis—also depends on such change being achievable. But the analysis advanced in *Dialectic of Enlightenment* leads to the abandonment of all hope in the possibility of progressive development. However, a concept of emancipation continues to play an important role even in this revised understanding of critical theory, though the notion of what emancipation might mean has been certainly greatly modified.

The understanding of emancipation adopted in "Traditional and Critical Theory" is an orthodoxly Marxian one. Horkheimer shares the classic Hegelian-Marxist vision of an emancipated society as a rational society. Such a society would result from a process in which humankind brought nature under its control through organized development planned in such a way that it benefited the species as a whole rather than simply individuals within it. But of course, according to the analysis advanced in *Dialectic of Enlightenment,* the very process of the domination of nature, far from leading to emancipation, in fact leads to ever greater domination of humankind's inner nature. The type of rationality necessary to domesticate and control the natural world leads to ever greater barbarism in human relations.

In the light of this analysis, Adorno and Horkheimer suggest an alternative conceptualization of emancipation. Unsurprisingly, this conceptualization envisages a different relationship between humankind and nature wherein emancipation lies through a "reconciliation" with nature (Adorno and Horkheimer 1979: 54). Emancipation requires a realization by humanity that it is *of* nature rather than *above* nature and a concomitant development by humanity of a noninstrumental, nontechnical relationship with nature. Humanity must somehow learn how to value nature in and of itself. But given that the critique of instrumental rationality advanced in *Dialectic of Enlightenment* is itself based on totalizing assumptions about humankind—in effect, a set of anthropological claims about humanity's relations with its material surroundings, as well as intraspecies relationships—all such depictions must remain at the level of hypothesis. Adorno and Horkheimer cannot point to any concrete examples of what types of institutions and relationships might characterize a more emancipated society. Such examples have never existed, and given the all-pervading effects of instrumental rationality, it is clear that they never could.

So the radically revised notion of emancipation advanced in *Dialectic of Enlightenment* is utopian in the negative sense: It has no relationship to the real world; it is literally unimaginable (Wellmer 1983: 92). To be sure, emancipation remains a kind of regulative ideal for Adorno and Horkheimer. But given that it is, by definition, indescribable and that any attempt to describe it inevitably succumbs to the very instrumentalist logic it endeavors to resist, it is hard to avoid the conclusion that the commitment of critical theorists to emancipation became merely metaphysical in character.

Technology

As discussed in Chapter 1, the version of critical theory developed by Horkheimer in "Traditional and Critical Theory" depended on a benign understanding of technology. Developments in the forces of production available to society—that is, more sophisticated technology—were regarded in a positive light; such developments created the possibility for a more emancipated society even if that potential was not always realized in the context of the class-ridden contemporary world. However, Adorno and Horkheimer's subsequent analysis totally reversed this understanding.

In *Dialectic of Enlightenment,* technology is regarded as the embodiment of the instrumental rationality that is exposed and criticized in the work. Thus technology is seen wholly negatively: It is a means to control and manipulate and is thus inimical to human freedom. Technological innovation in the name of human enlightenment leads to ever greater domination and, ultimately, the effacement of those very human characteristics that fueled efforts to attain enlightenment in the first place: "Machinery disables men even as it nutures them" (Adorno and Horkheimer 1979: 37). Indeed, in a dramatic inversion of the familiar enlightenment teleology of an inevitable advance toward a more rational and civilized society—a feature of both Marxism and liberalism—Adorno and Horkheimer postulate a deterministic progression toward an ever more oppressive society dominated by ever more destructive technology. According to this dystopian vision, technology, the material embodiment of instrumental rationality, is pushing humanity inexorably toward certain destruction. As Adorno was to argue memorably: "No universal history leads from savagery to humanitarianism, but there is one leading from the slingshot to the megaton bomb" (Adorno 1973: 320). And even those who recognize that this process is occurring are powerless to intervene and halt it.

CRITIQUE

There is no doubt that *Dialectic of Enlightenment* possesses a certain pathos. It reflects the bitterness and bewilderment of a group of left-wing

German Jewish intellectuals who felt they had been thoroughly betrayed in general by history, and in particular by the culture they had been brought up to venerate. But there can also be little doubt that the work contains much that is contemporarily relevant. It speaks powerfully to those troubled by the apparent paradox whereby the most advanced technology of the age is utilized to perfect the most unspeakable acts of barbarity. It speaks to those concerned by the damaging effects of humanity's exploitative relationship with the natural world on both humankind and nature. It also resonates with those who reject postmodern praise of popular culture and point to the apparently relentless dumbing down of contemporary society. Yet despite such prescience, the position taken by Adorno and Horkheimer in *Dialectic of Enlightenment* is flawed in important respects. The argument they advance is overly deterministic and ultimately yields to a paralyzing relativism in relation to politics. Furthermore, the authors of *Dialectic of Enlightenment* are forced into a position in which they cannot adequately account for the basis of their own critique of instrumental rationality.

One of the many paradoxes of *Dialectic of Enlightenment* is that a work that sets out to rescue the progressive impulses of enlightenment ultimately ends up as one of the most far-reaching dismissals of that tradition ever written. Another, related paradox is that two writers who emerged from a strain of Marxist thought that rejected the determinism so apparent in more orthodox (that is, party-aligned) Marxism eventually found themselves promulgating a version of determinism even more far reaching than the one that they originally rejected.

The crux of the argument put forward by Adorno and Horkheimer in *Dialectic of Enlightenment* can be summarized as follows:

- They equate enlightenment with humanity's attempts to dominate nature in order to provide for the sustenance and reproduction of the species.
- They argue that the very forms of rationality that come into play in the course of humanity's domestication of nature ultimately enslave humanity itself.
- They apparently regard this process of encroaching control and domination as inevitable.

As Habermas points out, Adorno and Horkheimer attribute the cause of the problems of their own epoch to "the anthropological foundations of the history of the species" (Habermas 1984: 379). *Dialectic of Enlightenment* therefore implies a telos—or perhaps anti-telos—to history: History is conceived in totally mechanistic and deterministic terms, as the inexorable march of instrumental rationality, from mythic prehistory to the gas chambers of Auschwitz.

The argument of *Dialectic of Enlightenment* is deeply problematic (for critiques by the successor generation of critical theorists, see in particular Habermas 1981; 1984: 366–399; 1991: 106–130; 1992a; Wellmer 1983). One basic flaw is the redefinition of enlightenment to encompass the whole history (and prehistory) of civilization. By expanding the meaning of the term to include literally everything, it becomes analytically meaningless. Nowhere is this better illustrated than in Adorno and Horkheimer's claim in the preface to *Dialectic of Enlightenment* that the work was written in order to redeem the hopes of enlightenment as they are more conventionally understood, that is, in terms of the history of ideas (Adorno and Horkheimer 1979: xi).

But how do the values of freedom, justice, and solidarity that are normally associated with enlightenment fit in to the worldview advanced in *Dialectic of Enlightenment?* In what sense can Adorno and Horkheimer describe them as enlightenment values? And if indeed they can, what is the relationship between the enlightenment analyzed in *Dialectic of Enlightenment* and the enlightenment of David Hume, Adam Ferguson, Voltaire, and Immanuel Kant? By so extending the meaning of the term, Adorno and Horkheimer deny themselves the vocabulary necessary to reflect on whatever recidivist elements exist within enlightenment thought while still keeping faith with the hopes of that tradition. Defenders of their work might well respond by arguing that this contradiction is precisely what they are seeking to expose. Another, less charitable response is that this particular contradiction is of their own making.

As well as being too broad, the understanding of enlightenment proffered in *Dialectic of Enlightenment* is also, paradoxically, too reductive. Adorno and Horkheimer reduce all forms of rationality to one: instrumental rationality. But those very values that the work was written to defend suggest a different sense of rationality—one that is not reducible to pure instrumentality. And indeed, in *Eclipse of Reason,* a book originally published in 1947 that delivers some of the main themes of *Dialectic of Enlightenment* in a more accessible form, Horkheimer does formally distinguish between instrumental rationality and substantive rationality, the latter being concerned with ends and not simply means (Horkheimer 1974: 3–91). But in *Eclipse of Reason* and, in an even more pronounced fashion, *Dialectic of Enlightenment,* the tendency is to reduce all rationality to its instrumental form. Given that almost all human activity—from the most basic urges for self-preservation to the most advanced scientific research— is seen as embodying instrumental rationality, then, by definition, it becomes extremely difficult for Adorno and Horkheimer to give an account of any other form of rationality. As I will discuss later, Adorno in particular attempted to give such an account through his aesthetic theory. However, even in the aesthetic realm, he argued that the hold of more substantive forms of rationality was extremely tenuous and uncertain. Thus Habermas seems to be correct when he argues that despite the intentions of its authors, the argument of *Dialectic of Enlightenment* tends to reduce all rationality to instrumental rationality and thus to produce a critique of rationality per se (Habermas 1984: 366–399; 1991: 106–130).

Quite apart from the dangers inherent in the slippage into an antirational position, another problem that arises from the deterministic and reductive approach to rationality adopted in *Dialectic of Enlightenment* is that it leaves the authors totally unable to account for the basis of their own critique. How can one advance a rational critique of rationality—for that is surely the aim of the work—if all worldly rationality is purely instrumental in nature? How, for example, can Adorno and Horkheimer account for their own social position as theorists? Do they enjoy some especially privileged position that gives them a certain critical distance form the machinations of instrumental rationality and allows them to expose and criticize its effects? If so, what is the basis of this position? Given their own outlook on these matters, their position must be social rather than biological, so can one presume that it relates to class, background, or education? But does this in turn not suggest that the insight they possess is, in principle at least, accessible to many more? And if this is indeed the case, then surely instrumental rationality is not as all-pervasive and totalitarian as they claim. Adorno and Horkheimer are unable to address these issues precisely because of the deterministic and reductive claims on which their theoretical position is based. But their own biographies—to say nothing of those people and practices existing in all societies whose behavior is not simply based on instrumental concerns or calculations—suggest that some of these central claims are hollow.

Apart from this failure of self-reflexivity, another conspicuous casualty of the unwarranted overgeneralization and oversimplification that characterize *Dialectic of Enlightenment* is the analysis of anti-Semitism contained within it. When examined in detail, the understanding proffered by Adorno and Horkheimer is wholly unconvincing.

As I have already discussed, *Dialectic of Enlightenment* argues that anti-Semitism is the outcome of the process of enlightenment; it is a symptom of the rise of instrumental rationality. Such a line of argument fails to address some of the most basic questions concerning this most intractable of phenomena. It cannot hope to explain why anti-Semitism has been a characteristic of so many different societies, at so many different stages in their development. If anti-Semitism is a product of modernity, why did it also feature in premodern times? Indeed, how is it that anti-Semitism is particularly associated with antimodern sentiment? Furthermore, why was it Germany that bore host to one of the most determined and certainly the most murderous strain of anti-Semitism (see and compare Goldhagen 1997,

Finkelstein 1997)? If we pursue the logic of Adorno and Horkheimer's argument, we must conclude that the virulence of anti-Semitism under the Third Reich is a sign that Germany was somehow more enlightened than other countries and that instrumental rationality had penetrated more thoroughly into German society than elsewhere.

When stated in these bald terms, the absurdity of their position becomes apparent. Jeffrey Herf provides a salutary and succinct rejoinder:

> They [Adorno and Horkheimer] mistakenly attributed to the Enlightenment what was in fact the product of Germany's particular misery. Germany did not suffer from too much reason, too much liberalism, too much enlightenment, but rather not enough of any of them. . . . Hitler's Germany was never more than partly and woefully inadequately enlightened. Auschwitz remains a monument to the deficit and not the excess of reason in Hitler's Reich. (Herf 1984: 234)

Dialectic of Enlightenment simply does not begin to grasp the historical specificity of the very barbarism that it was intended to explore.

An even more troubling feature of Adorno and Horkheimer's analysis is the downplaying of individual responsibility that is implicit in their argument. If Auschwitz is the inevitable outcome of enlightenment, and if instrumental rationality is too powerful to resist, then can we expect an individual Nazi to act in a different fashion? In the hermetic society the individual is a mere cipher, and if this is the case, can any individual really be blamed for his or her behavior? These questions highlight an ethical lacuna at the heart of *Dialectic of Enlightenment*. Despite the obvious intentions of the authors, their analysis generates a logic that renders them unable to differentiate meaningfully between different actions in the political realm. If "nothing complicitous with this world can have any truth," then surely everything that exists in the real world must be judged equally untrue or false. But if this is so, how are we to evaluate efforts at securing change in contemporary society?

Let us consider the ending of apartheid in South Africa. Although the citizens of that country cannot be adjudged to be free after the overthrow of the apartheid system, surely they are freer. Although the establishment of liberal democracy there offers no panacea, it is a better system than the totalitarian one that it has replaced. But although Adorno and Horkheimer as individuals would almost certainly have rejoiced in the downfall of the apartheid system, as theoreticians they seem to be unable to provide us with any grounds for favoring one particular set of social institutions over another. Here we have a bizarre inversion of the relativism to which contemporary poststructuralist approaches are prone. By arguing that there are no grounds to choose between different accounts of reality, poststructuralists are inevitably forced to accept that all accounts of a given reality are true.

They can make no judgment on these claims that is not arbitrary (Norris 1992; Hunter and Wyn Jones 1995). Similarly, by arguing that everything in the world is equally false, Adorno and Horkheimer can make no judgment as to why we might prefer some forms of behavior and some set of practices over others.

Here the impasse into which the analysis of *Dialectic of Enlightenment* leads its authors stands in bold relief. The determinism and reductionism of their argument is ultimately paralyzing. It was, of course, Antonio Gramsci who popularized the injunction that all those intent on changing society should attempt to face the world with a combination of "pessimism of the intellect" and "optimism of the will." This position has much to commend it given the propensity of radicals to view society with rose-tinted glasses. However, the limitations of this position are nowhere better illustrated than in *Dialectic of Enlightenment,* in which the pessimism is so thoroughgoing that it becomes absolutely debilitating. Any attempt to challenge the status quo already stands condemned as futile. The logical outcome of this attitude is resignation and passivity.

Adorno attempted to make a virtue of the detached attitude that he and Horkheimer adopted toward the political struggles of their own age by claiming: "If one is concerned to achieve what might be possible with human beings, it is extremely difficult to remain friendly towards real people." However, considering that it is only "real people" who can bring about a better society, Adorno's "complex form of misanthropy" ultimately leads only to quiescence (Wiggershaus 1994: 268). Thus, despite the clear similarities in the influences and interests of the founding fathers of critical theory and Gramsci, the resignatory passivity of the authors of *Dialectic of Enlightenment* led them to a position on political practice far more akin to that of Oswald Spengler or Arthur Schopenhauer than to that adopted by the Sardinian Marxist Gramsci, even as he languished in a fascist prison.

In view of the traditional Marxist emphasis on the unity of theory and practice, it is hardly surprising that Adorno and Horkheimer's rejection of any attempt to orient their work toward political activity led to bitter criticism from other radical intellectuals. Perhaps the most famous such condemnation was that of Lukács, who acidly commented that the members of the Frankfurt School had taken up residence in the "Grand Hotel Abyss." The inhabitants of this institution enjoyed all the comforts of the bourgeois lifestyle while fatalistically surveying the wreckage of life beyond its doors. Whereas Lukács's own apologias for Stalinism point to the dangers of subordinating theoretical activity to the exigencies of day-to-day practical politics, Adorno and Horkheimer sunder theory and political practice completely, impoverishing the theoretical activity itself. Their stance leads to an aridity and scholasticism ill suited to any social theory that aspires to real-world relevance.

Furthermore, the critical theorist's position on political practice is based on an underestimation of the potential for progressive change that exists even in the most administered societies. It is instructive to contrast the attitude of Adorno and Horkheimer with that of Raymond Williams, who delivers the following broadside against "high culture Marxists" such as the members of the Frankfurt School:

> When the Marxists say that we live in a dying culture, and that the masses are ignorant, I have to ask them . . . where on earth they have lived. A dying culture, and ignorant masses, are not what I have known and see. (R. Williams 1989: 8)

As I will discuss in Chapter 6, the evidence suggests that Williams is closer to the truth. People acting both individually and collectively, through social movements and state institutions, can actually influence the world around them in a progressive direction. Adorno and Horkheimer's pessimism is unwarranted.

One plausible explanation for the extraordinarily bleak worldview propounded in *Dialectic of Enlightenment* is extratheoretical. Given the historical context in which the work was written, its left-wing German Jewish authors were certainly more than entitled to adopt an apocalyptic view of contemporary society. Awareness of the particular historical context in which Adorno and Horkheimer were working is undoubtedly a key element in understanding the impasse in which critical theory found itself in the 1940s. However, it would be a mistake to view the deterministic pessimism of *Dialectic of Enlightenment* solely in terms of a legitimate reaction to the appalling brutality of the Holocaust, Stalinism, and World War II. This pessimism also reflects basic problems in the theoretical model on which critical theory is based. In other words, the impasse of *Dialectic of Enlightenment*—a work that, in effect, declares that a critical theory of society is impossible—not only is a reaction to Auschwitz but also reflects serious weakness in the intellectual basis of critical theory as set out in Horkheimer's "Traditional and Critical Theory."

PROBLEMS WITH
HORKHEIMER'S ORIGINAL FORMULATION

Several recent studies have focused on the weaknesses of Horkheimer's original formulation of critical theory and have argued that these weaknesses were enough to produce the subsequent theoretical impasse in the work of the Frankfurt School. Specifically, Axel Honneth criticizes the philosophy of history underlying Horkheimer's views of human action; Moishe Postone and Barbara Brick point to deficiencies in the political economy that underlies the work of the first generation of critical theorists; and Wolfgang Bonß emphasizes Horkheimer's underdeveloped understanding of the relationship between the two basic elements of critical theory—the specialized sciences (traditional theory) and the guiding framework of progressive social philosophy.

According to Honneth, Horkheimer's version of critical theory is blighted by the fact that it is "rooted in a philosophy of history that conceptually reduces the process of social development to . . . the domination of nature" (Honneth 1993: 187). Such a reduction gives rise in turn to an understanding of human social behavior that is far too narrow. Social behavior is regarded as being driven by the quest to dominate nature; it provides the impetus for human action. Furthermore, it is the process of human domination over nature that is perceived as harboring the potential for human emancipation, with "potential" being identified as the difference between the productive forces available to dominate nature and the prevailing relations of production that fail to utilize those forces fully and rationally.

Honneth charges that the notion that the perfection of scientific domination over nature is somehow best served via the institutions that radicals have historically associated with a rational society—planning, workers' control, and so on—is fallacious; there is no necessary connection between them. Indeed, Honneth argues that it is another form of human activity that provides the basis for the hope that emancipatory transformation of society is possible and hence for critical theory itself. This type of action is "a kind of activity that has not nature but 'society itself' as its object" (Honneth 1993: 195). It is "social struggle" or "critical activity" oriented toward changing society, not in order to improve the efficiency of human domination over nature, but in order to humanize that process.

Although Horkheimer's work clearly implies an understanding of human activity in this second sense, the philosophy of history on which his work is based cannot accommodate it theoretically. This has profound implications, for as Honneth argues: "This conceptual reductionism prevents Horkheimer from grasping the practical dimensions of social conflict and struggle as such" (Honneth 1993: 199).

The most striking result of this "sociological deficit" in Horkheimer's critical theory is that it leads him to locate the locus of critical, emancipatory potential in the wrong place. Horkheimer sees emancipation as arriving in the wake of scientific domination over nature. When this fails to occur—for example, in Auschwitz, where modern scientific techniques were utilized to commit mass murder—this leads him to despair at the very possibility of emancipation. Thus, according to this critique, Horkheimer's pessimism is a product of the particular philosophy of history on which his work is based and the resulting narrow conception of human activity that arises from it. Had he correctly recognized that critical activity is a different order of activity to the scientific-technical domination of nature, arising from a different set of social practices, the "pessimistic turn" might well have been avoided. Horkheimer might then have recognized the residual "resources of hope," to use Raymond Williams's phrase, that continued to exist despite the barbarity of the age.

Some of the critique advanced by Postone and Brick pursues themes similar to those developed by Honneth. The crux of their argument is that Horkheimer's pessimism was due to deficiencies in the understanding of political economy underlying his theory. Specifically, they argue that despite his Marxist leanings, Horkheimer adopted a concept of labor far narrower than the one posited by Marx himself. For Horkheimer, labor was identified with the domination of nature, whereas for Marx, labor mediated "the relations among people as well as between people and nature" (Postone and Brick 1993: 235). Crucially, Horkheimer goes on to locate the possibility of emancipation within this constrained understanding of labor: Emancipation is equated with increasing the efficiency of the labor process by bringing it under rational control and removing the contradictions in the relations of production that hinder the fullest utilization of the available means of production.

This understanding of emancipation is, of course, dependent on the existence of contradictions that require progressive change in social structures in order to be resolved. As I have already noted, without such contradictions, there can be no immanent critique and no possibility of emancipation. According to Postone and Brick, critical theory took its pessimistic turn when Horkheimer began to accept an argument made by Friedrich Pollock that there was no necessary contradiction between highly developed productive forces and totalitarian political structures. Pollock claimed that contrary to classic Marxist analysis, totalitarian societies had established the primacy of the political over the economic. He argued that under state capitalism, economic crises and contradictions could be ameliorated through state intervention without the need for major progressive reform (democratization and socialization) of the state's institutions.

By adopting the basic thrust of this analysis in his 1940 essay "The Authoritarian State," "Horkheimer now radically called into question any social uprising based on the development of the forces of production" (Postone and Brick 1993: 239). He began to view history as a process whereby the development of forces of production is accompanied by *increased* repression. According to Postone and Brick, Horkheimer "had fallen back to a position characterized by an antimony of necessity and freedom" where "freedom is grounded in a purely voluntarist fashion as an act of will against history" (Postone and Brick 1993: 239). Thus the possibility of a better world was not inherent or immanent within society but was an impossible demand that cut against the grain of history.

Postone and Brick argue that history has demonstrated the flawed nature of the political economic assumptions made by Pollock and subsequently used to underpin the analysis of *Dialectic of Enlightenment.*

> The most recent historical transformation of capitalism, which began in the early 1970s . . . can be viewed, in turn, as a sort of practical refutation of the thesis of the primacy of the political. It retrospectively shows that critical theorist's analysis of the earlier major transformation of capitalism was too linear and strongly suggests that the totality has indeed remained dialectical. (Postone and Brick 1993: 246)

As a result, Postone and Brick call for a rearticulation of critical theory on the basis of a political economy that is receptive to Marx's broader understanding of human labor and all its potentialities (see Postone 1993).

The focus of Wolfgang Bonß's critique is different. He highlights what he regards as serious deficiencies in the epistemological basis of Horkheimer's conception of critical theory as developed in "Traditional and Critical Theory." Horkheimer regarded critical theory as an interdisciplinary research project aimed at integrating research in the specialized disciplines of social science within a framework oriented by the work of progressive social theory. The aim of such an approach was twofold: to give traditional theory a more radical and critical direction and to ensure that radical metatheoretical reflection incorporated into itself the latest work in the empirical realm. Although Bonß is supportive of the intent behind this approach, he is critical of the way in which it was operationalized in the work of the Frankfurt School. He gives the following account of the division of labor between social theory (philosophy) and social science in the institute's work:

> [Social theory's] task is to transform the "big questions" into the standards of the individual disciplines and treat them comprehensively with the available methodological tools. Work in the individual sciences results in a transformation and securing of the universalizable concepts of social philosophy, which acquire a new form through their objectivation in the sciences and receive a deeper grounding. (Bonß 1993: 114–115)

The crucial point to note here is that despite the formidable criticisms leveled against traditional theory, the institute's own work accepted "the standards of the individual disciplines." Horkheimer therefore seems to ignore his own insight that the way these disciplines are configured in terms of their basic assumptions (their "standards") leads to reification and conformism. To suggest that the inherent structural deficiencies of traditional theory exposed in "Traditional and Critical Theory" can be overcome simply by placing the theoretical activity in another context is to ignore the ways in which disciplinary logics discipline those who work within them. Critical theory can only hope to be effective if it challenges "the standards of the individual disciplines"; if it accepts them, the critical theory project becomes epistemologically incoherent, as both of the parts that should form the whole—social theory and social science—must remain unintegrated and dialectical mediation between them impossible. Accordingly, Bonß delivers the following verdict:

> It becomes clear that the "capsizing" of interdisciplinary materialism . . . was neither accidental nor historically contingent. Given these weaknesses, the program—whose epistemological inconsistencies should be noted above all—could hardly have resolved the crisis of science, quite apart from the traumatic experiences of fascism and emigration. (Bonß 1993: 122)

Bonß goes on to argue that any contemporary attempt at critical theorizing must learn from this epistemological aporia that stands at the heart of the critical theory of Horkheimer (a point I will return to and develop in Chapter 5).

EMANCIPATORY POLITICS AFTER AUSCHWITZ

Working with Adorno, Horkheimer attempted to develop a theoretical account of the barbarity symbolized above all by Auschwitz. Whereas the critical theory of "Traditional and Critical Theory" was firmly Marxist in its outlook and assumptions, the position developed in subsequent years and set out most famously in *Dialectic of Enlightenment* broke away from these Marxist moorings. Although *Dialectic of Enlightenment* professes a loyalty to the ideals of the radical wing of the enlightenment tradition—that is, the ideals of the Marxists and socialists more generally—the book offers such a thorough critique of enlightenment that it is difficult to avoid the conclusion that Adorno and Horkheimer regarded those ideals (in any meaningful, social sense) as illusory.

The argument of *Dialectic of Enlightenment* is based on the claim that enlightenment is the process whereby humanity gains mastery over nature. This process is itself operationalized and articulated via instrumental rationality; the form of rationality concerned with technical control, manipulation, and domination—with means. Adorno and Horkheimer charge that the increased role that instrumental rationality plays as society develops leads to the atrophy of reason. Those forms of rationality concerned with the ends of human activity gradually become marginalized and redundant. The only forms of knowledge that are considered true knowledge are those that are quantified and calculable. In its ultimate expression of positivistic science, enlightened thought becomes solely concerned with charting or plotting repetition, and as concern with repetition is one of the motifs of the mythic, Adorno and Horkheimer claim that enlightenment reverts to myth.

The atrophy of reason that characterizes the deification of instrumental rationality has disastrous effects on the human subject. As reason atrophies, so does the moral consciousness of human beings. Instrumental rationality is incapable of justifying and defending moral behavior; its sole concern is the efficient achievement of given ends, be it developing water purification treatments or perfecting methods of mass slaughter. Thus the deadening and all-pervasive effects of instrumental rationality lead to the suppression of humanity's inner nature and of those qualities that are articulated in the ideals of radical enlightenment. The resulting damaged individuals, alienated both from themselves and from the rest of society, are easy prey to the irrational doctrines of fascism and Stalinism and the blandishments of the culture industry.

Thus the horrors of Auschwitz are seen by Adorno and Horkheimer as the result of humanity's attempts to dominate (outer) nature—a result of the very process of civilization itself. All of this is regarded in wholly deterministic terms, with no prospect for successful resistance and no real grounds for hoping that another way might be possible. Human agency ceases to exist in the world of *Dialectic of Enlightenment;* Auschwitz had demonstrated that emancipatory politics was an impossibility.

There is a bitter irony in all of this. Critical theory was intended to give a new, sophisticated voice to Marxist analysis, yet it found itself attacking the very intellectual tradition from which Marxism emerged—the enlightenment tradition—as the cause of the death camps of World War II. Critical theory aimed at a relationship with emancipatory political practice, yet it found itself in a position where all attempts at reforming society were dismissed as worse than futile. Critical theory aimed at rescuing the analysis of society from the aridity of traditional theory, yet it found itself arguing that all thought oriented toward society was irredeemably tainted and that the only thought that might retain any integrity was that oriented toward extrasocietal, extrahistorical remainders of the falsity of the real world. Critical theory aimed at developing an interdisciplinary research project, yet it was transformed into the most obstruse and rarefied form of philosophy. The promise of an epistemologically and methodologically advanced understanding of society, aimed at the transformation of its object, was wholly abandoned. The critical theorists saw themselves in terms reminiscent of a millennial religious cult—as a small group bearing witness to truth in a world where all around them had succumbed to falsity and evil. The difference, of course, is that whereas cultists expect to be rewarded for their steadfastness, Adorno and Horkheimer believed that redemption was an impossible dream.

The intractability of the theoretical impasse that Adorno and Horkheimer had constructed for themselves by writing *Dialectic of Enlightenment* is starkly demonstrated by their subsequent intellectual trajectories. Both returned to Frankfurt after the war, encouraged by energetic attempts by the U.S. occupation authorities to attract German émigrés back to reform the educational system and aid in the fostering of a liberal civic culture. There Horkheimer's professional career blossomed. He was appointed rector of Frankfurt University, becoming the first Jew to hold such a position at a German university, and was a prominent figure in academic life. But his intellectual contribution waned. As Habermas notes, "The late philosophy of Horkheimer is caught in a dilemma: *Dialectic of Enlightenment* cannot maintain the last word, but it blocks off the way back to the materialism of the 1930s" (Habermas 1993a: 73).

Horkheimer's response to this dilemma was twofold. First, he moved to distance himself from his early radicalism, which included actively seeking to bar his postwar students from gaining access to the *Zeitschrift für Sozialforschung* (Habermas 1980: 116). Second, in order to try to ensure that *Dialectic of Enlightenment* did not maintain the last word, Horkheimer turned to a version of theology. The appeal of theology was precisely that it does not depend on reason—the critique of *Dialectic of Enlightenment* having blocked an appeal to that quarter. Within this framework, Horkheimer attempted to develop a "philosophy of pity" relying purely on sentiment rather than any form of rationally based morality (Stirk 1992). However, this framework (which has interesting resonances with the work of Richard Rorty [1993]) remained fragmentary and undeveloped, and the elderly Horkheimer relapsed into a conventional, liberal veneration of bourgeois culture. Politically, this was accompanied by an uncritical attitude toward the Cold War. Horkheimer was generally sympathetic to the United States' intervention in Vietnam, and his attitude toward Chinese communism was, frankly, racist (Jay 1973: 353).

Inevitably, Horkheimer's high profile coupled with his apparent recantation of his radical past brought him into bitter conflict with the radicalized student body of the 1960s. Ernst Bloch spoke for many when he stated: "As far as Horkheimer is concerned, he became reactionary" (cited by Tar 1985: 206). Despite his own frosty relationship with Horkheimer, Habermas provides a somewhat rounder and more generous assessment, admitting to having "changed my opinion of Horkheimer after his death, when I read his diary entries" (Habermas 1980: 120). These revealed that Horkheimer lived in apprehension, even fear, following his return to Germany, continually searching for signs of a fascist revival: He never recovered from the historical tragedy in which he was embroiled.

Adorno's response to the impasse of critical theory was far more creative. One reason for this response was that *Dialectic of Enlightenment* did not represent the same break in his work as it did for Horkheimer. As Susan Buck-Morss (1977) points out, the main themes of the critique of instrumental reason had already been prefigured in Adorno's work—as well as the work of his close collaborator Benjamin—long before the publication of *Dialectic of Enlightenment.* Adorno's vision of the potential role of critical theory had always been more circumspect. Although—or perhaps because—Adorno had far more practical experience of work in the social sciences than Horkheimer, he always had less faith in their critical potential. For him, critical theory was always an essentially philosophical enterprise.

Another reason for Adorno's greater calm in the face of the impasse of *Dialectic of Enlightenment* was that his aesthetic theory allowed him an escape route not open to his coauthor. Adorno argued that "art may be the only remaining medium of truth in an age of incomprehensible terror and suffering" (cited by Bronner 1994: 190) and that the task of critical theory was to recover the truth sedimented in the aesthetic realm.

According to Adorno's aesthetic theory, the erosion of human subjectivity by instrumental rationality meant that this truth was not present in the content of art: Adorno regarded the intentions of the artist as essentially irrelevant (Wellmer 1983; Habermas 1984; Jameson 1990; Bronner 1994; Wyn Jones 1996a; the fullest exposition is in Zuidervaart 1991). Rather, truth—traces of that emancipatory moment that have been wholly expunged from society—could be found in the *form* of those types of art that escape, to some extent, the grip of the culture industry, namely, the avant-garde. These traces can be found in the tension between the different elements of an artwork. When viewed by observers who possess the necessary technical knowledge and who are cognizant of the work's artistic and societal contexts, this tension generates what may be termed a "tremor." This tremor serves as a reminder that an alternative might exist to the uniform barbarity generated by instrumental rationality; it exposes the fact that truth and freedom have been lost from the world.

Whatever the intrinsic interest of this approach and of the insights it generates in the aesthetic realm, it has little or no relevance politically. The only attitude it sanctions toward the social realm is one of pure negativity; the only attitude it sanctions toward political practice is a refusal to participate. Thus, socially and politically, the impasse remains. Adorno's later work can offer no assistance to the task of lending intellectual support to the practical struggle for emancipation. For him, even to dream that this might be possible was to succumb to a dangerous delusion.

3

Redemption: Renewing the Critical Project

The transformation in the attitudes of the first generation of critical theorists between the period of "Traditional and Critical Theory" and the aftermath of *Dialectic of Enlightenment* is perhaps nowhere better illustrated than in Horkheimer's address at the official opening of the new IfS building in Frankfurt in 1951 (the best account of the return of Adorno, Horkheimer, and Pollock to the Federal Republic is in Wiggershaus 1994). In his speech, Horkheimer "expressed the basic intention of Critical Theory in a way that transformed social change into a kind of ethical requirement for sociologists, like the Hippocratic Oath for doctors" (Wiggershaus 1994: 445). While continuing to contend that an intellectual orientation toward social change was necessary to allow research questions to be framed in the correct way, Horkheimer apparently now believed that this orientation involved no real-world political implications or commitments. So even if the need, even necessity, for social transformation was still admitted, such rhetoric was devoid of substance: It was formulaic and depoliticized. For the first generation of critical theorists, social change became a mantra in the literal sense, an instrument of thought that had little or no relevance to real political and social struggles. Thus Wiggershaus correctly characterizes the IfS in the postwar Federal Republic as a "Critical Ornament of a Restoration Society" (Wiggershaus 1994: 431). While the members of the Frankfurt School may have remained intellectually unreconciled with liberal capitalist society, they certainly provided no threat to it.

However, as if to confirm the persistence of the creative, rather than merely negative, potential of the dialectic, a new generation of critical theorists gradually emerged who were not content to remain bound by the contradictions and elisions within which the founding fathers had become entangled. This second generation was determined to rescue the critical project from what Goran Therborn has described as the "paralysed virtuosity" of its post–*Dialectic of Enlightenment* incarnation, and in particular from its political passivity (Therborn 1970: 96). Although part of the stimulus for their work was undoubtedly intratheoretical in nature—that is, aimed at addressing the aporias in the Horkheimer-Adorno legacy—there can be little doubt that it was real-world, extratheoretical developments that provided the driving force.

The global upsurge of radical student activism in the 1960s had a particularly profound impact in West Germany, a society that was in many ways deeply conformist and conservative. While this conservatism was undoubtedly reinforced by the ways in which the Federal Republic remained, de facto if not de jure, an occupied country whose very existence was defined by World War II and the subsequent Cold War, its root cause lay in the unmastered nature of Germany's recent past. In a society in which so many had acquiesced to, or actively supported, Nazi inhumanity, becoming "Hitler's willing executioners," pressure to conform to the postwar status quo was overwhelming. Nowhere was this more apparent than in academia, a sector that the Nazis had placed under strict party control and where many faculty members had benefited directly from the persecution of their Jewish and leftist colleagues. It is striking that Horkheimer and Adorno were among the very few academics hounded from their posts by the Nazis who managed to rebuild their careers successfully in the postwar Federal Republic, and even they were subject to a significant amount of resistance and resentment by their academic colleagues. In these circumstances, it is not surprising that the struggle between radical German students and the educational authorities was particularly acute and bitter.

The radicalization of the student body—a gradual process extending over a decade or more before the tumultuous events of 1968—created deep divisions within the institute. The old guard was hostile. As noted in Chapter 2, Adorno and Horkheimer regarded the idea that any group within society had the potential to initiate and inspire a genuinely emancipatory politics as a dangerous delusion. Their unease with the radical German student movement was compounded by the way that many of its leading figures cited the influence of the early work of the IfS and by the fact that Marcuse was a vocal supporter of their activities. Horkheimer was particularly disturbed. Not only was this pillar of establishment respectability embarrassed by the use of some of his more extreme Marxist formulations as student slogans—"He who wishes to speak of fascism cannot remain silent on the question of capitalism"—but he also appears to have been genuinely fearful that the students would provoke a reactionary backlash that could once again engulf Germany's fragile liberal polity.

Adorno was marginally more sympathetic to the students, yet even he was to declaim despairingly: "When I made my theoretical model, I could not have guessed that people would want to realize it with Molotov cocktails" (Jay 1984: 55). This type of comment may well be considered disingenuous to the extent that the Frankfurt School's apparently undifferentiated *theoretical* analysis of contemporary society—which can be summarized by adapting the well-known Third International slogan as "Soviet Marxism = Liberal Democracy = Fascism"—encouraged some of the most extreme manifestations of student radicalism. However, it does underline the extent of the distance between the old guard of critical theory and the would-be critical practitioners of the student movement.

There was no such distancing by the younger theorists who had studied with Horkheimer and Adorno after their return to Germany. Figures such as Albrecht Wellmer, Oskar Negt, and, most notably of all, Jürgen Habermas were prominent in their support for the general tenor of the students' demands, if not for every specific element of their program or practice (Wiggershaus 1994: 609–636). Horkheimer in particular attempted to discourage them—to the extent that he effectively drove Habermas out of the institute—but the members of this younger generation of critical theorists were not to be dissuaded. For them, the upsurge in radicalism was confirmation that emancipatory change remained more than simply an instrument of thought; it was an actually-existing potential that might be realized. The new radicalism was also a challenge to their thinking. How could their type of critical intellectual endeavor link up with progressive political practice? Could they actually provide the vision of a more emancipated society demanded by the students? What were the deep-seated sources of emancipatory impulse or instincts that had managed to defy the tyranny of instrumental reason and reemerge so dramatically? If the analysis of *Dialectic of Enlightenment* was too "one-dimensional," then what was the correct understanding of contemporary society?

In their attempt to address questions of this nature, the second generation of critical theorists gave new impetus to the critical theory project. In this chapter I will examine some of their arguments related to the theoretical issues that have been raised in the previous chapters. I want to emphasize, however, that the approach adopted is neither systematic nor comprehensive. The proliferation of work by second generation critical theorists, and indeed a subsequent generation of scholars, is so great that to attempt to produce an all-embracing survey would go well beyond the bounds of this study. Critical theory is now a truly international enterprise with "branches" or "outposts," to use IfS terminology, in most developed countries (on critical theory in Germany see Hohendahl 1991; on the United States see Kellner 1989: 176–223).

Furthermore, as I have demonstrated in the first two chapters, the legacy with which they have been working is hardly unified. Thus some scholars, such as Hauke Brunkhorst, Susan Buck-Morss, Oskar Negt, and Alexander Kluge, have attempted to develop themes in Adorno's work; others, often influenced by Marcuse and including Stephen Bronner and

Douglas Kellner, have attempted to reengage with the "Traditional and Critical Theory" version of critical theory; and the work of Habermas has generated a minor industry of its own. Inevitably this means that those theorists who see themselves as inheritors of the critical theory tradition have widely different understandings of the nature of the intellectual project in which they are engaged.

Rather than attempt the major task of theoretical taxonomy involved in identifying and explaining every contemporary variant of contemporary critical theory, I will adopt a different, more thematic approach. I will focus on how the central themes discussed in the previous chapters have been addressed by some of those thinkers whose work has figured prominently in efforts to renew critical theory. By focusing the discussion on theory, emancipation, and technology, I will not only illuminate some of the main routes through which critical theorists have sought to avoid the impasse represented by *Dialectic of Enlightenment* but also continue in the task of laying the groundwork for the discussion of security and strategy in Part 2.

THEORY: GROUNDING THE POSSIBILITY OF EMANCIPATION

Emancipation is arguably the one common concern of all critical theorists. It is the sine qua non of their thought. Indeed, Bronner, in the light of the fractured nature and varied concerns of contemporary critical theory, argues that the only plausible definition of this school of thought is "a *cluster of themes* inspired by an emancipatory intent" (Bronner 1994: 3, emphasis in original). Thus critical theory stands or falls by the possibility that emancipatory potential exists. Epistemologically, it is only this possibility that gives critical theory coherence and, indeed, purpose. Without it, critical theory cannot demur from the positivist/traditional theory emphasis on repetition, calculability, and predictability. Even Adorno, despite his utter pessimism concerning the real world, depended on the mimetic capacity of avant-garde art to express the possibility of the "totally other"—a more emancipated world—to give his theory critical purchase on that reality. This is also why, it might be added parenthetically, so many poststructuralist-inspired writers continually imply notions of emancipation despite their much-vaunted distaste for such metanarratives. Without the ability to claim that a better world is possible or even conceivable, there is no means by which the present can be criticized.

That said, the problem for critical theorists is to identify the locus of this promise of a better world—the site of emancipatory potential. The version of critical theory outlined in "Traditional and Critical Theory" located the possibility of emancipation in the realm of production. Specifically, it identified emancipation as the domination of nature within the context of a planned society in which the means of production were socialized. But as I discussed in Chapter 2, Horkheimer came to realize that the socialization of production (through state control, planning, etc.) had no necessary progressive consequences. Indeed, in conjunction with Adorno, he came to identify the process whereby humanity has gained instrumental mastery over nature with domination. In response, Horkheimer came to locate the source of emancipatory impulses in what he argued was an anthropologically based propensity for pity and human solidarity. Adorno, for his part, pointed to the "non-identical"—that which is beyond communication and which may only be grasped through art mediated by philosophy—as the site in which echoes of the possibility of emancipation might be located. None of these arguments on the "grounding"[1] of critical theory have satisfied most of its contemporary adherents. In this section I will elucidate and evaluate two of the main attempts that have been made to provide critical theory with a more secure basis, those of Habermas and Honneth.

Habermas on Communication

By locating the potential for emancipation in the sphere of production, the founding fathers of critical theory were adopting an understanding of emancipatory possibility entirely in accordance with—indeed, derivative of—that which featured in the classical version of Marxism (Postone 1993 disputes whether this in fact coincided with Marx's own views). Thus, when the impasse generated by *Dialectic of Enlightenment* led Jürgen Habermas to reassess the critical theory conception of emancipation, this also involved recasting the very Marxist legacy on which that tradition rests. Crucially, Habermas's "reconstruction of historical materialism"—the title of his 1976 book—is based on a move to distinguish between production, work, and labor on the one hand and interaction and communication on the other (for useful commentaries, see Honneth 1982, 1994; Outhwaite 1994). Habermas argues that these realms of social activity are characterized by two distinct types of human behavior: The realm of work or production is characterized by instrumental action and the realm of interaction is characterized by communicative action. He further charges that Marxism tends to reduce communicative action—activity oriented toward the generation of mutual understanding—to instrumental action, "the productive activity which regulates the material interchange of the human species with its natural environment" (Habermas 1986b: 169). This reduction becomes all too apparent in the tendency of Marxists, including the Horkheimer of "Traditional and Critical Theory," to equate progress in terms of the efficient utilization of the forces of production with general progress in human relations, that is, emancipation. According to Habermas:

> To set free the technical forces of production . . . is not identical with the
> development of norms which could fulfil the dialectic of moral relation-
> ships in an interaction free of domination. . . . *Liberation from hunger and
> misery* does not necessarily converge with *liberation from servitude and
> degradation;* for there is no automatic developmental relation between
> labour and interaction. (Habermas 1986b: 169)

This realization spurred Habermas to investigate the basis of emancipation
within the realm of interaction, a project that ultimately bore fruit in the
publication of the two-volume study *The Theory of Communicative Action*
(1984, 1987) and in his subsequent work.

Habermas's analysis of communicative action is enormous in both its
sheer volume and its scope (the best critical overview of his work is
Outhwaite 1994; also useful is White 1988). It is also still very much a
work in progress. Habermas is continually revising his ideas, in part as a
response to the massive critical scrutiny afforded to his every utterance and
also as a result of his own attempt to extend his analysis into new areas—
most recently, for example, law (Habermas 1996). Although this great output serves to underline his status as *the* towering figure in contemporary
social theory, it also makes his work almost impossible to summarize in a
form that respects both its subtlety and its breadth. Nevertheless, two
moments in his work are particularly relevant to this discussion. The first
relates to Habermas's notion of universal pragmatics and the claim that
truth is inherent in language, and the second relates to the analysis of society that he then develops as a result of this conception of language.

Habermas's basic claim concerning communication, and indeed his
basic argument concerning the locus of emancipatory promise, is summarized in his *Knowledge and Human Interests:*

> The human interest in autonomy and responsibility is not mere fancy, for
> it can be apprehended a priori. What raises us out of nature is the only
> thing whose nature we can know: language. Through its structure, autono-
> my and responsibility are posited for us. Our first sentence expresses
> unequivocally the intention of a universal and unconstrained consensus.
> (Habermas 1986b: 314)

Although Habermas's subsequent writing has largely superseded the
work from which this quotation is taken, he has still maintained this basic
line of argument. In *The Theory of Communicative Action,* for example, he
proclaims that "reaching understanding is the inherent telos of human
speech" (Habermas 1984: 287). Although this is certainly subtly different
from the previous position—note how "consensus" has become "understanding"—the broad claim is the same. Habermas argues that there is
something inherent in speech that acts, in effect, as a promissory note for

the possibility of a better world. The nature of this "something" is delineated via his universal pragmatics.

"Universal pragmatics" is the name given by Habermas to his attempt to "identify and reconstruct the universal conditions of possible understanding" (Habermas 1979: 1).[2] He argues that speech actions—note that here he reduces consideration of communication to the analysis of speech—necessarily involve a series of presuppositions if they are to be valid (Habermas 1979: 1–68). Specifically, four "validity-claims" are isolated by Habermas: If a speech act is to be valid, this presupposes that the utterance is meaningful, true, justified, and sincere. Given the complexity of Habermas's arguments in this regard, Anthony Giddens provides a welcome, succinct summary of their main thrust:

> When one person says something to another, that person implicitly (sometimes explicitly) makes the following claims: (1) That what is said is intelligible—that is to say, that it obeys certain syntactical and semantic rules so that there is a "meaning" which can be understood by the other. (2) That the propositional content of whatever is said is true. The "propositional content" refers to the factual assertions which the speaker makes as part of what he or she says. (3) That the speaker is justified in saying whatever is said. In other words, certain social rights or "norms" are invoked in the use of speech in any given context of language-use. (4) That the speaker is sincere in whatever is said—that he or she does not intend to deceive the listener. (Giddens 1990: 128)

These validity-claims are presupposed in *all* speech acts—lying, for example, depends on these presuppositions.

The implications of this argument, if correct, are far reaching. If everyday linguistic and communicative activity does indeed depend on "intersubjectively criticizable validity claims," then, inter alia, language use depends on the existence of an intramundane form of rationality (i.e., existing immanently in actually existing social practices) (Cooke 1994: xii). The existence of this communicative rationality allows Habermas's thought to steer between the Scylla of poststructuralist skepticism concerning reason and the Charybdis of positivism's constriction of the realm of rationality to a calculus of means.

Against poststructuralist arguments that reason is merely the cloak to an instrumental will to power (to employ a Nietzschean trope with obvious echoes in the work of Adorno), Habermas can point to what Maeve Cooke terms a "nonrepressive conception of reason—that is, a conception that provides standards for the critique of irrational or unjust forms of individual and social life while avoiding possibly repressive metaphysical projections" (Cooke 1994: ix). The standard of critique is provided by the fact that the possibility of unforced understanding is inherent in speech—

indeed, speech depends upon it. (As Bronner explains, "Everyday speech, even of the most distorted sort, [must] both anticipate and presuppose an undistorted form of communication" [Bronner 1994: 293].) Thus any structures or practices that hinder this process of mutual understanding are open to criticism and revision. Note that such a critique is procedural in focus rather than concerned with advocating a particular end point—thus eluding the postmodern criticism that Marxist-inspired social theory attempts to impose a metanarrative on its subjects (Lyotard 1986: xxiv; Hunter and Wyn Jones 1995).

Although positivism is not hostile to notions of rationality per se, it does confine its scope to the instrumental realm—to questions of means (see Horkheimer's critique of traditional theory outlined in Chapter 1). Ends are treated as normative questions that are not susceptible to rational arbitration. But of course, the presuppositions of speech as reconstructed by Habermas and as sketched above themselves contain normative elements. Normative elements form part of the rational core of speech. Thus communicative rationality splits asunder positivist attempts to constrict the bounds of rationality.

Communicative rationality also provides critical theorists with the assurance that the possibility of a better world—specifically, a world of unconstrained communication leading to unforced understanding—is already immanent within the present. Speech is the locus of the emancipatory promise. But what are the processes within society that hinder this type of communicative action? By which practices could the already-existing progressive potential of speech be realized? And what are the prospects for such a realization?

Habermas's answers to these questions are developed in the sociological analysis of *Theory of Communicative Action,* as well as in his subsequent work. His basic argument is that developmental processes in Western societies increasingly threaten the human capacity for intersubjectively achieved understanding. This judgment arises from Habermas's basic conceptual model of the evolution of modern society. This model is based on a distinction between *system* and *lifeworld*. These refer, respectively, to the material and cultural domains of society (or "base" and "superstructure" in Marxist terminology). The system is the realm of the market and state bureaucracy: structures that articulate themselves via money and power—what Habermas characterizes as the system's "steering media." The lifeworld is defined negatively by Habermas as "the totality of action domains which cannot be bent to conform to a description of media-steered sub-systems" (Honneth and Joas 1991: 257). More positively, lifeworld refers to the interrelated realms of society, culture, and subjectivity. Or in Habermas's own words, "Processes of cultural reproduction, social integration and socialization are the structural components of the lifeworld"—

thus, the lifeworld is a "culturally transmitted and linguistically organized stock of interpretive patterns" through which individuals orient themselves (Habermas 1987: 124). Further, and crucially, it is the realm of communicative action and intersubjectively achieved mutual understanding.

According to Habermas's analysis, society is facing a pathological development whereby the system is increasingly colonizing the lifeworld. Honneth summarizes his argument as follows:

> Habermas's theory of society leads to a diagnosis of the times according to which the power of self-steering systems has grown to such an extent that they threaten the communicative achievements of the lifeworld: under the corrosive force with which the steering media of money and bureaucratic power currently invade everyday culture, the human potential for reaching understanding in language is dissolving. (Honneth 1994: 259)

This analysis leads Habermas to advocate a politics of resistance to the colonization of the lifeworld, a politics that is, of course, ultimately concerned with defending the conditions for intersubjective understanding. In a passage in the second volume of *The Theory of Communicative Action*, which, significantly, immediately precedes his attempt to rearticulate critical theory in the light of his general analysis of society, Habermas writes:

> The point is to protect areas of life that are functionally dependent on social integration through values, norms, and consensus formation, to preserve them from falling prey to the systemic imperatives of economic and administrative subsystems growing with dynamics of their own, and defend them from becoming converted over, through the steering medium of law, to a principle of the law, to a principle of sociation that is, for them, dysfunctional. (Habermas 1987: 372–373)

Furthermore, Habermas wishes to control the steering media themselves by subjecting the technocratic cultures that surround them to public scrutiny and control—in other words, by rendering them susceptible to communicative processes of intersubjective understanding.

As even this rather crude summary indicates, Habermas's work is quite dazzling in its eclecticism and ambition. Through his "communicative turn" Habermas provides what at first sight appears to be a coherent and plausible account of the intramundane locus of emancipatory promise. Furthermore, he claims to identify the tendencies within modern society that stifle the achievements of humanity's rational potential. Habermas would certainly claim that he has provided a new paradigm in which critical theory can transcend some of the limitations highlighted in *Dialectic of Enlightenment*. Although this is hotly disputed by those who remain more enamored of Adorno's work than they are of that of his former student (e.g., Bernstein 1994), many critical theorists have accepted the broad thrust of

Habermas's work and contented themselves with developing—or disputing—particular aspects of it.

A number of important points have emerged from the massive literature stimulated by Habermas's work (see, in particular, Thompson and Held 1982; Honneth and Joas 1991; Benhabib and Passerin d'Entrèves 1996). Some are of particular relevance to the central theme of this section.

A major reservation is that doubt has been cast on the ability of Habermas's theory of communicative action to bear the normative weight that he wishes to rest upon it. Bronner provides the following commentary, which, although it is rather brutal in its disregard for the myriad qualifications and categorical subtleties that Habermas builds into his work, nevertheless summarizes these concerns:

> "Communication" lies at the root of the undertaking. It is seen as presupposing an unrestrained discourse, the willingness of each to place himself or herself in the position of the other, the discipline to engage in a rational justification of claims, and a willingness to bracket self-interest so that the "better argument" can win out. Concretely, however, every discourse is necessarily "constrained" both in terms of the agenda and those participating in the discussion. Also, if each is able to put himself or herself in the place of the other, then . . . there will remain very little to discuss. Finally, even if participants are sometimes willing to engage in a rational justification of claims, history suggests that there is no reason whatsoever why the "better argument" should intrinsically prove victorious without extra-discursive activities being brought into play. (Bronner 1994: 305)

So even if there are, as Habermas claims, normative elements inherent in the presuppositions of speech, the question remains: How important is this?

Further doubt has been cast on the basic categories upon which Habermas has constructed his theory of society. In particular, the differentiation between work and interaction and the identification of the former with instrumental action and the latter with communicative action seem to set up a series of unnecessarily antinomic dualisms. How useful is it to imply that instrumental and communicative activity are somehow governed by separate logics and practices? After all, "just as every moral norm can be employed for strategic purposes . . . so are political and economic activities often inspired by morality and ideology" (Bronner 1994: 304). Is it not better to recognize and reflect on the fact that discourse oriented toward success (characteristic of work) and discourse oriented toward understanding (characteristic of interaction) are invariably mutually implicated rather than distinct?

Such mutual implication underlines the problematic implications of Habermas's tendency simply to ignore work—the sphere of production and labor—and concentrate his theoretical attention solely on interaction. One need not make grandiose claims about the dignity of labor to recognize that the realm of work cannot simply be reduced to simple relations of instrumentality; one need not be an economic reductionist to accept that people's positions in the realm of production have major implications for their role and status within society; and one need not posit that the proletariat is a universal class uniquely placed to emancipate humanity to argue that emancipatory politics can be generated through people's experiences in the realm of work.

Interaction does not occur in a vacuum; rather, it occurs in a context that is at least partly structured by people's economic activities—indeed by their relationship with nature. Thus to refuse to engage seriously with economic relationships—as if these relationships do not also embody social, political, moral, and even aesthetic elements—is to constrain the critical edge of critical theory. Even in terms of Habermas's own theory, it is clear that inequalities inherent in the structures of economic accumulation have major distorting effects on the pursual of mutual understanding. Simply to decry those effects without attempting to expose their causes or search for remedies—effectively Habermas's position—seems to cast doubt on the whole theoretical enterprise. This is all the more so because Habermas himself, in standard Marxist fashion, is candid in his recognition of the primacy of productive relationships (Habermas 1994: 117).

Further baneful effects of dubious categorical distinctions are also evident if we consider the separation of system and lifeworld, which has underlain so much of Habermas's theory of society since the early 1980s.

Bronner charges that lifeworld is ultimately "little more than a vague anthropological postulate for the understanding of the non-institutional features of everyday life" (Bronner 1994: 304). As a result, neither lifeworld nor its antonym, system, is "ontologically grounded nor historically articulated" (Bronner 1994: 305). This in turn leads to an overly abstract and ahistorical theory of society that is unable to account for—or intervene in—*particular* forms of life or social struggle. Nowhere is this more apparent than in a consideration of the adequacy of Habermas's theoretical framework to what has historically been the central problematic of international relations, interstate relations. Writing in 1983, John B. Thompson noted:

> It is striking . . . that a "society" or a nation-state remains the *pierre de touche* of Habermas's account. Nowhere does he examine in detail the international system of nation-states, the multi-national alliances which greatly affect economic development and threaten one another's survival with the accumulated means of waging war. It is at best incomplete to interpret the conflicts and protest movements of our societies from within a framework that filters out the confrontation of nation-states and the politics of mass destruction. (J. Thompson 1983: 293)

Although some of Habermas's recent works, such as the 1994 volume *The Past as Future,* pay more attention to interstate relations, his comments in these works do not seem to relate to—or arise from—his theory of society. They reflect a general left-liberal sensibility rather than any specific or conscious attempt to apply a critical theory perspective to interstate relations (see, for example, Habermas 1994: 76–83). This should come as no surprise given that key concepts such as lifeworld and system do not seem to provide Habermas with any useful opening onto this realm.

Craig Calhoun broadens this line of criticism when he argues that Habermas's theory of communicative action is so abstract as to render it unable to account for particular sociocultural identities (Calhoun 1995: 193–230). Such is Habermas's concern with the general and universal that he fails to give sufficient or due weight to the specific identity contexts in which communicative action takes place. This unease is given more concrete form in the work of perhaps the most creative of the latest generation of German critical theorists, Axel Honneth.

Honneth on Recognition

Although Honneth certainly concurs with the broad thrust of Habermas's communicative turn—the attempt to locate emancipatory potential and politics in the realm of interaction rather than work—he disagrees with Habermas's emphasis on language. Honneth's worry is that in understanding communication solely in terms of speech (viewed generically and abstractly), Habermas fails to meet what Honneth regards as "an unrenounceable premise" of the "Frankfurt tradition of social theory" (Honneth 1994: 255). According to Honneth, "Critical theory in its innermost core—whatever its congruence with other forms of social critique may be—is dependent upon the quasi-sociological specification of an emancipatory interest in social reality itself" (Honneth 1994: 256). That is, contemporary critical theory must be able to identify "empirical experiences and attitudes which indicate, already pretheoretically, that its normative standpoints" have a "basis in social reality" (Honneth 1994: 260). But Honneth is unconvinced that Habermas's emphasis on speech and his diagnosis of the ills of modern society in terms of the denial of the immanent possibility for unforced mutual understanding actually grasp those real-world pretheoretical experiences that generate emancipatory impulses.

Furthermore, Honneth argues that Habermas's tendency to understand pathological tendencies within society by reference to the levels of development of human rationality means that he has no analytical handle on problems that do not fit into this framework. For example, Honneth notes that the breakdown of community—a concern of many political theorists and activists—"is only indirectly related to changes in human rationality" (Honneth 1994: 264–265). As a result, Habermas cannot give a convincing account of why this breakdown might be occurring nor, indeed, why it is important.

Honneth's response to the problems he claims to have identified in Habermas's work is to attempt to reconstruct the communicative turn in a way that satisfies the basic premise that critical theory must be able to ground its critique in real-world experience. He asserts that

> the emancipatory process in which Habermas socially anchors the normative perspective of his Critical Theory is not at all reflected as such in an emancipatory process in the moral experiences of the subjects involved; for they experience an impairment of what we can call their moral experiences, that is, their "moral point of view", not as a restriction of intuitively mastered rules of language, but as violation of identity claims acquired in socialization. (Honneth 1994: 261)

He states more concretely:

> Normative presuppositions of social interaction cannot be fully grasped if they are defined solely in terms of the linguistic conditions of reaching an understanding free from domination; rather what must be considered above all is the fact that the assumption of social recognition is precisely what subjects associate with normative expectations when entering communicative relationships. (Honneth 1994: 263)

Honneth's contention is that human beings have "intuitive notions of justice" premised on respect for their "dignity, honour, or integrity" and that they "encounter each other within the parameters of the reciprocal expectation that they receive recognition as moral persons and for their social achievements" (Honneth 1994: 262). When these expectations are not met this has serious consequences:

> Because the experience of social recognition presents a condition on which the development of the identity of human beings depends, its denial, that is, disrespect, is necessarily accompanied by the sense of a threatening loss of personality . . . [and resulting] shame, anger, or indignation. (Honneth 1994: 263)

By shifting the communicative paradigm from a theory of language ("linguistic-theoretic") to a theory of recognition ("intersubjectivity-theoretic"), Honneth argues that he can demonstrate which intramundane experiences generate emancipatory political action, thereby—he believes—providing a more convincing underpinning for the critical theory project itself:

> Those feelings of injustice which accompany structural forms of disre-
> spect represent a pretheoretical fact on the basis of which a critique of the
> relations of recognition can identify its own theoretical perspective in
> social reality. (Honneth 1994: 263)

The sociological presumption of recognition of identity becomes, for
Honneth, the locus of emancipatory promise and potential.

The logic of Honneth's argument concerning the grounding of critical
theory leads him to develop an alternative analysis of society to the one
proffered by Habermas. In place of the latter's emphasis on the system/life-
world relationship and the structural distortions of the possibility of
unforced mutual understanding, Honneth focuses on "the societal causes
responsible for the systematic violation of the conditions of recognition"
(Honneth 1994: 264). He argues that the task of critical theory becomes the
unmasking of those structures and practices within society that "are constituted such that they do not provide the amount of recognition necessary . . .
in forming an identity" (Honneth 1994: 265). In particular, Honneth concentrates on the

> three forms of social recognition which can be regarded as the commu-
> nicative presuppositions of a successful formation of identity: emotional
> concern in an intimate social relationship such as love or friendship,
> rights-based recognition as a morally accountable member of society, and,
> finally, the social esteem of individual achievements and abilities.
> (Honneth 1994: 265–266)

One interesting consequence of this attempt to refigure the communicative paradigm toward relations of recognition is that it returns the experience of human labor to a position of prominence in critical theory because
economic activity is central to human social relations and moral experiences (Honneth 1994: 266–268).

Honneth's attempt to reintegrate labor into critical theory is only one of
several positive elements of his theoretical framework. Another important
advantage that arises from his intersubjectivity-theoretic version of the
communicative turn is that it provides critical theorists with the analytical
tools to understand how apparently particularistic struggles for the recognition of localized identities can form part of a broader process of emancipation. Of course, Honneth is aware that "the struggle for recognition"—the
title of his 1995 book—is "an extremely ambivalent source of motivation
for social protest and resistance" (Honneth 1994: 268). It can give rise not
only to the pacifistic internationalism that, for example, overwhelmingly
characterizes Welsh nationalism (Wyn Jones 1995, 1996b) but also, as
Honneth himself points out, to the neo-Nazi groups that have developed in
Germany. Thus a crucial question that critical theorists must address is

how a moral culture could be so constituted as to give those affected, dis-
respected and ostracized, the individual strength to articulate their experiences in the democratic public sphere, rather than living them out in the
countercultures of violence. (Honneth 1994: 269)

The importance of this question need hardly be underlined in a world con-
vulsed by barbaric manifestations of identity politics, such as ethnic cleans-
ing. Honneth's theoretical model certainly provides an innovative means by
which it might be framed.

Honneth's work is not without its problematic aspects, however. Peter
Osborne, for example, provides a short but devastating critique of the particular analysis of contemporary society developed in *The Struggle for
Recognition* (1996). Because the focus of this section is the grounding of
critical theory rather than the detailed analysis of particular versions of a
critical theory of society, neither Honneth's argument nor Osborne's critique need be pursued. It will suffice to introduce two arguments that have
important implications for the application of Honneth's work to the discussion of security.

First, although Honneth aims to uncover and analyze the *struggle* for
recognition, his argument seems to be based on the assumption of an essential harmony between the identity claims of individual subjects. That is, his
argument is premised on the notion that the full development of an individual's identity can take place without impinging upon the identity of another.
But is this really the case? For example, the Bosniac national identity,
based as it is on a multiethnic, multiconfessional civic nationalism, must
surely conflict with the exclusive ethnic nationalism of many Bosnian
Croats and Bosnian Serbs. These identities are fundamentally incompatible.
In this case at least, the successful development of identity for one group
can take place only at the expense of another, thus calling into question
Honneth's presumption of an essential—or at least potential—harmony
between identity claims.

Second, it is not clear that Honneth is sufficiently cognizant of the
extent to which interests and identities are entwined and, indeed, the extent
to which the latter are often an expression of the former. Bill McSweeney
focuses on this relationship in his discussion of the so-called troubles in
Northern Ireland. Discussing the seemingly intractable conflict between
unionists and nationalists, Protestants and Catholics, he writes:

In each case, the roots of identity can be traced to the pursuit of interests
and to the dominance of particular interests over some others which might
have defined the group identity differently. In each case also, the identities
which emerged from these struggles gradually acquired a primordial character which entered interactively into the definition of interests, inhibiting
any attempt to expose their human fabrication and to separate the instru-

mental interests at stake at any time from the symbolic meaning which they sustained. (McSweeney 1996a: 174)

Among the implications of this is that the struggle for recognition is in many if not all cases also a struggle between different material interests. Therefore, to conceive such conflicts solely in terms of (narrowly understood) identity is to ignore some of the most basic sources and dynamics of tension and contention.

Because Honneth's project is still in its formative stages, it is too early to judge whether his arguments concerning the grounding of critical theory will prove to be a substantial improvement over those developed by Habermas. There are certainly lacunae at the heart of his project of which Honneth himself is well aware. For example, he has not demonstrated, even to his own satisfaction, that "the expectation of social recognition belongs to the structure of communicative action" (Honneth 1994: 263), or, in other words, that his ideas on recognition are part of the communicative turn in critical theory initiated by Habermas.

The question arises whether we should be concerned by the inability of critical theorists to provide a fully satisfactory account of the intramundane basis for the belief that emancipatory transformation is possible. Honneth himself believes that demonstrating the grounding of the emancipatory promise of critical theory is absolutely vital:

> Without proof—however this may be provided—that the critical perspective is supported by a need or a movement within social reality, Critical Theory cannot be continued in any way today; for it no longer distinguishes itself from other models of social critique by claiming a superior sociological explanatory substance or in its philosophical procedures of justification, but solely by its attempt (which still has not been abandoned) to give the standards of critique an objective foothold in pretheoretical praxis. (Honneth 1994: 257–258)

So, for Honneth, without an adequate account of grounding, the critical theory project fails.

However, Bronner argues that this belief is unwarranted. Like Habermas and Honneth, Bronner is critical of the emphasis that Adorno and Horkheimer, in *Dialectic of Enlightenment,* place on "pure negation." Bronner argues that this stance, by definition, makes verifying the claims of critical theory impossible, and creates the dangers of dogmatism and detaching the theory from "practical interests, institutions, and actual movements" (Bronner 1994: 324). But in an implicit criticism of Habermas, he argues that the correct response to the problems inherent in a position of pure negation is not to concentrate on grounding as a philosophical problem or puzzle. After all, as he reminds his readers:

Foundations [read groundings] were precisely what critical theory sought to deny. They smacked of "traditional theory" with its finished claims, fixed systems, and attempts to subsume the particular in the general. (Bronner 1994: 323)

For Bronner, the real problem "was less a matter of 'grounding' in the abstract than an inability to deal concretely with concepts like democracy and the rule of law, socialism and equality, internationalism and cosmopolitanism" (Bronner 1994: 324). Seen in this light, grounding becomes a "matter for political and social theory rather than philosophy" (Bronner 1994: 325).

Bronner's own solution to the grounding issue seems to rely more on history than on political and social theory. Rather than attempting to anchor emancipatory potential in the presuppositions inherent in communication—whether this is understood in terms of a theory of language or recognition—Bronner believes that a review of the historical record is sufficient to justify certain institutions and practices over others:

It is enough to look back at *real systems* and see that, with few historical exceptions, the extent to which the liberal rule of law is employed is the extent to which grievances are open to consistent forms of equitable redress. It is enough to note that the extent to which reciprocity is denied is the extent to which popular sovereignty is subverted, inequality is legitimated, and the subject's security is lost. It is enough to know from the past that the arbitrary exercise of power is grounded in terror. (Bronner 1994: 325)

Furthermore, in a statement that resonates with the sentiments of the early critical theory of "Traditional and Critical Theory," Bronner argues:

The interests of critical theory in justice and happiness are validated by those who suffer from their denial. They need not "justify" their experience of oppression, only the manner in which they seek to mitigate it—and that because, in fact, they will assuredly bear the burden for its failure. (Bronner 1994: 326)

Critical theory must be partisan in its concern for the oppressed and the marginalized.

Although the 1930s exiles were unable—and, as their subsequent history perhaps indicates, unwilling—to transform their concern for the downtrodden into practical suggestions for the transformation of their situation, Bronner is adamant that:

Critical theory cannot ignore substance in the name of form; it must prove willing to confront power and offer criteria for judging how one response to exploitation or oppression might work better for the exploited than another. (Bronner 1994: 327)

Indeed, Bronner believes that the critical theory project may become invalidated if it concentrates on metatheoretical issues—such as grounding—at the expense of more practically oriented theoretical concerns.

Bronner's comments are well taken. They are a salutary warning against the persistent tendency of critical theory to collapse into "nothing more than an academic exercise" (Bronner 1994: 325). Although metatheory is important, as Bronner recognizes, its importance must be measured in terms of its contribution to the generation of theory, which is oriented toward real-world social transformation. It is this social transformation that is the point of critical theory and it is according to its adequacy for this task that critical theory must be judged. As Nancy Fraser more elegantly argues: "It is in the crucible of political practice that critical theories meet the ultimate test of vitality" (Fraser 1989: 2). Furthermore, in good dialectical fashion, it is important that those critical theorists who choose to concentrate their efforts in metatheoretical activity remind themselves that just as theory offers insights for practical struggle, the converse is also true.

Nevertheless, Bronner's argument that the historical record in effect speaks for itself on issues of grounding is too complacent. Consider, for example, his short account, quoted earlier, of what history proves (Bronner 1994: 325). Bronner argues that history demonstrates that the liberal rule of law and accountability (democracy) is demonstrably superior to any previous or present alternative. This would seem to be not only plausible but irrefutable. But note his subsequent comment that "the extent to which reciprocity is denied is the extent to which popular sovereignty is subverted, inequality is legitimated, and the subject's security is lost" (Bronner 1994: 325). What Bronner seems to be suggesting, contrary to Habermas and Honneth, is that there is no need to worry unduly about the source(s) of expectations concerning reciprocity; it is enough to recognize that popular sovereignty, equality, and security are the necessary prerequisites for reciprocity in the real world.

Bronner's argument should, however, be considered in the light of the Marxian critique of capitalism of which critical theory is an intellectual heir. Marxist political economy argues that capitalism generates inequality and insecurity and that the reified separation of economics and politics into separate spheres—a move characteristic of capitalism—undermines the claim of liberal democracies to be polities based on popular sovereignty. The important point to note in the present context is that none of this critique is based on pointing to historical or contemporary examples of an actually-existing alternative order. History certainly does not prove the superiority of a mode of production alternative to that of capitalism.

Neither can the Marxian critique of capitalism be reduced to an immanent critique in the sense of juxtaposing the present order to the justifications that are supplied for it—for example, "This is a society that claims to be based on equality, yet this principle is not enacted in relation to this particular group (women, linguistic minority, etc.) within it." Rather, as Norman Geras has persuasively argued in *Marx and Human Nature* (1983), Marx and his adherents have also argued on the basis of another form of critique, a critique that—often implicitly—measures the present on the basis of a conception of actually-existing but not yet actualized human potential.

The debate over grounding is in essence a debate about delineating both the source and the character of this potential. By abandoning the latter form of immanent critique and concentrating solely on the former—a move that is implicit in Bronner's position—critical theory would be narrowing the basis of its critique in an unwarranted and unhelpful fashion. As the Marxian critique of capitalist political economy illustrates, accounts of human potential form an important part of the critical theorist's theoretical armory.

If this argument is correct, there is certainly justification for critical theorists to pursue the issue of grounding, and as we have seen, there remains much work to be done. Although both Habermas and Honneth offer interesting insights, their work contains significant drawbacks. Habermas is a theorist whose ideas on grounding appear to be of limited relevance to those societies in which the basic struggle for survival is still very obviously ongoing. Honneth appears to be resting a rather elaborate edifice on some questionable assumptions. Indeed, it may well be, as Postone argues (1993), that a return to Marx's broader notion of labor—a concept that contained those features that Habermas has separated out under the heading "interaction"—remains the best way forward for critical theory in this respect.

Nevertheless, however unfinished and preliminary the theories of grounding developed by critical theorists are—and their theoretical precepts should remind them that they will always be engaged in a work in progress—this should not preclude others from relating their insights to empirical examples. This is the task I will undertake in the following chapters.

THEORY AND PRACTICE

The first generation of critical theorists signally failed to produce a convincing account of the relationship between their theoretical activity and political practice. As I have already stressed in the previous chapters, there were contingent historical circumstances that made this failure all too understandable. Nevertheless, the fact remains that their theoretical endeavor, oriented as it was toward human emancipation, could not account for its own role—real or potential—in generating the conditions for progressive social change. With the collapse of faith in the proletariat as both subject and object of revolutionary transformation, critical theorists were unable to identify an addressee for their work—a target audience to which critical theory, in however mediated a form, could be or might become relevant. As a result, neither could they provide an account of their own social role qua theorists. Adorno's solution, which was to argue that critical theorists were producing "messages in a bottle" for addressees at a time and place unknown, was certainly a striking and indeed poignant image. However, it merely deferred the issues rather than resolved them.

As I have already discussed, much of the impetus for attempts to renew the critical theory project was generated by the perceived failure of the old guard to relate their thinking to radical political activity. One of the challenges for the successor generations was thus to provide more plausible accounts of the theory-practice nexus. In this section I will consider their efforts in reference to the work of Habermas.

Habermas's work has been characterized by a somewhat paradoxical oscillation between, on the one hand, ambitious claims about what his work successfully demonstrates or proves at the theoretical level and, on the other, a series of cautious and modest claims about his theory's practical political import. For example, in the context of his work on discourse ethics, work that develops directly out of his theory of communicative action, Habermas admits to making

> an outrageously strong claim . . . that there is a universal core of moral intuition in all times and in all societies . . . [and that] these intuitions have the same origin. In the last analysis, they stem from the conditions of symmetry and reciprocal recognition which are unavoidable presuppositions of communicative action. (Habermas 1992b: 201)

And yet, despite this boldness, in the course of the same interview in which he makes this comment, Habermas also argues that "philosophers are not the teachers of a nation," and that "only rarely" can they "be useful people" to society as a whole (Habermas 1992b: 199).

Habermas's emphasis on the attenuated societal relevance of theoretical activity is a recurrent feature of his work, from his 1963 essay "Theory and Practice" to his most recent interviews (Habermas 1992b). Habermas wishes to underscore his belief that social theorists possess no special insight that should lead to their views being accorded a privileged position in the area of political activity. Some of the impetus for this argument can no doubt be attributed to a well-founded desire on Habermas's part to distance himself from some of the dogmatic excesses of those leftist ideo-

logues who, despite their radical rhetoric, have tended to accord themselves
a role bearing more than a passing resemblance to that suggested by Plato
for the philosopher-kings of *Callipolis*. However, although the more cir-
cumscribed role that Habermas posits for theorists, and indeed for intellectuals more generally, may betoken a welcome humility and sense of perspective, it is questionable whether his account of the relationship between
theory and practice is adequate.

In another interview (it is striking that it is from this source that his
views on the theory-practice nexus emerge most clearly) Habermas discusses his own multiple roles in the following terms:

> [I try] to keep various spheres separate: first of all these political-journal-
> istic things, then "real" philosophizing. . . . After that, scientific work in a
> narrower sense; and finally teaching and, when the time is ripe, a political
> praxis which goes beyond journalism. In the last ten years I have also had
> to play the role of institutional director. I keep these various kinds of work
> separate, but I am not saying that this is the kind of division of labour in
> which one thing has nothing to do with another, or in which it is a matter
> of a combination of various roles. I would rather play each of these roles
> in such a way that the others remain visible at the same time. (Habermas
> 1992b: 127)

This general position is further clarified through a consideration of
Habermas's comments on John Rawls. According to Habermas, the
acclaimed author of *Theory of Justice* has not

> systematically cared when he speaks as a philosopher and when he speaks
> as a committed liberal in his society. This is what philosophers should
> also do; forget about their professional role and bring what they can
> do better than others into a common business. (Habermas 1992b:
> 199–200)

But what is the "common business" to which Habermas refers? And what
does he believe that philosophers—in particular, critical theorists—"can do
better than others"? Or rather, who should critical theorists be talking to,
and what should they be talking to them about?

Habermas's account of his own audience is typically modest and self-
deprecating:

> I work as a philosopher and sociologist, and therefore the people to whom
> my work is addressed primarily occupy positions in the scientific and edu-
> cational system: now and again I dabble in political journalism and write
> in daily and weekly newspapers, or in so-called cultural periodicals. In
> both cases it tends to be the left intellectuals who are interested in what I
> write—and of course my old sparring-partners on the other side.
> (Habermas 1992b: 184)

This account, however, does less than justice to Habermas's own prominence as a public intellectual in Germany. Indeed, his own biography suggests that the impact and influence of the theorist can reach well beyond the rather narrowly conceived academic and intellectual circles whom he claims to be attempting to address (see Robert Holub 1991; Habermas 1993b).

In terms of Habermas's own theory, we can understand his various public interventions as contributions to the debates—or communicative action—taking place in the various overlapping lifeworlds that exist within and overflow the geographical space known as Germany. But what is the status of these contributions? The comments cited earlier in this section ("Philosophers are not the teachers of a nation") suggest that Habermas does not believe that his own eminence as a social theorist should lead to his political views being accorded any special attention. This interpretation is supported by comments such as "Everyday moral intuitions have no need of the clarification of the philosopher" (Habermas 1992b: 199). Thus Habermas seems to be implying that he and other theorists are entering the debates of the lifeworld(s) simply as ordinary citizens—their theoretical expertise should not allow them to trump political arguments. Nevertheless, this implication is belied by numerous other statements in Habermas's oeuvre in which he posits a more prominent role for theorists and theoretical activity. In "Theory and Practice," for example, Habermas describes his ambition to "develop the idea of a theory of society conceived with a practical intention" (Habermas 1992b: 168), whereas in *The Theory of Communicative Action,* he argues that the task of critical theory involves "bringing to consciousness potentialities that have emerged within the maturing historical situation itself" (Habermas 1987: 382).

The question arises whether Habermas is contradicting himself in suggesting, on the one hand, that philosophers—including critical theorists— "are not teachers of a nation" while arguing, on the other hand, that critical theory should "perform the task of making possible enlightening interpretations of situations, which affect our self-understanding and orientate us in action" (Habermas 1992b: 168). I think not. Rather, what he seems to be saying is that political discourse cannot be reduced to a philosophical exercise. Theory and theorists can inform political debates. Positively, they can raise the level of those debates by pointing to unrealized possibilities or probable but unintended consequences of certain forms of action. But practical political questions cannot be settled at the level of theory. Indeed, any attempt to do so is likely to lead to highly undesirable, dogmatic outcomes. In summary, for Habermas, theory and practice are not identical, but neither are they totally autonomous enterprises. Nor should they be collapsed one into the other. Rather, both interact dialectically with each other.

This is a plausible position and one that is certainly closer in spirit to that propounded in the early articulation of critical theory than the *Dialectic of Enlightenment* version. However, it remains underdeveloped in at least two important ways. First, Habermas has not paid enough attention to the role of intellectuals. In his understandable desire to privilege democracy and democratic procedures, Habermas has been reticent in admitting that even within participatory democracies, some will play a leading role in the conceptualization and articulation of political possibilities. If critical theory is to have a practical impact, this role needs to be explored and explicated.

Whereas this deficiency can certainly be addressed and accommodated within Habermas's theoretical framework, a second objection raises more fundamental questions. Quite simply, Habermas's conceptualization of public debate and the possible contribution of critical theorists to this debate is too consensual. He seems to imply—to exaggerate only slightly—that after intellectuals contribute their insights to the "public sphere,"[3] the "force of the better argument" will somehow prevail and these insights will be taken up and become influential. But what is missing here is any notion of struggle—of how ideals and interests intermingle and interact, of how movements take up, adapt, and utilize ideas as part of an interactive process within and between societies. In other words, Habermas's understanding of politics is underdeveloped.

This represents a serious problem in Habermas's understanding of the relationship between theory and practice. It also highlights a problem at the heart of Habermas's understanding of his key concept of lifeworld. Habermas uses the term in two distinct ways. In the usage encountered earlier, it refers to "relatively informal ways of life, contrasted with market and administrative systems" (Outhwaite 1996: 369)—that is, the ensemble of relationships now commonly referred to as "civil society" (Cohen and Arato 1992). Its second usage refers to those background, taken-for-granted, or "commonsensical" assumptions on the basis of which communicative activity occurs (Habermas 1992b: 109–110, 205). Notwithstanding these different meanings that Habermas attaches to the term, the problem is that in neither case does he seem to recognize that the lifeworld is suffused with politics. It hardly needs to be underscored that lifeworld in the civil society sense is very much a realm of political struggle. But the same is equally true of lifeworld understood in the second sense. Yet Habermas seems to ignore how and why certain opinions come to be regarded as common sense; he thus glosses over the relationship between knowledge and interests.

Although one may sympathize with Habermas's motives in defending a strong (procedural) notion of truth, especially in light of the contemporary tendency simply to reduce knowledge to interests, one may ask whether this defense has led him to develop an apolitical theory of society. Indeed, this line of criticism could well be pushed further. Could it be that in his reconstruction of historical materialism, Habermas ultimately develops an ahistoric theory that effectively ignores material interests? Even if this verdict is too sweeping, there can surely be little doubt that Habermas's theory of society pays too little attention to politics in its conception of the lifeworld. To regard politics as somehow extrinsic to the lifeworld is naive, yet by making comments such as "Politics has become an affair of a functionally specialized subsystem," Habermas seem to suggest that politics is a *systemic* phenomenon (Habermas 1991: 360). Although not everything can be reduced to politics, little can be understood without reference to it.

In the light of both its underdeveloped notion of the role of intellectuals and theorists and its lack of understanding of how politics revolves around the interplay of ideas and interests, Habermas's conceptualization of the relationship between theory and practice is inadequate. These are important gaps in the development of a critical theory of security. In Chapter 6, I will develop an alternative conceptualization based on the work of Antonio Gramsci and on the historical experience of the relationship between the theory and practice of alternative (critical) notions of security.

EMANCIPATION: CONCRETE UTOPIAS

Politics involves making choices: choices between different visions of the ends pursued and choices between different means of pursuing them. But choices are seldom clear-cut. Means and ends may conflict, short-term goals may contradict longer-term objectives, and of course, actions often have unintended consequences. Thus part of the task of theory with emancipatory intent is to delineate and clarify the choices being faced in the practical realm and to examine and illuminate conflicts and contradictions between them. In this way, theory can give direction to action; theory and practice can be consciously unified in praxis.

But in order for this to happen, theoretical reflection cannot remain at the very abstract level. In contrast to the refusal of Adorno and Horkheimer to supply descriptions of an emancipated order—a refusal they often justified in terms of the Judaic prohibition on the portrayal of Jehovah (see Jay 1984: 20)—critical theorists must go beyond generalized exhortations concerning emancipation, empowerment, freedom, and happiness. If critical theory is to have practical relevance, it must reflect on what emancipation means in terms of actual institutions and relationships. As radical German students demanded in the 1960s, critical theorists should seek to outline positive visions of concrete utopias (Wiggershaus 1994: 623).

The work of the first generation of critical theorists does not offer much specific guidance in the task of outlining what emancipation might mean in practice, but the preceding discussion of their work suggests three points that those attempting to overcome this failing should bear in mind. First, and most obviously, visions of concrete utopias must be consistent with whatever deeper notions of the grounding of emancipatory potential are deployed. Thus, for example, if the possibility of emancipation is grounded in the economic realm, then, logically, depictions of a more emancipated order cannot simply concentrate on (narrowly defined) political institutions. Second, descriptions—indeed, prescriptions—of a more emancipated order must focus on realizable utopias. Critical theorists must not lose sight of the fact that the coherence of their project is dependent on their utilization of the critical potential of immanence. If they succumb to the temptation of suggesting a blueprint for an emancipated order that is unrelated to the possibilities inherent in the present—a tendency that Marx and Engels argued was characteristic of "utopian socialists" such as Robert Owen (Marx and Engels 1948: 44–46)—then critical theorists have no way of justifying their arguments epistemologically. After all, to justify a utopia that is not already present in some form within the prevailing order requires the existence of an Archimedean point according to whose standards this utopia might be envisioned—a possibility rejected by critical theorists.

Thus immanent critique (understood in broad terms) remains a vital part of the metatheoretical armory of critical theory. Furthermore, it is highly unlikely that a vision of an emancipated order that is not based on immanent potential will be politically efficacious. Unless anchored in a realistic assessment of actually existing possibilities, emancipatory ideas are hardly likely to convince their target audience (whoever they might be) that progressive change is not only desirable but also plausible and achievable, and therefore worth the effort or risk of trying to secure. Thus, for both epistemological and purely instrumental reasons, concrete utopias must be based on practices that have some basis in preexisting behavior.

Finally, in addition to basing their visions of concrete utopias on realizable, immanent possibilities, critical theorists should also restate their understanding of emancipation as a process rather than an end point, a direction rather than a destination (Nye 1987: 245–247; Booth 1991b). Such an understanding is, of course, inherent in a dialectical approach that regards each order or condition as the bearer of its own negation. Indeed, one of the defining features of the Western Marxist tradition of which critical theory forms a part is its hostility toward the tendency of "orthodox Marxism" (a term that may be historically obsolete but remains a useful shorthand) to succumb to some notably undialectical notions about the future. The idea, for example, that history would effectively come to an end once the proletariat had gained power may well have been given credence by Marx's own work, but for critical theorists, and Western Marxists more generally, it flew in the face of the basic principles of Marx's method. Each order is susceptible to criticism. Even if a more emancipated order is brought into existence, the process of emancipation remains incomplete. There is always room for improvement; there is always unfinished business in the task of emancipation.

One of the benefits of explicitly recognizing emancipation as a process whose culmination or fulfillment remains forever deferred is that it deflects Adorno and Horkheimer's objection to calls for critical theory to detail which arrangements it regards as preferable to those that currently prevail. The authors of *Dialectic of Enlightenment* argued that by supporting particular structures and practices, theory becomes reified and loses its critical edge. The experience of Marxism as an official state ideology confirms that this argument contains a kernel of truth. But the lessons that Horkheimer and particularly Adorno drew from this experience effectively threw out the baby with the bath water. They argued, as part of their more general critique of instrumental reason, that the only response to this danger of reification was to adopt a position of resolute and unrelieved negativity—a move whose basis and consequences were criticized in Chapter 2.

In contrast, I would argue that if one adopts an explicit understanding of emancipation as a process rather than an end point, the undoubted dangers of reification are minimized. If emancipation is understood in terms of a journey that is never completed, then the theoretical justifications—as opposed to psychological and other justifications—for complacency and conformism are removed. With these basic injunctions in mind, I will now examine efforts to delineate the broad contours of concrete utopias as found in the works of Habermas and Ulrich Beck.

Habermas on Democracy and Emancipation

The overall thrust of Habermas's thinking on the contours of emancipation is procedural. Indeed, he explicitly argues that "the only utopian perspectives in social theory which we can straightforwardly maintain are of a procedural nature" (Habermas 1992b: 206–207; see also Habermas 1994: 112–113). The procedure that he identifies as being the "necessary condition" of an emancipated society is democracy. Through the extension of democratic decisionmaking, Habermas wants to transform the relationship between lifeworld and system. He wishes to reverse the colonization of the former by the latter by bringing "impulses from the lifeworld" to bear on the system. By doing this, the "socially integrating power of solidarity" generated through "autonomous, self-organized public spheres" can assert itself over the system-steering media of money and bureaucratic power (Habermas 1991: 364).

But what of the practicalities of bringing about such a transformation? In truth, Habermas seems unable or unwilling to move beyond the most vague assertions. He certainly does not provide a sketch of a more emancipated order that might serve as a set of coordinates for activists attempting to achieve progressive change within the complex constellations of interests and identities that form contemporary society. Thus, for example, when pressed by an interviewer to discuss the type of political institutions that might be congruent with a more emancipated order, Habermas is no more specific than the following:

> I am convinced that the competition of parties which have become more and more independent of their bases, and which carry on the business of providing legitimation in an essentially manipulative way, must be changed. I suspect that *another* kind of separation of powers would have to be introduced. (Habermas 1992b: 182)

The interviewer and the readers are left only to guess as to what this might actually mean in concrete terms. Habermas is equally vague when discussing the type of economic order necessary to allow a transformed relationship between lifeworld and system. He admits: "I cannot imagine that this [transformation] would be possible without a gradual abolition of capitalist labour market" (Habermas 1992b: 183). However, he gives no inkling as to what might replace that market.

In this context it is instructive to note Habermas's response to a question posed to him in an interview conducted in 1984:

> [Question:] Aren't you in a way logically committed to some programmatic account of the social order your work is concerned to bring about, beyond your diagnostic analysis of the present order which you reject? Could you contemplate your producing one day an equivalent for us of Hegel's *Constitution of the German Nation* or Kant's *Scheme for Perpetual Peace?* . . . Hasn't the highest philosophical vocation traditionally embraced this kind of concrete thought too?
> [Answer:] The examples are too grand, but I must take your admonitions to heart. (Habermas 1992b: 184).

This mea culpa notwithstanding, although Habermas has continued with his "diagnostic analysis of the present order," he has still not generated any sustained reflections on the order that his work is "concerned to bring about." Habermas has still not moved beyond generalized exhortations that never ultimately address how broad principles can be operationalized. Thus the political limitations (and hence relevance to security studies) of Habermas's critical theory of society are manifest.

Beck on Ecological Enlightenment

More useful for security studies is the work of Ulrich Beck, and for two
reasons. First, Beck's version of critical theory is less philosophically oriented than Habermas's, and as such, his more sociologically and politically
focused critique may provide a more concrete vision of emancipation than
that proffered by Habermas. Second, Beck's now influential characterization of contemporary society as a "Risk Society" (Beck 1992a) and his dissection of the ecological threats facing humanity have important implications for the discussion of security in Chapter 4.

There is scope for debate about Ulrich Beck's exact relationship to the
Frankfurt School, but it is not the purpose of this book to explore the range
of influences and contacts, both intellectual and professional, that tie Beck
to critical theory. Nevertheless, enough linkages can be identified that render plausible the claim by Scott Lash and Brian Wynne in their introduction
to *Risk Society* that Beck is engaged in the development of a critical theory
of society appropriate for the post–welfare state world (Beck 1992a: 8).

The essence of Beck's argument is that the technological evolution of
contemporary society is causing a shift "From Industrial Society to the Risk
Society," to cite the title of one of his articles (Beck 1992b). Modern industrial society has always been characterized by risk, which Beck understands
as threats to human physical security arising from "decisions that focus on
techno-economic advantages and opportunities and accept hazards as simply the dark side of progress" (Beck 1992b: 98). A society based on instrumental or purposive rationality, to adopt terminology already utilized in
this book, generates numerous unintended consequences—from factory
accidents and pneumoconiosis to industrial smog and Aberfan-type disas-
ters—that threaten human health and life. However, in industrial society the
actual and potential social and political effects of these risks were contained by "the emergence of a system of rules for dealing with industrially
produced risks and insecurities" (Beck 1992b: 99).

This system, an amalgam of public and private insurance schemes and
agreements, created a "social compact against industrially produced hazards" that generated "present security in the face of an open uncertain
future" (Beck 1992b: 100). Although this "security pact" may have been
based on a "calculus of risk" that exemplified a type of "ethics without
morality, the mathematical ethics of the technological age" (Beck 1992b:
100), it did provide the prevailing politico-economic order with legitimacy
in the eyes of the vast majority of the population. As green commentators
never tire of pointing out, the left never challenged some of the most basic
assumptions of industrial capitalism concerning the desirability of unre-
strained growth and the nature of humanity's relationship with the natural
world (e.g., Gorz 1994; Eckersley 1992).

According to Beck, "the foundations of the established risk logic are being subverted or suspended" (Beck 1992b: 101) as a result of a series of technological challenges to the ecology, such as those caused by nuclear power and the chemical and biotechnology industries. These technologies have the potential to wreak destruction on such an unimaginably large scale that they subvert any risk calculus; there is no social and political order that could deal with the consequences of a worst-case scenario. As a result, legitimation for this new risk society cannot be generated through the same type of security pact that characterized industrial society. Rather, "political stability in risk societies is the stability of not thinking about things" (Beck 1992b: 101). It is only in this way that the tension between popular expectations for the continuation of "a level of security founded on the perfection of techno-bureaucratic norms and controls," on the one hand, "and the spread and challenge of historically new hazards which slip through all the meshes of law, technology and politics," on the other, can remain hidden (Beck 1992b: 104).

If this silence is not maintained—if the nonthinking begin to think—then, given the intimate interrelationship between technology and the political and social order, the potential for upheaval is tremendous. According to Beck, the catalyst for a process whereby the dependence of society on a uniquely hazardous techno-economic logic may be unmasked is the failings of the technologies themselves. Accidents, near misses, the emergence of new hazards, the realization that technologies previously deemed safe are in fact hazardous (chlorofluorocarbons and the ozone layer, for example)—these all serve to undermine the legitimacy of the prevailing order. They undermine the claim of experts—long dominant in developed societies—to a monopoly of wisdom, a result that has far-reaching implications. As Beck says: "The exposure of scientific uncertainty is the liberation of politics, law and the public sphere from their patronization by technocracy" (Beck 1992b: 109). But which groups within risk societies are best placed to challenge the prevailing techno-economic order and emancipate humanity from its grip? And what types of institutions and practices could replace this order?

Beck argues that one of the novel features of the new threats facing humanity is that they do not respect the traditional state and class boundaries. Of course there are winners and losers, and the weakest suffer disproportionately, but nevertheless, traditional axes of conflict are subsumed within conflicts between different regions and between different economic sectors—with competing alliances of capital and labor confronting each other. One result is that the traditional antisystemic movements, such as workers' parties and trade unions, are unlikely to provide the main source of opposition to the risk society.

Beck argues that it is those social movements often termed "new" or "critical" that can—and indeed are—exposing the tensions that underlie contemporary societies (see Ray 1993; Kellner 1989: 218–233). The "civil courage of individuals and the vigilance of social movements," combined with the "sensationalist greed of the mass media," can ensure that the inevitable catastrophes that occur in contemporary societies will serve to expose the hazardous and hazard-generating nature of the techno-economic foundations upon which these societies have been constructed (Beck 1992b: 116). Such a concatenation will

> threaten markets, make sales prospects unpredictable, devalue capital and set streams of voters in motion. Thus the evening news ultimately exceeds even the fantasies of countercultural dissent; daily newspaper reading becomes an exercise in technology critique. (Beck 1992b: 116)

Social movements have already had a major impact, in Beck's opinion. In his native Germany, for example, they have ruptured "an authoritarian everyday culture which, historically, has enabled all official nonsense and insanity with its anticipatory obedience" (Beck 1992b: 117).

Of course, even if social movements in Germany have challenged the traditional culture of deference toward bureaucrats and experts, they have not—as yet—challenged the basic contours of that country's political economy. To ensure such a far-reaching transformation, Beck advocates a project of "ecological enlightenment" to be fought out at the micro and broadest macro levels and to span every aspect of life (Beck 1992b: 118). The aim of this emancipatory project—here echoing Habermas—should be the democratization of society:

> Industrial society has produced a "truncated democracy", in which questions of the technological change remain beyond the reach of political-parliamentary decision-making. As things stand, one can say "no" to techno-economic progress, but that will not change its course in any way. It is a blank check to be honoured—beyond agreement or refusal. That is a manufactured "natural force" in civilization, an "industrial middle ages", that must be overcome by more democracy—the production of accountability, redistribution of the burdens of proof, division of powers between the producers and the evaluators of hazards, public disputes on technological alternatives. (Beck 1992b: 118–119)

More concretely, and thus in contrast to Habermas, Beck argues that such a radical democratization can be achieved by two sets of reforms.

First, Beck wants society to recognize that the role, scope, and institutional expression of politics are changing as part of a more general process of societal transformation: "Monopolies are breaking up—the monopolies of science on rationality, of men on professions, of marriage on sexuality, and of politics on policy" (Beck 1992a: 232). Specifically, the political process as conventionally understood—that is, the governmental structures of sovereign states—is losing much of its power. This is occurring both domestically, where power is being lost to the media, the legal system, and to quasi-governmental bodies, and internationally, where transnational actors of various kinds are undermining the sovereignty of the state.

Beck is relatively sanguine about this process inasmuch as he is no fetishist of the sovereign state. By the same token, however, he regards it as vital that transparency and accountability are extended to these new centers of decisionmaking power and that the principle of the division of powers is entrenched across the new political landscape. To this end he recommends that the independence of the legal system and the media should be fully recognized. More originally, Beck also wishes to ensure that the possibility for self-criticism is "institutionally protected" in order to facilitate "alternative evaluations, alternative professional practice, discussions within organizations and professions of the consequences of their own developments, and repressed skepticism" (Beck 1992a: 234).

Second, Beck wants to ensure the democratization of techno-economic development, thus bringing technology under the control of society and ending the present situation, in which the opposite is the case (see Beck 1992a: 228–231). This aim can be secured by informing, empowering, and emboldening the public sphere. Beck believes that through informed public scrutiny of scientific developments, the public sphere can ensure that the unintended consequences and civilizational implications that orthodox science currently excludes from its calculation—often precisely because they are incalculable—are given due consideration. This would allow society to end its dependence on the judgment of experts and judge for itself how best to "counter the incapacitation and expropriation of daily life in the civilization of threat" (Beck 1992b: 120).

Beck's sketch of an alternative order is interesting and important. But certain aspects of it may not be convincing. For example, can public scrutiny ever be organized and institutionalized in such a way that it can control the trajectory of apparently autonomous techno-economic development? Even to pose this question is to highlight what is undoubtedly the major failing of contemporary left-wing theorizing in general; that is, its inability to provide a plausible account of alternative modes of political-economic organization to those modes that characterize capitalism. Nevertheless, Beck's analysis of and prescriptions for society relate to the experiences, perceptions, and aspirations of many ordinary people in developed societies. Furthermore, his account of the relationship of technology and society is arguably more sophisticated and rounded than those provided by the leading lights of the Frankfurt School. The next section will explore this relationship in more detail.

TECHNOLOGY

In the previous chapters I outlined two diametrically opposed views on the nature of technology and, specifically, the relationship between technology and society. In Chapter 1 I examined Horkheimer's essentially benign view of technology that underlies the argument of his essay "Traditional and Critical Theory." Horkheimer equates technological progress with progress itself in that it improved prospects for human emancipation—understood in terms of the rational, planned domination of nature. This view was subsequently rejected by Horkheimer, who in the course of his collaboration with Adorno came to regard technology in entirely negative—indeed apocalyptic—terms. As the discussion of *Dialectic of Enlightenment* in Chapter 2 illustrated, Adorno and Horkheimer saw technology as the product of a form of rationality whose hegemony was wholly inimicable to human freedom.

But both of these views are deeply problematic. The former is remarkably unreflective and uncritical. By treating technology as if it were simply a neutral medium, "Traditional and Critical Theory" effectively ignores one of Marx's basic arguments, namely, that the dialectical relationship between the forces and relations of production acts as the motor of history. The argument of *Dialectic of Enlightenment* goes to the other extreme and adopts a conception of technology that is far too reductionist and deterministic. This in turn leads to an abject fatalism. By viewing technology as the material manifestation of a form of rationality that is all-consuming, Adorno and Horkheimer effectively relegate human beings to the role of ciphers who have lost all capability to think and act for themselves. In effect, human subjectivity is denied. Thus the possibility that technology could be developed and utilized for human ends is dismissed tout court.

But this position ignores the fact that at least some forms of technology have significantly reduced human suffering. In no facet of life is this more true than in medicine. As noted in Chapter 2, Adorno and Horkheimer's response was to argue that "the serum which a doctor gives a sick child is obtained by attacking defenceless animals" (Adorno and Horkheimer 1979: 223). This, of course, has historically been the case: Other sentient beings have suffered appallingly for causes often far less deserving than children's health. But to divine from this undoubtedly important realization that our technological destiny is to subside into a condition of unmitigated oppression and suffering is unwarranted. Consider the example proffered by the authors of *Dialectic of Enlightenment*.

The first point to note is that the serum does provide succor to the child; that is, the dark side of this episode is balanced by a positive outcome. Thus the example is not simply one of unrelieved horror, and to portray it as such is a gross misrepresentation. Furthermore, real world experience has shown how an increasing awareness of animal suffering during the testing of products designed for human consumption—and increased concern about the moral implications of this suffering—has gradually led to pressure on those developing such products to seek out alternative ways of testing them. Although there may not be an end to all animal testing in the foreseeable future, there has been progress: Moral learning has taken place, and new technologies are being developed as a result. This outcome underlines the ahistorical nature of Adorno and Horkheimer's example. The undeniable fact that the health of children has been purchased in part at the expense of animal suffering does not necessarily mean that it will always be so.

Despite the emphasis by critical theorists on the insights provided by a dialectical approach, their work on technology, at least as exhibited in the two classic texts studied in the previous chapters, has been notably undialectical. They have consistently failed to recognize the dialectical interaction between technology and society, which mold and shape each other. This is true of the approach adopted in "Traditional and Critical Theory" and its implication that technology is neutral and can simply be shaped to the will of society. It also true of *Dialectic of Enlightenment* and its suggestion that technology totally determines society (indeed, one might suggest that the book's title is a misnomer). What is needed, therefore, is a critical approach that goes beyond the one-dimensionality of traditional critical theory conceptualizations of technology and develops a dialectical understanding of its subject. This is precisely what Andrew Feenberg has attempted to develop in his *Critical Theory of Technology* (1991).

Feenberg reconstructs the basic assumptions underlying the various conceptualizations of the relationship between technology and society. The resulting taxonomy distinguishes between two main views: the *instrumental* and the *substantive*. On the basis of a critique of both views, Feenberg develops his own critical understanding of technology. It is important to note that in his reconstruction and critique of prevalent views of technology, he addresses and criticizes the work of other critical theorists, including Adorno and Horkheimer, Marcuse, and Habermas. His own work may be regarded as an attempt to develop an understanding of technology that is more consistent with the basic precepts of critical theory than are those proffered by the leading critical theorists. In the remainder of this section I will summarize Feenberg's reconstruction of the instrumental and substantive views of technology as well as his own critical understanding.

The instrumental view of technology is by far the most influential, at least in Western societies. It sees technology as basically neutral; in Feenberg's words, "as subservient to values established in other social spheres i.e. politics and culture" (Feenberg 1991: 5). In other words, technology can serve a "plurality of ends" depending on the particular circumstances of its use (Feenberg 1991: 12). A simple illustration of this view can be found in the argument of the U.S. National Rifle Association (NRA) against gun control, an argument encapsulated in the slogan "It's not the gun, it's the person holding the gun." The implication of the slogan is that the gun itself is neutral; it can be used for good purposes, such as defending family and home, or for nefarious activity, such as crime. Another example can be found in the field of military strategy and its recurrent arguments against the banning of offensive weapons. The argument here is that weapons are not inherently offensive or defensive; rather, it depends on the attitudes and outlooks of those controlling their use. "What is not a weapon in the wrong hands?" is a question that vexed those involved in the interminable debates on disarmament in the League of Nations during the 1920s.

The instrumental view is predicated on the "common-sense" notion that "technologies are 'tools' standing ready to serve the purposes of their users," that is, that they are neutral in themselves (Feenberg 1991: 5). As I discussed in Chapter 1, this was the view of technology underlying Horkheimer's early critical theory. It is also the view of Habermas (his most sustained discussion of technology can be found in Habermas 1970: 81–122; Feenberg 1991: 176–179).

Feenberg argues that the substantive view of technology is in essence a deterministic attitude that "attributes an autonomous cultural force to technology that overrides all traditional or competing values." Thus "substantive theory claims that what the very employment of technology does to humanity and nature is more consequential than its ostensible goals" (Feenberg 1991: 5). No matter what the intentions of those inventing or introducing a new technology, it will determine social and cultural relations in a particular way.

For a military-related example, consider the invention of the conoidal bullet. The bullet was first developed for hunting and dueling, and for many years military chiefs opposed its introduction into warfare. However, they were eventually forced to accept its deployment, which ultimately precipitated a radical change in military tactics. Units on the battlefield could no longer be arranged in centrally controlled massed ranks because these became too vulnerable; instead, troops had to be dispersed into small units and given operational autonomy (see De Landa 1991: 11–125). This example fits particularly well with Feenberg's description of technological determinism that he sees as based on two theses:

> 1. The pattern of technical progress is fixed, moving along one and the same track in all societies. Although political, cultural, and other factors may influence the pace of change, they cannot alter the general line of development, which reflects the autonomous logic of discovery.

2. Social organization must adapt to technical progress at each stage of development according to the "imperative" of technology. This adaptation executes an underlying technical necessity. (Feenberg 1991: 122–123)

Military leaders could not resist the introduction of the conoidal bullet, and once it occurred, military organization was eventually forced to adapt to the imperatives of the new technology. In one of his more deterministic moments Marx once asked Engels the rhetorical question "Is our theory that the organisation of labour is determined by the means of production confirmed anywhere more splendidly than in the man-slaughtering industry?" (Holloway 1983: 131). Despite the fact that Marxists have regularly succumbed to technological determinism, the substantive approach is perhaps more usually associated with such figures as Martin Heidegger (1977) and Jacques Ellul (1964).

The substantive approach is predicated on a deterministic, even fatalistic, view of technology. Technology is regarded as an autonomous force, and as such, it is a destiny that cannot be avoided or escaped. As I discussed in Chapter 2, this view was emphatically the conception of technology adopted by Adorno and Horkheimer in *Dialectic of Enlightenment.*

Feenberg rejects both the instrumental and substantive views of technology. He regards the former view as hopelessly simplistic. To use an earlier example, "the army is not merely accidentally related to its weapons, but it is structured around the activities they support" (Feenberg 1991: 65). It is not simply a coincidence that military organizations tend to change their operational structures and especially tactics and strategies when new technologies are introduced. Similarly, the number of violent deaths in a society, despite the NRA's arguments to the contrary, are not somehow accidentally related to the ease of access to firearms within that society. Easy access to guns can undermine the previously prevalent social and cultural values. In reality, subjects—be they armies or individuals—and means are related.

But in advancing the significance of the subject/means relationship Feenberg is not simply accepting the substantive position that technology is autonomous and that a particular set of social values or social relations are embodied within a given technology: He is not saying that the means of action (e.g., weapons) ultimately controls the subject of action (e.g., army). Rather, developing his critical theory perspective, Feenberg regards the means and subject as *"dialectically* intertwined" (Feenberg 1991: 65, emphasis in original). He provides a succinct explanation of this position:

Critical theory argues that technology is not a thing in the ordinary sense of the term, but an "ambivalent" process of development suspended between different possibilities. This "ambivalence" of technology is distinguished from neutrality by the role it attributes to social values in the design, and not merely the use, of technical systems. On this view, technology is not a destiny but a scene of struggle. (Feenberg 1991: 14)

The important term to note is "ambivalence." Technology does have a logic in that it simultaneously creates and constrains the choices available to society; however, technology does not predetermine which of those particular choices is made. That decision is social and as such reflects a whole series of social, cultural, and power relations. The fact that these relations are potentially contestable leads to the argument that technology is a "scene of struggle."

Feenberg reformulates this argument in a more formal fashion by arguing that each technology contains within it a number of neutral "technical elements" (springs, pumps, etc.) but the way in which these particular elements are configured together reflects certain values. These values arise from the socially hegemonic pattern of alliances and power relations. The values then embodied in the technology often serve the function of supporting or legitimating the position of the hegemonic groups within society. Thus the critical theory position developed by Feenberg rejects the instrumental view that technology is simply a neutral means. It also rejects the substantive view of technology as destiny: Such technological determinism is, in the words of Raymond Williams, a "form of intellectual closure of the complexities of social process" (R. Williams 1982: 67–68).

The critical theory perspective, as developed by Feenberg, views technology as an ambivalent process that contains within it a number of possibilities. The decision as to which of these possibilities is ultimately realized is a social decision and thus reflects a whole complex of (potentially contestable) social, cultural, and power relations. In Chapter 5 I will use this view of technology to reconceptualize strategy in terms of the interrelationship between the (ambivalent) possibilities of technologies and particular strategic cultures.

RENEWING THE CRITICAL PROJECT

In this chapter I have analyzed various attempts to renew the critical theory project and redeem its early promise from the impasse generated by the totalizing "critique of instrumental rationality" underlying *Dialectic of Enlightenment*. By concentrating on issues related to theory, emancipation, and technology, I not only have delineated the main thrust of contemporary critical theory, in particular as found in the work of Habermas, but have done so in such a way as to lay the foundation for the discussion in Part 2 of this book.

It has been argued that many aspects of contemporary critical theory remain problematic. In particular, the attempts by Habermas and subsequently Honneth to ground the normative claims of critical theory in actually existing social practices, though viewed as ultimately unconvincing, are still creative, interesting, and instructive, and certainly an improvement on the ideas in the work of both Horkheimer and Adorno. Furthermore, Habermas's account of the theory-practice nexus has been regarded as deficient, exposing a lack of appreciation of the role of intellectuals in society and a conception of politics that is too narrow and too consensual. The tenor of the discussion of Habermas's ideas concerning the contours of a more emancipated order has also been critical; in particular, it has been suggested that his account of concrete utopias is too abstract to enjoy much political relevance.

Other manifestations of contemporary critical theory have been seen in a more positive light. Beck's critique of the risk society and his suggestions concerning the possible structures of a more emancipated order have been applauded for their realism and possible utility as part of the theoretical underpinnings of progressive political practice. Similarly, Feenberg's critical theory of technology has been applauded for its sophisticated and plausible account of the relationship between technology and society and for the insights it offers into the possibilities for progressive transformation.

The overall picture that emerges from this discussion is mixed. Contemporary critical theory has strengths, but some elements of it—and important elements at that—are unconvincing. Important work remains to be done. In particular, the task of providing an adequate account of intramundane emancipatory potential is unfinished. Nor is there yet a convincing account of the relationship between critical theory and emancipatory political practice.

However, the view that critical theory is an unfinished project—that it is work in progress—should not be regarded as surprising. After all, given critical theory's conception of thought as being historically situated and reflecting particular constellations of interests, it should be apparent that, logically, critical theorists must view their own work as perpetually unfinished. As society changes over time—as interests and identities alter—so must theory if it is to retain any critical purchase and perspective. The unfinished and in some aspects unconvincing character of critical theory should not deter attempts to apply its insights to particular issues. The notion that every metatheoretical and theoretical issue must be resolved before applying a theory to a particular empirical case is based on an undialectical and ahistorical conception of theory that is wholly at odds with that of critical theory. The logic of the critical theory position must be that by applying the theoretical and metatheoretical insights to concrete questions, analysts not only generate new ways of viewing those particular questions but also become more aware of the potential and pitfalls of the theoretical framework itself. Theoretical development and empirical application are two sides of the same coin. Indeed, if Nancy Fraser is indeed correct to argue that "it is in the crucible of political practice that critical theories meet the ultimate test of vitality," then it follows that through its application to concrete problems and issues, critical theory can continue to make progress at the metatheoretical level.

Furthermore, even though critical theory does not have all the answers—indeed, can never have all the answers—in Part 2 I seek to demonstrate that an approach based on its precepts and principles can generate innovative ways of thinking about the theory and practice of security and strategy.

NOTES

1. The obvious metaphor to use here is that of foundations. However, the static nature of foundations often leads hostile commentators to suggest that those who use this metaphor are inferring some sort of Archimedean point by which critical theory orients itself. Although critical theory explicitly rejects any notion of an Archimedean point, I refer to "grounding" rather than "foundations" in the hope that this implies less immobility.

2. In his recent work, Habermas has tended to use the term "formal pragmatics" rather than "universal pragmatics." See his comments in Outhwaite 1996: 129ff.

3. This phrase is associated with Habermas's work *Structural Transformation of the Public Sphere* (1989), first published in German in 1962. The concept has been subsumed within his more recent analysis of society in terms of the system/lifeworld relationship. He now uses "public sphere" to refer to those "higher-level, concentrated communicative processes" that are particular manifestations of the lifeworld (Habermas 1991: 359).

PART 2

Traditional and Critical Security Studies

4

Theory:
Reconceptualizing Security

Writing in 1982, an extraordinarily prescient E. P. Thompson predicted a sudden end to the Cold War, arguing:

> I think we may now be living, this year and for many years ahead, through episodes as significant as any known in the human record. . . . There would not be decades of détente, as the glaciers slowly melt. There would be very rapid and unpredictable changes; nations would become unglued from their alliances; there would be sharp conflicts within nations; there would be successive risks. We could roll up the map of the Cold War, and travel without maps for a while. (E. Thompson 1982a: 1, 34)

Since the tumultuous events that eventually ended the stasis of Cold War, we have indeed entered an era of bewildering upheaval. As E. P. Thompson correctly predicted, this era has continued to be characterized by change, uncertainty, and conflict; it remains an era, even now, through which we are traveling "without maps."

The concepts and theories that were the dominant source of orientation and direction during the Cold War have lost whatever limited relevance they once enjoyed. In response, the last few years have witnessed a sustained and determined attempt to rethink some of the basic categories of thought concerning world politics and to delineate the contours of this new era. As a result, much of what has previously passed muster as timeless wisdom has been fundamentally problematized and challenged. Nowhere has this been more apparent than in notions of security. Analysts of differing persuasions have entered the fray and subjected this centrally important concept to unprecedented scrutiny (the literature is enormous, but especially useful are Brown, Lynn-Jones, and Miller 1995; Lipschutz 1995; Lynn-Jones and Miller 1995; Tickner 1995; Baldwin 1997; Brown et al. 1997; Krause and Williams 1997; Bilgin, Booth, and Wyn Jones 1998; Buzan, Wæver, and de Wilde 1998). In this chapter I intervene in this debate from

93

a perspective based on the understanding of the critical theory tradition developed in Part 1. I also draw on the work of a scholar who has already begun to develop a critical theory–influenced approach to security, namely, Ken Booth (1991a, 1991b, 1991c, 1994, 1995, 1997a).

Through a critical engagement with some of the most important and influential conceptualizations of security—in both traditional and more recent alternative work—I will seek to build up a distinctly critical understanding of security. It is argued that in light of the increasingly untenable nature of the scientific-objectivist epistemology underlying the traditional approach to security and the political indeterminacy of the poststructuralist-inspired interventions in the debate, it is only critical theory that can supply the necessary theoretical sophistication and normative direction for attempts at rethinking security. It is on this foundation that a new critical security studies can be developed. This critical approach has the potential not only to generate a theoretical understanding of the contemporary world and its pathologies but also to signpost possible routes through which this reality may be transcended through political practice. Thus, although we may well be destined to travel without maps, a critical reconceptualization of security at the core of critical security studies can help generate a sense of direction.

THE INADEQUACY OF TRADITIONAL SECURITY STUDIES

I begin this chapter by outlining the metatheoretical assumptions underlying the mainstream of postwar security studies and providing a critique of them. I should first note that the nomenclature is a potential source of confusion. Specifically, the label "security studies" has only recently become widely and internationally adopted as a replacement for "national security studies" (in the United States) and "strategic studies" (particularly in the United Kingdom). Generally speaking, this rebaptism appears to have been a typically 1990s piece of repackaging: Although the name change was intended to signify a sensitivity to the changed security environment after the collapse of the Soviet bloc, the substance of the enterprise remains very much the same (Krause and Williams 1997; see also Booth and Herring 1994: 120–131). In a deliberate echo of Horkheimer's work, I will refer to the mainstream approach to postwar security studies/strategic studies/national security studies as traditional security studies.

There are obvious difficulties and potential pitfalls awaiting any attempt to generalize about a major body of thought, let alone a body of work as vast as traditional security studies. Perhaps the main danger lies in oversimplification. It appears almost inevitable that any attempt to distill a set of arguments to their essence—an operation that is necessary in order to make generalizations—will lead to the disregard of nuance, richness, and diversity in favor of simplistic caricature. Nevertheless, it is plausible to argue that despite the often hotly contested differences that have divided traditional security studies into rival camps, the work of almost all the participants in these debates share broadly similar ontological and epistemological assumptions (M. Williams 1992a; Reus-Smit 1992; Krause and Williams 1997). That is, all have a similar view of the world with which they are trying to engage, and all share a similar conception of what constitutes knowledge about that world. In the former case, those who have adopted the traditional approach to the study of security have viewed the world from a *statist* perspective. In the latter case, all the arguments have been premised on a *scientific objectivist* understanding of knowledge (Reus-Smit 1992: 2). Therefore, the differences between various groups of strategists are actually based, whether the protagonists are aware of it or not, on a broad measure of agreement on the metatheoretical basis of enterprise in which they are engaged. In this section I will briefly explain and criticize both the ontological and the epistemological foundation of this agreement.

Statism is a view of the world that regards states—conceived in unitary and often anthropomorphized terms—as the only truly significant actors in world politics. Statism also involves a normative claim—and herein lies the justification for referring to "statism" rather than "state-centrism"—that, in political terms, states should be accorded a high, if not the highest, value in themselves. The statism of traditional security studies is a product of the fact that the whole approach is itself based on the foundations of a realist understanding of world politics. As John Garnett argues: "Perhaps the most pervasive assumptions underlying contemporary strategy are those associated with the theory of political behaviour known as realism" (Garnett 1987a: 9; see also Gray 1982a: 188). Statism is one of the central tenets—if not *the* central tenet—of all forms of realism. It is, however, open to criticism on both empirical and normative grounds.

Empirically, realists regard statism as being justified, indeed necessary, because this perspective reflects the reality of international relations: States are placed at the center of the analysis of world politics because they are at the center of the international stage, particularly when security issues are concerned. For realists, international relations is defined in terms of the interaction of states. Thus one arrives at the tautological argument that states are at the center of the study of international relations because international relations is about the interrelationship of states. But even leaving aside any qualms about the logical status of such an argument, we are left with a far more fundamental question. How realistic is the realists' statism?

While very few scholars, whatever their theoretical perspective, would want to doubt the importance of states in world politics, statism, with its tendency to make unitary conceived states the exclusive focus of analysis, seems, empirically speaking, to be highly problematic. One of the major consequences of the fetishization of the state is the construction and reification of the so-called inside/outside dichotomy based on the concept of sovereignty. This dichotomy resonates throughout the realist view of international politics (Walker 1993). One of the implications of this binary opposition is a rigid differentiation between the substate and the suprastate "levels of analysis." Although the latter is seen as the preserve of international relations specialists, the former is considered to be within the purview of other disciplines and largely irrelevant to the concerns of international relations. Realists argue that although domestic politics within a state may be interesting, one does not need to know anything about it in order to understand that state's international political behavior. A state (any state) will behave in certain statelike ways no matter what its internal composition because of the constraining influence of international anarchy. Thus Colin S. Gray can confidently proclaim: "The strategic theorist does not know, cannot know, who will be in office, who will be aligned with whom. . . . But the theorist does know how statesmen behave and why they behave as they do" (Gray 1992: 627).

Although no one can doubt the elegant simplicity of this position, crucial questions remain: Is the realist's statism analytically useful? Can the internal politics of the state be ignored, thus allowing analysts to concentrate their attentions solely on the determining influence of the international "realm of necessity"? The experience of the end of the Cold War, undoubtedly the greatest change in the international security environment in decades, suggests not.

The failure of any international relations specialist working within the realist paradigm to foresee the end of the Cold War and the remarkably peaceful disintegration of the Soviet Union has been much commented upon (among the voluminous literature, see, for example, Gaddis 1992–1993; Wohlforth 1995; Waltz 1995; Mearsheimer 1995; also the symposium on the end of the Cold War and theories of international relations in *International Organisation* Vol. 48, No. 2 (1994), pp. 155–277). According to Gray:

> The fact that most realists or neorealists did not predict the fall of the House of Lenin in the 1980s was a failure in prescience, not of paradigm. The ending of the Cold War has occurred for reasons fully explicable without strain by realist argument. (Gray 1992: 629)

Many realist writers have tried to provide ex post facto explanations for the end of the Cold War. Working from realist precepts, they argue that the reforms of Mikhail Gorbachev were, in the words of Kenneth Waltz, "an externally imposed necessity" (Lebow 1994: 266). But these arguments are not persuasive. The reforms instituted in the Soviet Union after 1985 went far beyond what was necessary if Gorbachev and his colleagues were simply concerned with adjusting to relative economic decline. As Richard Ned Lebow trenchantly observes:

> None of . . . [the realists] insisted that the Soviet Union's relative decline demanded a leader who would introduce Western-style democratic reforms, hold relatively free elections, acknowledge the legal right of republics to secede from the Soviet Union, encourage anti-communist revolutions in Eastern Europe, agree to dissolve the Warsaw Pact, withdraw Soviet forces from the territories of its former members, accept the reunification of Germany within NATO. . . . Such recommendations, let alone a prediction that all this would soon come to pass, would have been greeted derisively as the height of *un*realism. (Lebow 1994: 264)

The reforms in the Soviet Union were literally unthinkable for those trapped within a realist mind-set.

Quite simply, to understand the end of the Cold War, one cannot merely concentrate on state/system interaction. Rather, the focus must also embrace an analysis of events within the state and of transnational, but nonstate, interaction. Crucial to any understanding of events after 1985, for example, are the Western European peace movement, the Eastern European dissidents, and their interaction; the influence of Western alternative security thinking on the Soviet leadership; the rise of nationalism among subservient nationalities in Eastern Europe; the collapse of confidence in the shibboleths of Marxism-Leninism; and many other factors not amenable to interrogation within the traditional realist framework (Risse-Kappen 1994; see also Chapter 6). As Lebow observes, "Soviet foreign policy under Gorbachev is outside the realist paradigm. To explain it, the analyst must go outside the paradigm and look at the determining influence of domestic politics, belief systems, and learning" (Lebow 1994: 268).

In a comment apparently aimed at post–Cold War critics of the traditional approach to security, Colin S. Gray states: "People who have not functioned competently as strategic thinkers on the old agenda, are simply going to perpetuate familiar means-ends errors as they transition to exciting new topics on a new agenda" (Gray 1992: 626). Considering that exponents of the traditional realist approach championed by Gray completely failed to anticipate, let alone satisfactorily understand or explain, the most significant recent transformation in the security environment, it is apparent that this charge has a somewhat double-edged quality. If the traditional approach's statism means that it is analytically fragile in the face of such a massive, tectonic shift as the end of the Cold War, it seems highly unlikely that scholars and analysts who persist in holding to these views have any-thing of significance to contribute to any new agenda. (This is not of course to deny the continuing importance of states and the military dimension of world politics in the new agenda.)

A less familiar, though no less pervasive, corollary to these empirical claims regarding states is the realist assumption that states have normative value in themselves. This assumption is often left implicit by authors work-ing within this tradition and particular proponents of its neorealist variant. Yet, as Christian Reus-Smit convincingly demonstrates, the realists' pro-clivity to view the so-called nation-state as an "idealised political commu-nity" plays a vitally important simplifying role in their worldview (Reus-Smit 1992; this argument is also made in Walker 1997 and Wheeler 1996).

Reus-Smit is not claiming that the realist view of the state is analogous to the view adopted by romantic nationalist philosophers in the nineteenth century, that is, as some kind of organic entity to whose interests all indi-viduals and all other forms of community should become instrumental and subservient. Rather, his argument is that the ideal of the state as a unified and relatively homogeneous (nationally, ethnically, and ideologically), coherent, and peaceful community "is fundamental to the logical structure and coherence" of traditional security studies (Reus-Smit 1992: 14). For proponents of this view, the nation-state is a sovereignty-bounded realm within which order, justice, liberty, and prosperity (the good life) is possi-ble. In the well-known words of Osgood and Tucker, the state is the "indis-pensable condition of value" (Osgood and Tucker 1967: 284). The pro-found implications of this claim for security discourse are summarized by Reus-Smit:

> Once the nation-state is seen as a unified political community, it is assumed that there exists such a homogeneity of interests and identifica-tion within that community that security can be reduced to a minimal con-ception of state survival which is seen as synonymous with aggregate individual security. . . . Political action . . . is thus explained in terms of a unity of purpose among citizens coalescing around a common desire to limit threats by maximising military capabilities. (Reus-Smit 1992: 17)

Here the important simplifying effects of the assumption of an ideal-ized political community are laid bare. If it is assumed that there is an essential harmony of interests between individuals and their state, then ana-lysts working within the traditional paradigm can claim that their privileg-ing of the state is justified because state security is a precondition for indi-vidual well-being within that state. In other words, a normative justification for focusing on the state as the referent object of security discourse emerges based on the claim that states are the agents that provide citizens with security at the domestic level. According to this view, the main (existential) threat to their security emanates from other states that are perceived, in purportedly Hobbesian fashion, to view their neighbors rapaciously, ready to pounce at the slightest sign of weakness. Thus the security of the state is regarded as synonymous with the security of its inhabitants.

Once this idealized view of the state is measured against the empirical evidence, the privileging of the state that is characteristic of the traditional approach to security appears highly problematic. In much of the world, states, far from fostering an atmosphere within which stability can be attained and prosperity created, are one of the major sources of insecurity for their citizens. As J. Ann Tickner points out:

> In an international system which, in parts of the South, amounts to domestic disorder and stability of international borders, often upheld by the interventions and interests of great powers, the realist assumptions about boundaries between anarchy and order is turned on its head. (Tickner 1995: 181)

Even if a very narrow, military understanding of security is applied, it is apparent that the arms purchased and powers accrued by governments in the name of national security are far more potent threats to the liberty and physical safety of their citizens than any putative external threat. This is true not only of states in the disadvantaged South but also of those in the North. When a broader definition of security that includes nonmilitary threats is applied, it is clear that many states are deeply implicated in the creation of other forms of insecurity for their own populations, for example, in such issues as food and environmental security.

Viewed empirically, apparently aberrant "gangster states" are closer to the norm of state behavior than the Eurocentric notion of the "guardian angel" state, which is central to the traditional approach to security, would suggest (Wheeler 1996). Furthermore, radical understandings of global politics suggest that those few developed states that provide their citizens with a good deal of security (however defined) can do so only because of their dominant, privileged position within the global economy (some of these arguments are summarized in Hobden and Wyn Jones 1997). However, the very structure of this global economy creates and reinforces the gross disparities of wealth, the environmental degradation, and the class, ethnic, and gender inequalities that are the sources of insecurity in the South. In other words, the relative security of the inhabitants of the North is purchased at the price of chronic insecurity for the vast majority of the world population. Radical critics also suggest that the ideological function of the statism of the traditional approach is actually to discipline those within the state who deign to challenge the status quo (Reus-Smit 1992; Campbell 1992). For example, dissident voices on both sides of the iron curtain argued that "the principal axis of the Cold War conflict lay, not between the superpowers, but between states and civil society" (Reus-Smit 1992: 22). So, far from being a necessary condition for the good life, statism appears to be one of the main sources of insecurity—part of the problem rather than the solution.

If this analysis is correct, then empirical justifications for realism's state-centric ontology are highly dubious. Furthermore, it appears that one of the main functions of the statist discourse that lies at the heart of traditional security studies is to provide an ideological justification for the political and economic status quo. This point is particularly striking when it is contrasted with the epistemological position upheld by those who champion the traditional approach to security. This epistemology aims to describe the world "as it is," claims to distinguish sharply between fact and value and between subject and object, and seeks objective knowledge of the world, untainted by the analyst's own standpoint and predilections. It is not surprising, then, that the charge that a particular (pro–status quo) bias is smuggled into, or even embedded in, traditional analysis is anathema to its proponents.

Historically, there have been varying degrees of epistemological self-consciousness among traditional security specialists. However, in line with developments in the study of international relations in general, the period since the late 1980s has witnessed a growing awareness among analysts of the metatheoretical issues at stake. This increased awareness has been prompted both by attempts among mainstream scholars to develop more sophisticated theoretical underpinnings for their work (Waltz 1979 was particularly influential) and by trenchant criticism from those beyond that mainstream (see Keohane 1986; Smith, Booth, and Zalewski 1996). The net result of these developments for traditional security studies has been an increasingly self-conscious embrace of the "scientific" epistemology particularly associated with neorealism (for critical theory–inspired critiques of neorealism, see R. Cox 1981; Ashley 1981; Linklater 1995). Thus, for example, Gray has proclaimed that "strategists may be termed and should acknowledge that they are, without apologies, neo-realists" (Gray 1982a: 188).

Stephen M. Walt posits the "scientific method" as the foundation stone for his conception of the study of security:

> Security studies seeks *cumulative knowledge* about the role of military force. To obtain it, the field must follow the standard canons of scientific research: careful and consistent use of terms, unbiased measurement of critical concepts, and public documentation of theoretical and empirical claims. . . . The increased sophistication of the security studies field and its growing prominence within the scholarly community is due in large part to the endorsement of these principles by most members of the field. (Walt 1991: 222)

As Krause and Williams point out, proponents of this view seek to work within the "strictures of a particular conception of science and knowledge: the search for timeless, objective, causal laws that govern human phenomena" (Krause and Williams 1997: 37). Indeed, Walt's description of the epistemological basis of traditional security studies provides a paradigmatic example of the traditional theory criticized in Horkheimer's essay "Traditional and Critical Theory."

It is interesting that the case for rejecting the traditional conception of theory underpinning traditional security studies is strengthened by precisely those scientific discoveries and technological developments that gave the field its central focus. I am referring, of course, to the development of nuclear weapons; there is no doubt that nuclear weapons and their implications lie at the heart of traditional security studies. Ken Booth has correctly described the theory of nuclear deterrence as the "jewel in the crown" of postwar strategic studies (Booth 1987: 254). Ironically, the development of these weapons was made possible by a series of breakthroughs in scientific knowledge that undermined the very model of science upon which their later study was premised.

The scientific discoveries that enabled the development of nuclear weapons formed part of a paradigm shift away from the Newtonian understanding of the physical world toward the Einsteinian paradigm (the novelist Martin Amis has referred to nuclear weapons as "Einstein's monsters" [Amis 1988]). The Newtonian paradigm posits a rigid distinction between subject and object, observer and observed, and regards the physical world as governed by cast-iron laws, which, even if not presently understood, are potentially discoverable. These are, of course, the very premises that Horkheimer associated with traditional theory: The Newtonian paradigm underpinned the conception of the natural sciences that traditional theory adopted as a model in the study of the social world. However, the new quantum physics, popularly associated with the work of Albert Einstein, rejects the Newtonian view that there is a world out there existing independently of our observations. Following Werner Heisenberg's uncertainty principle, physicists discovered that the very act of observation influences the behavior of the object being observed. At one fell swoop this discovery undermined the rigid distinction between subject and object, and hence fact and value—or, in Horkheimer's words, the "separation of value and research, knowledge and action, and other polarities" (Horkheimer 1972: 208)—that form the epistemological foundations of all traditional theory, traditional security studies included. Thus, even while Horkheimer was arguing against the adoption of the natural science model for the study of the social world, developments in the study of physics in the 1920s and 1930s were undermining that model even for the study of the natural sciences themselves!

There are serious weaknesses in the theoretical underpinnings of the traditional approach to security. The statism of traditional security studies not only appears to be empirically unhelpful but also to act as an ideological justification for the prevailing status quo—a status quo in which the vast majority of the world's population are rendered chronically insecure. Furthermore, the scientific objectivist conception of knowledge adopted by the field not only is vulnerable to the critique that Horkheimer launched against traditional theory but also appears to have been undermined by the very scientific discoveries that acted as the catalyst for its development.

In the next three sections I will challenge the reified and constricted conceptualization of security that has been built on these metatheoretical foundations. I will also discuss and take issue with some of the alternative understandings that have been advanced in recent years. In these sections I argue for the deepening, broadening, and extending of the traditional concept of security.

DEEPENING SECURITY

In addition to criticizing the attempt to draw a rigid distinction between subject and object, Horkheimer's critique of the epistemological basis of traditional theory takes issue with the way that traditional theory tends to isolate (through cetirus paribus assumptions) particular practices from the totality of which they form a part. This procedure is institutionalized and further entrenched through the formation of academic disciplines, each with its own professional infrastructure. The result is the development of reified knowledge structures in which the dialectical interaction of the different elements of the social totality—and, in particular, their potential for change—is ignored. Traditional security studies provides a fine exemplar of that tendency to which Horkheimer objects.

Traditional security studies has tended to abstract military issues from their broader context by making a series of often implicit assumptions about that context based on realist premises, for example, those concerning the role and value of the state. It is not surprising, therefore, that analysts intent on undermining this traditional approach to the theory and practice of security have challenged this reified view of their subject. Thinkers such as R. B. J. Walker and Ken Booth stress the relationship between notions of security and deeper assumptions about the nature of politics and the role of conflict in political life (R. Walker 1990, 1997; Booth 1991a, 1991b, 1991c, 1997a). For both scholars, notions of security are derived from these deep-seated assumptions.

This connection was regarded as self-evident by some classical military theorists, most notably Carl von Clausewitz, who recognized that strategy is subordinate to political considerations and that war is a reflection of society (Clausewitz 1968: 101–168; Gat 1989: 215–250). However, despite the constant invocation of Clausewitz, this relationship became largely obscured during the development of postwar (i.e., traditional) security studies. In contrast, alternative thinkers have attempted to foreground the background assumptions of the traditional approach to security in order to subject them to appropriate critical scrutiny.

Deepening the conceptualization of security not only provides an important means for criticizing traditional security studies, but it also is a vital part of reconstructing the approach on an alternative, more critically oriented basis. R. B. J. Walker argues that attempts at rethinking security

> must be harnessed to an attempt to work through more persuasive answers to those questions about the character and location of political life to which the state and states system have seemed such a natural response for many for so long. (R. Walker 1997: 63)

This, in effect, is a demand that the reconceptualization of security must be undertaken in conjunction with a deeper attempt to think through what emancipation might mean in terms of alternative institutions and practices—an issue addressed in a later section of this chapter.

In the interim, it is enough to note that those who seek to deepen the conceptualization of security point out that traditional thinking about security is all too often based on understandings of world politics that are reified and unreflective. Consequently the intimate relationship between security and political theory more generally must be restated, and critical approaches to security must anchor their work in attempts to delineate the contours of alternative forms of world politics.

The next two sections focus respectively on the key axes of the contemporary debate over the conceptualization of security: whether the security agenda should be broadened to incorporate other, nonmilitary issues and whether the agenda should be extended away from a statist view of what constitutes the correct "referent object" for security discourse. I want to note that this differentiation between broadening and extending is my own. In most of the literature, the term "broadening" is used to denote both incorporating nonmilitary issues onto the security agenda and defining the correct referent object for security discourse (for example, Buzan 1991; R. Walker 1990, 1997). Given the bewildering proliferation of categories that is characteristic of international relations and of social theory in general, it may seem somewhat indulgent to introduce yet another distinction into the literature. However, a distinction that enables a clear differentiation between these two meanings of broadening security is not only logical but, more important, analytically useful. As the following analysis demonstrates, whereas many, if not most, contemporary writers have favored attempts to broaden security by moving away from a narrowly military focus, the debate over the need to abandon the state as the referent object for consideration of security has been far more contentious. It is thus desirable to be able to differentiate clearly between both issues.

BROADENING SECURITY

Barry Buzan's *People, States and Fear* (1991) can be viewed as the high-water mark of the traditional approach to the study of security. While remaining grounded in a scientific objectivist epistemology and, ultimately, in a state-centric ontology, Buzan produced a rich, suggestive, and sophisticated discussion of the concept of security. It is arguable that Buzan could go no further and remain tied to those metatheoretical assumptions. As Bill McSweeney has convincingly argued, Buzan's subsequent attempts to develop some of the central ideas of *People, States and Fear,* in particular in his work on European security (Wæver et al. 1993), cast considerable doubt on some of the basic underpinnings of the original work (cf. McSweeney 1996b and Buzan and Wæver 1997).

This argument has been vindicated by the fact that Buzan's most recent attempt to theorize security—in *Security: A New Framework for Analysis* (1998), written in collaboration with two of his Copenhagen School colleagues, Ole Wæver and Jaap de Wilde—clearly represents a significant break with both the epistemological and ontological foundations of *People, States and Fear.* Nevertheless, given the work's status as the high point of traditional security theory and its centrality to recent debates concerning the conceptualization of security, the next three sections will take the book's arguments as their starting point. I will also refer to Buzan's subsequent work when it is relevant to the alternative position that I am developing here.

In this section I will examine the basis for Buzan's original case for broadening the conceptualization of security beyond the traditional concern with military threats. I will then examine the debate that developed in response to his argument that it is useful to view other issues and problems in world politics through the lens of security.

The arguments advanced in *People, States and Fear* for moving beyond a purely military focus for the security agenda are inextricably bound to Buzan's wider attempt to delineate and define the scope of security studies and strategic studies (see also Buzan 1987; Buzan, Wæver, and de Wilde 1998; Buzan and Herring 1998). According to Buzan, strategic studies should be concerned with the study of the military aspect of the security agenda and specifically with the impact of military technology on international relations (this point is discussed at length in Chapter 5). What he terms international security studies should concern itself with more broadly defined threats to the "security of human collectivities" (Buzan 1991: 19). Specifically, Buzan identifies threats to security as emanating from five main sectors: political, societal, economic, environmental, and military (see also Buzan, Wæver, and de Wilde 1998: 49–193).

Buzan's original call for a broader security agenda was made in less than propitious circumstances. The first edition of *People, States and Fear* was published in 1983, the year in which Ronald Reagan made his infamous "evil empire" speech and the Soviets appeared to live up to the sobriquet by shooting down a South Korean Boeing 747 over Soviet air space, killing all 269 people on board. The second Cold War was at its zenith. Reflecting on his own reaction to the first edition, Steve Smith comments that, despite being impressed by the intellectual argument for a broader agenda, Buzan's concerns seemed somewhat "utopian and removed from the world that was the subject of my teaching and analysis. But," he goes on, "Buzan was right, as the events since the publication of the first edition have proved" (Smith 1991: 325).

Certainly, there can be no doubt that, as Smith recognizes, the end of the Cold War has added legitimacy and credibility to demands for a broader security agenda: the collapse of the Soviet bloc and the numerous problems that have emerged since its demise, which have highlighted the inadequacy of adopting a narrowly military conceptualization of security. Whereas in the past calls for a broader conception were confined to (marginalized) peace researchers, world society thinkers, and a few of the more intellectually adventurous international relations scholars such as Buzan himself and Ullman (1983), they have now become commonplace in the mainstream of traditional security studies (e.g., Crawford 1991; Matthews 1989).

Most analysts are now willing, at least rhetorically, to admit nonmilitary issues onto the security agenda. In the introduction to a reader put together by the editors of the most prominent and prestigious journal in the field of security studies, *International Security,* Sean M. Lynn-Jones and Steven E. Miller argue that the end of the East-West confrontation has

> revealed in its wake . . . a different set of dangers, not really new but previously overshadowed by Cold War preoccupations. . . . No longer will the field of international security be overwhelmingly fixated on how to deter the Soviet Union or how to reduce the risk of nuclear war between the superpowers. The newly revealed agenda is broader in its focus, giving much greater attention to previously neglected sources of conflict. (Lynn-Jones and Miller 1995: 4)

The "previously neglected sources of conflict" focused on in the text are environmental threats, threats arising from international migration, and threats emanating from resurgent nationalisms.

Of course, attempts to interlink issues of peace and war with wider questions of economic and social equity and justice are hardly novel. Indeed they have been a recurring feature in the statements of various international organizations. Article 55 of the UN charter, for example, links the creation of "friendly and peaceful relations among nations" with the resolution of "economic, social, health, and related problems," as well as respect for human rights (*Charter of the United Nations* 1987: 30). However, two sets of critics have objected to current attempts to broaden the concept of security traditionally utilized in the field of security studies. On the one hand, traditionalists have argued that such a move will lead to a loss of focus; on the other hand, some commentators have pointed to the dangers of viewing as security issues problems such as those associated with environmental degradation.

The traditionalist argument has been put forward forcefully by Walt (1991). In his programmatic essay confidently titled "The Renaissance of Security Studies," Walt criticizes Buzan on the grounds that introducing nonmilitary issues onto the security agenda undermines the field's "intellectual coherence." However, as Ken Booth and Eric Herring point out, there appears to be a major inconsistency in Walt's argument. Walt's own proposed research agenda, although wishing to uphold a restrictive conception of security, includes such issues as the role of domestic politics, the power of ideas, and the influence of economic issues. The serious consideration of any of these issues would wholly undermine the traditional, parsimonious approach he appears to advocate (Booth and Herring 1994: 126–127). Indeed, it seems inevitable that Walt will be forced into a contradictory position because of the inherent limitations of his conception of security.

If analysts adopt the narrowly military focus advocated but not apparently practiced by Walt, they will have little or no analytical purchase on many of those factors that create and accentuate conflict situations. For example, the dynamics of the (military) security situation in the former Yugoslavia cannot be understood without reference to the processes of identity formation and disintegration occurring in the region. To put it bluntly, if those who purport to be experts in security issues continue to conceptualize security in such a restrictive manner, then from Pristina to Belfast, and from Algiers to East Timor, they will continue to miss much of what is most relevant to the contemporary security agenda.

Arguments that a broader understanding of security threaten the intellectual coherence of the field are unconvincing. As Booth and Herring argue: "When studying any human phenomenon it is preferable to have open intellectual boundaries (which risk only irrelevance) rather than rigid ones (which risk ignorance)" (Booth and Herring 1994: 20). Ultimately, it is vital to underscore that all disciplinary boundaries are only a necessary convenience, valuable as a source of both intellectual and administrative orientation and organization but unhelpful if they are regarded as more than that. When these boundaries become reified, even fetishized, they can become a hindrance to the very understanding that they were intended to promote. Given that, as Adorno argues, "all reification is a forgetting" (Jay 1973: 267), it is surely right to worry more about what lies beyond the artificial borders of traditional security studies—that which has been forgotten—than about any alleged loss of focus or intellectual coherence.

A second, and perhaps more serious, challenge to scholars seeking to broaden the understanding of security has arisen from analysts who object to the securitizing of problems such as those relating to the environment and migration (e.g., Deudney 1990; Huysmans 1995). For these critics, there is a real danger involved in the process of "hyphenating security," that is, the attachment of different appellations, such as "economic" or "identity," to the term "security." This danger lies in the militarization and confrontation-oriented attitude conjured up by the traditional conception of security as "national security." For example, Daniel Deudney argues that environmental problems cannot be solved via the national security mind-set and that indeed this very mind-set is inimical to the development of "environmental awareness and action" (Deudney 1990: 461).

There are a number of possible responses to these criticisms. One response arises from arguments that emphasize the link between notions of security and deeper assumptions concerning the nature of politics. Walker, for example, argues that the concept of security will inevitably expand to include issues that are not military in nature. This expansion will occur because the questions regarding security are closely implicated in the legitimation of the sovereign state, that is, in deeper notions of politics. Thus:

> In the end it has never been possible to pin security down to concrete practices or institutions with any great precision, no matter how insistent the voices of military and defence establishments might be. The whole point of concepts of security that are tied to the claims of state sovereignty is that they *must* expand to encompass everything within the state, at least in its ever potential state of emergency. (R. Walker 1997: 76)

As a result:

> Concerns about [broadening] the practices of security policy into other spheres of political life may well be founded . . . but the extent to which practices of security are already part of the broader social, political, economic and cultural arenas is not something that can simply be wished away. (R. Walker 1997: 76)

The implication of this argument is that, contrary to Deudney's view, the terrain of security should not simply be abandoned to traditional, militarized conceptualizations. Rather, because the concept of security is inevitably broadened as a result of its connection to deeper issues concerning the legitimacy of various forms of governance, its meaning (that is, what is signified by attaching the appellation "security" to a particular issue) must be disputed.

The meaning of the term "security"—its signification—lies at the heart of Ole Wæver's innovative "speech act" approach. This approach focuses on the ways in which attaching the label "security" to a particular problem gives that problem special status and legitimates the "extraordinary measures" taken by state representatives to deal with it (Wæver 1994: 6). (Wæver's arguments have since moved beyond their original formulation. These changes will be reviewed later.) Security discourse is used to identify some threats as being "existential," that is, part of the "drama of survival." In this way, "Issues [become] phrased as 'no way back': after we have lost our sovereignty/identity/the sustainability of the eco-system, it will be too late; therefore it is legitimate that we take extraordinary measures" (Wæver 1994: 10ff.). These measures can include state-sanctioned killing, suspension of civil rights, confiscation of private resources, and so on.

Wæver has responded directly to Jef Huysmans's worries about the broadening of the concept of security. He argues that the intention of such a move is not to trigger a traditional security-type response to "new" security issues (Wæver 1994: 19). Rather, Wæver believes that analysts are justified in broadening security precisely because politicians already use the term in relation to problems that are nonmilitary in character but are still regarded as existential threats to the political order—the state (Wæver 1995: 51–53). In short, because state elites attach the label "security" to nonmilitary issues, analysts need to focus on their reasons for doing so. What power is signified or called upon by the use of the term? Analysts must broaden their conceptualization of security because the term has already been broadened in practice.

But that said, Wæver also seems to accept much of the force of Huysmans's and Deudney's misgivings. He writes:

> Security, as with any concept, carries with it a history and a set of connotations that it cannot escape. At the heart of the concept we still find something to do with defense and the state. As a result, addressing an issue in security terms still evokes an image of threat-defense, allocating to the state an important role in addressing it. This is not always an improvement. (Wæver 1995: 47)

Because he regards the effects of attaching the label "security" to an issue as fixed ("a conservative approach to security is an intrinsic element in the logic of both our national and international political organizing principles"

[Wæver 1995: 56–57]), Wæver advocates the "desecuritization" of as many issues as possible (Wæver 1995: passim). To desecuritize an issue is to remove it from the realm of the politics of survival and thus to render it amenable to more cooperative forms of behavior.

Although Wæver's argument is premised on assumptions different from those of Deudney and Huysmans, he arrives at similar conclusions. For Deudney in particular, "security" cannot escape its association with the theory and practice of so-called national security. Thus the concept, with all its attendant baggage, should not be used as a prism through which other issues are viewed. For Wæver, however, "security" is already broad because it is used by state elites to justify extraordinary measures taken in a range of issues that are perceived as a threat to their political order's survival. But Wæver also argues that it would be preferable if the term—because of its baggage—were used in relation to as few issues as possible. Thus Wæver also ultimately wishes to narrow the usage of "security" or, more correctly, "securitization."

Politically speaking, Wæver's strategy of desecuritization has real limitations. What of those problems that *are* a threat to survival? Should groups abandon the mobilization potential that is undoubtedly generated by using the term "security"? One presumes not, but then are existential threats to security simply to be abandoned to traditional, zero-sum, militarized forms of thought and action?

These questions highlight two significant weaknesses in Wæver's original formulation of the speech act approach: (1) its state-centrism and (2) the apparent unwillingess to question the content or meaning of security.

State-centrism is the point at issue in the next section. Suffice it to say here that in his initial formulation of the speech act theory of security, Wæver attempted to yoke his insights concerning securitization to a thoroughgoing state-centrism (Wæver 1994, 1995). As we have seen, he was interested only in how states securitized issues in order to justify extraordinary measures by states: Wæver viewed the grammar of security as inherently statist. In doing so he actually undermined much of the usefulness of the speech act approach. Its (potential) great strength is that it encourages analysts to interrogate the politics of how particular threats are securitized in order to mobilize and legitimate particular responses to them.

States, or even state elites, are not the only actors who use the grammar of security in this way. All kinds of social groups, at both sub- and suprastate levels, attempt to securitize many different types of issues, often with far-reaching sociocultural, political, and economic implications. Consider, for example, how the peace movement of the 1980s identified nuclearism as a threat to security (e.g., Falk and Lifton 1982; E. Thompson 1982b) and generated massive public support for its cause despite bitter opposition from governments. Or the way in which some Welsh-language activists have identified the flow of substantial numbers of so-called lifestyle migrants from England to rural Wales as a threat to the survival of the language and thus, in their view, to Welsh nationhood.

Adopting a speech act approach to the politics of security as practiced by groups other than the state is a fruitful avenue for exploration. Yet Wæver's state-centrism initially led him to attempt to delegitimate any effort in this direction. Significantly, however, this position has now been reversed. In his collaborative study *Security: A New Framework for Analysis,* Wæver and his co-authors, Buzan and de Wilde, have decoupled the speech act approach from state-centrism, correctly acknowledging the distinction between "a state-centric approach and a state-dominated field [of study]" (Buzan, Wæver, and de Wilde 1998: 37).[1]

It is arguable, however, that a more fundamental problem remains in Wæver's particular understanding of speech act theory itself. Wæver seems to regard the content of security as fixed; that is, he believes that the implications of calling an issue a "security problem" cannot be challenged, only the objects to which that label is applied. In the earlier, avowedly state-centric version of speech act theory, Wæver viewed the consequences of securitization as inherently conservative: "The language game of security is . . . a jus necessitatis for threatened elites, and this it must remain" (Wæver 1995: 56). This broad thrust has been retained (including the state-centrism?) in the latest formulation of the theory, which argues that to securitize an issue is to render it "so important that it should not be exposed to the normal haggling of politics but should be dealt with decisively by top leaders prior to other issues" (Buzan, Wæver, and de Wilde 1998: 29). But the notion that the implications of securitization—the meaning of security—are fixed can be challenged at both the empirical level and at the level of the theory of language.

Empirically, there can be no doubt that the theory and practice of traditional security have come under unprecedented scrutiny over the past twenty or so years. In particular, notions of "common security" have been advanced based on the argument that there can be no long-term resolution of threats through unilateral, militarized, zero-sum action. Rather, it is only a holistic and empathetic approach to security that can hope to ameliorate threats (the emergence of such an approach can be traced through the following independent, international commissions: the Commission on International Development Issues [1980]; the Independent Commission on Disarmament and Security Issues [1982]; the Commission on Global Governance [1995]). Moreover, the experience of the end of the Cold War demonstrates that such a conception of security can become influential (a point returned to and developed further in Chapter 6). This suggests that contrary to the opinions of Wæver or indeed Deudney, the meaning of security is not necessarily fixed but is open to argumentation and dispute.

Theoretically, this criticism of Wæver is buttressed by a Habermasian understanding of speech acts. Habermas's "universal pragmatics," which forms the general framework for his understanding of speech acts, was outlined in Chapter 3. His specific views on speech acts are summarized by Outhwaite:

> Contra conceptions of language as just a factual representation of states of affairs, or their negative counterpart in which it is seen as mere rhetoric, [in Habermas's approach] the three validity-claims of truth, normative rightness and expressive truthfulness or sincerity are given equal importance. (Outhwaite 1994: 131)

This understanding of speech acts has major implications for alternative approaches to the theory and practice of security. It suggests that when the label "security" is attached to particular issues, it generates validity-claims that are open to redemption or refutation through argumentation.

Thus, for example, if a state treats the continued existence of a minority language within its borders as a threat to national security (as is the case with Turkey and Kurdish, and as was the case until recently with the United Kingdom and Irish), this behavior is susceptible to critique on the grounds of truth, rightness, and sincerity. In this case, the truth of the claim that a minority language is a threat to the state may be questioned. The normative rightness of persecuting a minority culture in the name of national security may also be called into doubt, as well the sincerity of those advocating this policy (whose interests are really being served by such a claim?).

Another example of how validity-claims are brought into play through the use of the term "security" is a decision by a government to base another state's nuclear weapons on its territory to counter a threat that it perceives as emanating from a third country (as was the case with the deployment of U.S. cruise missiles in the United Kingdom in the early 1980s). In this case the questions that might arise during the process of redeeming the validity-claims implicit in this scenario would include: Does the third country really pose a threat to the state deciding to host nuclear weapons? What is the evidence concerning both material capabilities and intentions? Could not nuclear weapons and nuclearism pose a greater threat to security than any putative aggressor? Is it right to threaten death and destruction to millions of innocents in the name of national security? Should a state be privileged in this way? Is the decision to deploy nuclear weapons a sincere response to a perceived threat, or is it a result of intra-alliance politics? Or does it reflect pressure from a self-interested military-industrial-academic complex?

As these examples demonstrate, once security discourse is viewed in terms of a series of validity-claims subject to redemption through argumentation rather than a take-it-or-leave-it package of militarized assumptions and responses, a more fluid picture emerges than the one presented by Wæver or Deudney. Understood in Habermasian terms, the speech act of security cannot simply be narrowed by prior definition to exclude all threats other than those that are military in nature—rather, the breadth of the concept is subject to debate. Similarly, the meaning—the implications—of securitizing a particular issue cannot be regarded as fixed. However, I am not arguing that it is easy to challenge the traditions that are attached to a particular concept. Simply to talk about something differently does not necessarily lead to different forms of behavior: Practice cannot simply be reduced to theory. But argumentation and disputation can have— and have had—profound effects even on the practice of security (a theme pursued in Chapter 6).

When anchored in Habermasian pragmatics, the speech act approach to security supports arguments for broadening the understanding of the concept and certainly undermines attempts at closure as a result of prior definition rather than argumentation and discussion. More generally, the focus on how arguments concerning truth, rightness, and sincerity are brought into play by security discourse provides powerful theoretical support for the project of critical security studies.

EXTENDING SECURITY

People, States and Fear is an arresting title; it is also a somewhat misleading one. "States and Fear" is a more accurate representation of Barry Buzan's ultimate focus in that work. To be sure, Buzan does pay some attention to the security of individuals, as well as security at the suprastate levels of particular regions and of the international system itself. However, in the final analysis, his interest in these other levels centers on their impact upon states.

Buzan offers two main justifications for adopting this state-centric perspective. Empirically, he argues that the security dynamics at the international and substate levels are all mediated through the state:

> It is the job of government, indeed almost the definition of its function, to find ways of reconciling these two sets of forces. The fact that no other agency exists for this task is what justifies the primacy of national [i.e., state] security. (Buzan 1991: 329)

So once again, the argument is that states should be the "conceptual focus of security" because they "have to cope with the whole security problem" (Buzan 1991: 329). Allied to this argument is Buzan's contention that states can in fact provide individuals with security. Buzan is aware that states are often a mortal danger to their own citizens. However, he holds that the problem is not states themselves (that is, states qua states) but rather particular kinds of states. Individual security can be obtained when there are "strong states" (states with a high degree of internal stability and cohesion) coexisting in a "mature anarchy" (a developed international society) (Buzan 1991: 57–111).

Because these arguments are sophisticated variants of those discussed and criticized earlier in this chapter, the counterarguments need not be repeated here. Indeed, I have already noted that Buzan's subsequent work has involved a marked distancing from many of the tenets underpinning *People, States and Fear,* including, perhaps above all, its state-centrism. In *Security: A New Framework for Analysis,* state-centrism is explicitly rejected as "a narrow self-closing definitional move" (Buzan, Wæver, and de Wilde 1998: 37).

Interestingly, resistance to shifting the referent away from the state has also been expressed by some of those who view security from a poststructuralist perspective. R. B. J. Walker, for example, objects to the notion that the globe should be made the referent object for security through such conceptions as "cooperative or common or world security" (R. Walker 1997: 77). His objections revolve around his contention—to my mind correct—that the basic political and philosophical point at issue in arguments about referents is the relationship between the universal and the particular in politics. This argument, he believes, cannot simply be side-stepped by embracing the universal at the expense of the particular. Indeed, Walker argues: "It is because of its insistence of the absurdity of this move, in fact, that the old junker of political realism can remain on the road, and keep some of its critical potentials alive in some places" (R. Walker 1997: 77).

Walker's general line of argument reflects the now familiar poststructuralist suspicion of the universal as an inevitable precursor of homogenization and a denial of "difference." Proponents of common security, which may be Walker's target, would of course refute the characterization that their position denies the value of diversity; rather, they view common security as a procedural means of coping with that diversity. They might also legitimately point out that some threats are truly global in nature, for example, global warming and the threat of nuclear winter. Whatever the merits or demerits of Walker's arguments on this particular point, in light of his insistence that attempts at "re-visioning security" need to go hand in hand with rethinking "the political" and an understanding of the "contemporary transformations of political life," it is hard to believe that he would object to extending security discourse away from the state to other referents.

Whatever its theoretical justification—be it realist or even poststructuralist—state-centrism has been subjected to strong criticism by those who argue that the state should not be the privileged referent object of security discourse. These critics have sought to extend the security agenda by shifting the focus away from states to other levels of analysis.

A number of alternative referent objects for security have been proposed by scholars working from an alternative defense perspective and by those engaged in the practice of social movements. Some have argued that the conceptual focus should be placed on individuals (Booth 1991a; Smith 1991). Others have suggested that the apposite focus is society, particularly some notion of civil society (Shaw 1994a; Reus-Smit 1992). Yet others have proposed that ethnonational and religious identities are crucial referents for conceptualizing security (Wæver et al. 1993). Another suggestion is that there should not be one referent object for security but rather different referents at different times, in different locations, and in relation to different issue areas. This is now the position of Buzan and Wæver (Buzan, Wæver, and de Wilde 1998; also Baldwin 1997).

One of the most prominent advocates of making individuals the referent of security is Ken Booth. In his "Security and Emancipation" (1991a) he argues against privileging the state as the referent object of security on the grounds that to do so is to confuse means with ends. States are, or at least can be, a means for providing security, but ultimately it is only with reference to individuals that the notion of security has any meaning: "It is illogical therefore to privilege the security of the means as opposed to the security of ends" (Booth 1991a: 320). Following from this, Booth argues that "individual humans are the ultimate referent" (Booth 1991a: 319).

Ken Booth's argument is an important corrective to state-centrism. It is, however, open to the charge that it is based on a kind of liberal individualism that conceives human beings in reductionist, atomistic terms (Shaw 1994a: 96–100). Such an interpretation may well be encouraged by Booth's usage of the term "means" in relation to human collectivities. In some circumstances it may be useful to conceive such collectivities—families, communities, nations, or states—in this way. For example, when considering threats to so-called basic human needs—that is, the basic material prerequisites of life—then it may well be legitimate to view any collective group as a means by which individuals' basic needs can be satisfied. However, there is another context in which conceiving human collectivities in such instrumental terms is unhelpful, and that is in relation to identity.

Identity is a central aspect of the human experience. Even when it is conceived in traditional terms, it is clear that questions relating to the formation, recognition, expression, and disintegration of different forms of identity—of which national identity is only one of the most prominent—should be of vital concern to those interested in security issues. When the conceptualization of security is deepened, broadened, and extended, identity is even more self-evidently important.

Moreover, identity is not simply a means in any crude instrumental sense. As the discussion of Axel Honneth's work in Chapter 3 suggests, the successful development and recognition of an individual's identity may be regarded as an end in itself. Furthermore, identities are by definition collective phenomena. An individual's identity is created, negotiated, ascribed, and denied through interaction with others. As a result, to reduce questions relating to identity to individuals or aggregations of individuals—that is, to view them in terms of liberal individualism—is misleading. Where identity is concerned, the whole is more than the sum of the parts. Therefore, in relation to questions of identity—one of the key variables in any discussion of security—if Booth's focus on individuals is taken as a form of liberal individualism, then this interpretation is problematic and limiting.

However, Booth's emphasis on the individual as the "*ultimate* referent" for security is better understood in the light of the discussion of Horkheimer's notion of emancipation in Chapter 1. Horkheimer believed that critical theory should be concerned with the corporeal, material existence and experiences of human beings. In so arguing he was not denying the importance of class, the state, or other collectivities. Indeed, it is clear that Horkheimer did not think that the existence and experiences of individual human beings could be understood without viewing them as part of such contexts. Rather, what he continually stressed was that in analyzing the various dynamics within societies and their institutions, theorists should never lose sight of their effects on and implications for individual human beings. Thus, for Horkheimer—as for Booth—the individual is always the ultimate referent for critical theory.

In this sense, the emphasis on the individual does not acquire the limiting and reductive implications that might accrue from Shaw's false "liberal individualist" reading of Booth's "Security and Emancipation" (and Booth 1997a suggests very strongly that this "Horkheimerian" interpretation is closer to his original intention than Martin Shaw's reading [1994a] or that found in Buzan, Wæver, and de Wilde 1998). Apart from the normative importance of having the individual as ultimate referent, thus hopefully avoiding the tendency of traditional theorists to "concern themselves with • 'man as such' [rather] than human beings in particular" (Schmidt 1993: 30), there are also analytical benefits. Namely, by making the individual the ultimate referent, the security analyst is encouraged to understand the various contexts that impinge upon an individual's security and simultaneously is discouraged from their reification and fetishization.

The importance of the latter injunction is highlighted by moves of a number of contemporary theorists to make social groupings other than the state the referent object for security discourse. For example, Wæver, Buzan, Kelstrup, and Lemaitre (1993) focus on ethnonational groupings (see also Wæver 1994). Implicit in Samuel Huntington's "The Clash of

Civilizations" is the grandiose notion that civilizations should become the conceptual focus of security (Huntington 1993). Surveying this work, Krause and Williams express the concern that a "shift . . . to a prima facie focus on structures of exclusionary group-identity will merely replicate the inside/outside structure of anarchy in a different form" (Krause and Williams 1997: 48; see also Booth 1991a: passim; Shaw 1994a: 100–103). However, highlighting the individual as the ultimate referent reduces the danger of reification. A focus on individuals brings the analyst face-to-face with the complexities of human identity. Identity never occurs in the singular. At a minimum, people have a gender identity and something else. The human condition is one of overlapping identities; that is, each person has a number of different identities, all (potentially) in flux, and all of which come into play at different times and in different situations. Thus a focus on individuals strongly discourages any tendency to reify human identity; it points instead to the complex, multifaceted, and even fluid nature of identity.

This discussion underlines the need for an analytical framework that is sensitive to difference and diversity but understands that such distinctions are not primordial forces: a framework that recognizes that inside/outside, self/other dichotomies—no matter how and why they have been constituted—do have a certain reality but simultaneously avoids their reification. But is such a framework possible? Is it not true that notions of group identity, even if tied to an understanding of the individual as the ultimate referent, are so vague and amorphous that it "hardly provides us with a clear capacity for thinking about security" (Krause and Williams 1997: 48)? I suggest that this worry is overstated and that once analysis moves from the abstract to the particular, what seems to be problematic at the broad conceptual level appears to be far less so in practice (a point illustrated by the analysis of southern Africa in Booth and Vale 1997).

When analysis is historicized and particularized through the analysis of specific issues in specific areas, it becomes apparent that the appropriate referent object varies from case to case. In some areas, in regard to certain issues, the appropriate referent may well be national identity or civil society. In other circumstances, these categories may be irrelevant or meaningless. Smaller, more localized communal identities may then be the appropriate referent object, or it may be far larger referents that are most apposite (e.g., it may be appropriate to consider some notion of "woman" in relation to an issue such as rape). In other words, the problem of what group to privilege as the conceptual focus of security discourse can be resolved only through concrete analysis (Booth and Vale 1997; for further theoretical support for this position, see Baldwin 1997).

To extend the concept of security in the manner advocated in this section is to initiate a radical rupture with the state-centric perspective of traditional security studies. Rather than make the state the referent for security discourse, security analysts should concentrate their attention on "real people in real places" (Booth 1995: 123), making individual human beings the ultimate referents for their discussion. However, adopting such a position is not inconsistent with believing that it is impossible to understand an individual's security situation apart from the wider social contexts that a particular person inhabits. It is the nature of these particular contexts and the particular issue being focused upon that should define the relevant social grouping(s) that the analyst uses as the conceptual focus for her or his discussion.

Statism is the security blanket of traditional security studies. Its removal will create discomfort; familiar intellectual reference points will disappear. The picture (or pictures) of reality that will be generated once the blanket is cast aside will undoubtedly be far more complex and confusing than those drawn by traditional security studies. However, understanding this complexity is a prerequisite for bringing about comprehensive security. Statism, whether its theoretical justification is realist or poststructuralist, is a hindrance to those intent on pursuing this goal.

SECURITY AND EMANCIPATION

Apart from its statism, another feature that anchors *People, States and Fear* firmly to the traditional approach to thinking about security is its scientific objectivist epistemology. This epistemological position is premised on a claim that it is potentially possible to draw clear dividing lines between subject and object, fact and value, description and prescription. In Buzan's case, this position goes hand-in-hand with an explicit commitment to neorealism. Summing up his approach to security in *People, States and Fear,* Buzan comments:

> Some might even see International Security Studies as a liberal reformulation of Realism, emphasising the structural and security-oriented approach of Neorealism, and applying it across a broader agenda. I would support such a view. (Buzan 1991: 373)

Thus, although Buzan's position on the most apposite conceptualization of security is markedly different from that adopted by, for example, Walt or Gray, his position on what constitutes an acceptable theory of security is fundamentally similar.

There are serious problems with the epistemological underpinnings of neorealism, not the least of which is the obsolescence of the very scientific paradigm they seek to emulate. However, it is important to emphasize that these problems do not merely have repercussions at the abstract plane of high theory; in this case at least, the inadequacy of scientific objectivist epistemology has disturbing implications at a more concrete level.

In *People, States and Fear,* Buzan presents security as yet another "essentially contested concept." Despite his obvious preference for strong states and mature anarchy, he offers no theoretical grounds for judging rival accounts of security nor for deciding on the relative importance of security as compared with other values (Booth 1991a: 317; Smith 1991: 335). As Steve Smith points out, this leaves Buzan "dangerously close to relativism in choosing between rival accounts of security, and close to conservatism when it comes to asserting the importance of security, as opposed to other moral claims" (Smith 1991: 335). Despite his liberal sensibilities, Buzan's conceptualization of security provides him with no theoretical grounds for disputing, say, Radovan Karadzic's claims that Bosnian Serb security depends on the creation of an ethically pure territory. Because Smith realizes there are political and ethical lacunae at the heart of Buzan's project, he argues that the conceptualization of security should be based on some notion of emancipation. Given that "all theory is *for* someone and *for* some purpose" (R. Cox 1981: 128), Smith suggests that theories of security must be for those who are made insecure by the prevailing order, and their purpose must be to aid their emancipation.

During the course of this argument, Smith explicitly endorses the work of Ken Booth, one of the few scholars engaged in the study of security who have placed a commitment to emancipation at the center of their work. In his 1991 article "Security and Emancipation," Booth describes the interrelationship of the two elements of his title:

> "Security" means the absence of threats. Emancipation is the freeing of people (as individuals and groups) from those physical and human constraints which stop them carrying out what they would freely choose to do. War and threat of war is one of those constraints, together with poverty, poor education, political oppression and so on. Security and emancipation are two sides of the same coin. Emancipation, not power or order, produces true security. (Booth 1991a: 319)

Such a formulation obviously raises at least as many questions as it answers. In particular, the issue of what people "would freely choose to do" is undoubtedly one on which social theorists of various persuasions would disagree vehemently. There is also the vexed question of the relationship between theory and practice. How does an emancipatory approach to thinking about security interact with and impinge upon emancipatory praxis (see Chapter 6)?

I raise these concerns not to call into question the validity of Booth's explicit emphasis on emancipation (Booth [1999] outlines his thinking of emancipation in much more detail). Rather, returning to the metaphor in the E. P. Thompson passage at the start of this chapter, I do so to suggest that the recognition of the interrelationship between security and emancipation is not the end of the journey toward the development of an alternative and improved conceptualization of security. In fact, it is only a preliminary, if vitally important step. However, it is a step onto unfamiliar terrain for security analysts. Citizens and politicians are traveling without maps in the post–Cold War era; once security specialists renounce the old verities of traditional security studies and embrace a commitment to emancipation, they, too, have very few familiar markers upon which they can take their intellectual bearings. How, then, can critical security studies be developed that generates new maps—maps that can plot a way forward not only for a discipline but for society as a whole? I argue that this requires progress on two fronts.

First, those intent on developing critical security studies must embed their work in the general critical theory project. Successive generations of critical theorists have developed sophisticated and suggestive perspectives (both positive and negative) on the potential for and contours of emancipation. These provide a formidable resource upon which critical security studies can draw. The need for such an intellectual grounding becomes all too apparent when one analyzes the work of those scholars who have attempted an alternative approach to security on the basis of some form of poststructuralism. For although the critical edge, to say nothing of the intellectual coherence, of their work depends on some notion of the possibilities for progressive alternatives—that is, emancipation—the metatheoretical underpinnings upon which their work is built do not provide them with the concepts or, indeed, the theoretical language with which emancipation can be discussed. Their discussion of emancipation—what it means at either the abstract or the concrete level—is therefore left implicit or always deferred.

Consider, for example, the work of writers heavily influenced by poststructuralism who have already been discussed in this chapter. In the final paragraph—itself significant—of R. B. J. Walker's essay "The Subject of Security" the author observes:

> If the subject of security is the *subject* of security, it is necessary to ask, first and foremost, how the modern subject is being reconstituted and then ask what security could possibly mean in relation to it. It is in this context that it is possible to envisage a critical discourse about security, a discourse that engages with contemporary transformations of political life, with emerging accounts of who we might become, and the conditions under which we might become other than we are now without destroying others, ourselves or the planet on which we all live. (R. Walker 1997: 78)

Implicit in this passage is a notion of improving and, however contingently, the possibility of moving toward a better world than the present: that is, some notion of emancipation.

A close reading of Ole Wæver also reveals similar concerns in his discussion of the merits and demerits of securitizing and desecuritizing issues as part of what seems to be, in the broadest sense of the word, a progressive political project. In a revealing, if slightly opaque, footnote, Wæver agonizes:

> For understandable but contingent institutional reasons, post-structuralists have emerged on the academic scene with the political program of tearing down "givens," of opening up, making possible, freeing. This invites the reasonable question: opening up for what? Neo-nazis? War? How can the post-structuralist be sure that "liberating minds" and "transcending limits" will necessarily lead to more peaceful conditions, unless one makes an incredible enlightenment-indebted "harmony of interests" assumption? For someone working in the negatively-driven field of security, a post-structuralist politics of responsibility must turn out differently, with more will to power and less de-naturalization. (Wæver 1995: 86)

Again, Wæver seems to be hinting at some notion of emancipation—or, at the very least, some means beyond the purely arbitrary of deciding whether and how some forms of society are more acceptable (emancipated) than others.

There are certainly important differences between Walker and Wæver in their treatment of security, differences that should not be ignored or downplayed. However, both betray the same incapacity to go beyond these vague and oblique references to an underspecified notion of emancipation.[2] Is this a coincidence? Is it a reflection of the fact that deconstruction is a necessary prelude to reconstruction? Can we expect more concreteness and specificity in the future? I argue not. The poststructuralist hostility toward metanarratives and the concepts of totality and the universal—coupled with the emphasis on (even fetishization of?) difference and otherness—leaves its adherents without the necessary intellectual tools to conceptualize progress, development, and emancipation.

Although many, if not most, poststructuralist-inclined thinkers have broadly progressivist political inclinations, they are not in a position to justify these commitments theoretically (this argument is elaborated in relation to the 1991 Gulf War in Norris 1992 and in the context of contemporary Welsh politics in Hunter and Wyn Jones 1995). Thus Walker and Wæver are snared in the same "performative contradiction" (the phrase is Habermas's) as the leading lights of poststructuralism. Michel Foucault, for example, was a brave and tireless campaigner for prison reform. Yet his analysis of society (in this case, like that of Adorno) portrayed a world of unremitting and undifferentiated domination, giving him no theoretical grounds for arguing why one prison regime was preferable to another. His practice was emancipatory, but his theoretical output undermined the grounds for his actions by pointing to the alleged futility of all efforts to change society for the better.

In these circumstances, even if the argument of the preceding chapters is accepted and the arguments of critical theorists with regard to emancipation are seen as defective or incomplete, it must surely be right to anchor critical security studies in an intellectual tradition that is attempting to take this crucial issue seriously. Especially given that the main alternative involves a prior theoretical condemnation of all attempts at emancipation as merely generating new forms of domination, even though it simultaneously depends on implicit notions of emancipation to give its concrete analysis a critical edge.

In addition to anchoring critical security studies in the tradition of critical theory, the second move by which the concept of emancipation can become less of a terra incognita is through concrete analysis of particular issues and areas. After all, when the concept is considered abstractly, it is impossible to outline what form emancipation takes beyond fairly broad generalizations. Although such generalizations are necessary in that they clarify what the broad issues in question are—such as the potentialities (understood in terms of social practices) that emancipation can unleash— they are not sufficient. It is only when specific, historical examples are addressed that the discussion of emancipation can proceed to the consideration of particular institutions and forms of life.

This work is still very much in its infancy, a fact that is hardly surprising given that critical security studies itself is a very recent development. However, a number of relevant studies have already appeared, some by researchers with a specific security focus and others the work of those seeking to apply critical theory to particular aspects of the study of world politics.

Among the former, Ken Booth and Peter Vale have attempted to apply a critical security studies perspective to southern Africa (Booth 1994; Vale 1986). In a joint essay published in 1997, they apply a series of "disarmingly simple" questions to the region:

> Who should be the agents for differently conceived security practices? What institutions in particular settings will best advance regional security from a critical security perspective? What should the relationships be between regional and global structures and processes? What conditions can be created to deliver comprehensive regional security? . . . What would a condition of comprehensive regional security look like? (Booth and Vale 1997: 329–330)

As Booth and Vale admit, their answers to these questions are "contestable and complex" (Booth and Vale 1997: 330). Nevertheless, by showing that emancipation can be considered in concrete terms even (indeed, especially) in an area that enjoys the dubious distinction of being "the most distressed and insecure region in contemporary world politics" (Booth and Vale 1997: 329), the authors provide convincing testimony that by adopting such a perspective analysts are not escaping from real-world problems but are directly addressing them.

Booth and Vale's analysis of southern Africa ranges widely from possible force postures to the impact of migration on regional stability and the potential for regional political and economic cooperation. Given the critical stress on deepening the conceptualization of security, a process Booth describes as "investigating the implications and possibilities that result from seeing security as a concept that derives from different understandings of what politics is and can be all about" (Booth 1997a: 111), it is not surprising that the authors are also concerned about exploring the potential for alternative forms of political community in the area. In light of the failure of all sovereign states in southern Africa to provide their citizens with security—understood both broadly and in narrowly military terms—Booth and Vale discuss the possibility of encouraging the development of "non-statist states committed to regionalism and human diversity both internally and externally," what they term "rainbow states" (Booth and Vale 1997: 352, 353).

It is precisely at this point that the second potential source for understanding emancipation in concrete terms comes into play, namely, the work of those scholars attempting to apply the insights of critical theory to the study of world politics. Andrew Linklater is one of the foremost exponents of this approach. In his 1990 book *Beyond Realism and Marxism* Linklater wrote of the need "to construct a broader vision of the meaning and preconditions of emancipation," which he characterized as the extension of the "realm of social interaction which is governed by universalisable moral principles" (Linklater 1990b: 24, 26). His subsequent work has sought both to clarify and to elaborate upon this theoretical understanding of emancipation and also to seek out and highlight the (immanent) potential for emancipatory political transformation.

Linklater's theoretical explorations have been heavily influenced by Habermas's "discourse ethics"; Karl-Otto Apel's work on the subject also playing a significant supplementary role (Linklater 1996a: 85–88; 1998a: 77–144). Notwithstanding the criticism of Habermas advanced in Chapter 3, it cannot be denied that his recent study *The Transformation of Political Community* (Linklater 1998a) builds on these foundations to argue a powerful case for a "universal dialogic community." Linklater contends that the development of such a community would underpin the "triple transformation" of society, that is, the development of structures and practices that are simultaneously more universal, more sensitive to cultural difference, and characterized by greater material equality. The parallel "praxeological" elements of his work relate this understanding of emancipation to changing conceptions of sovereignty and citizenship. In particular, Linklater argues that the process of European integration contains within it the possibility for a move toward a "post-Westphalian era" (Linklater 1996a: 81–85; 1998a: 179–212; 1998b).

Linklater's work serves as an important reminder that the two approaches to understanding the interrelationship of emancipation and security—the study of critical theory approaches to emancipation and the more concrete analysis of particular political developments—should not be regarded as separate enterprises. Rather, they complement each other. The study of concrete examples generates insights that are useful on the more abstract level and vice versa. There is a dialectical relationship between both approaches from which proponents of critical security studies, as well as critical international theorists more generally, can profit.

NOTES

1. In the analysis of the dynamics of securitization in the various sectors, this concession appears to be clawed back to the extent that the authors effectively seem to regard states and identity groups as being the only successful "securitizing agents," that is, the only entities whose use of the grammar of security can generate the broader resonance needed to make the "securitizing move" successful—according to the authors' criteria (see Buzan, Wæver, and de Wilde 1998: 49–162). In this regard, as indeed in others, the book represents a less radical departure from their previous work (in particular Wæver et al. 1993) than may first appear to be the case.

2. The same issues are raised in Wæver's recent collaborative work with Barry Buzan and Jaap de Wilde (Buzan, Wæver, and de Wilde 1998). In that book, the authors take great care to distance themselves from the critical security studies approach and make great play of their refusal to "define some emancipatory ideal" (p. 35). Simultaneously, however, they also proclaim the need "to understand the dynamics of security and thereby maneuver them" (p. 35) and argue that one of the benefits of their approach is that it "becomes possible to evaluate whether one finds it good or bad to securitize a certain issue" (p. 34). This confusion is almost certainly a reflection of the work's metatheoretical underpinnings—in this case a somewhat contorted amalgam of constructivism and more traditional (in a Horkheimerian sense) approaches. But whatever its source, the resulting failure to seriously engage with the issue of why some outcomes are preferred to others means that the authors' preference for desecuritization receives almost no theoretical support or justification. Ironically, in light of their position on critical security studies, Habermasian discourse ethics could well supply the buttress their position requires.

5

Technology: Reconceptualizing Strategy

As Chapter 4 has demonstrated, an expanded conceptualization of security is rendered necessary, even perhaps inescapable, by at least two impulses. First, it is made necessary by empirical practice. All attempts by traditional security specialists to constrain the realm of what is conceived of as the legitimate concern of security studies are subverted by the actual usage of the term in everyday security discourse. Note, for example, the way in which a broader conceptualization has been long been in use in Southeast Asia (discussed in Booth and Trood 1998). Both politicians and social movements regularly use the term in relation to threats across a whole range of what Buzan has termed "sectors." As even many security specialists are beginning to acknowledge, attempts to constrict the realm of security studies to the study of military security are untenable. To do so is to ignore a whole range of issues that most governments, let alone individual human beings, regard as real security concerns.

The same argument also holds true for all attempts to constrict the term to a particular privileged referent object, namely, the state. To adopt Wæver's terminology, other actors *securitize* and are *securitized*. Once again, this is a point that is slowly being grasped by Western academic international relations security specialists. For example, as was noted in Chapter 4, Buzan, through his collaboration with the Copenhagen School, has tried to develop society as an additional referent object, even though this effort creates substantial problems for his original conceptualization of security. The same author now also admits the need for an "opening up to the fact that the domestic agenda has become the primary military forum in some parts of the world" (Buzan and Herring 1998). The increased attention that has been paid to "internal conflicts" (i.e., intrastate conflicts), such as the war in the former Yugoslavia and the rise of so-called warlordism in some Third World countries, has led more mainstream security specialists to focus on referents other than the state (see, for example, Herbst 1996–1997; Howe 1996–1997).

Efforts to uphold a constrictive definition of security as national security defined in statist, militarized terms seem bound to fail, despite the efforts of the traditionalists (see, for example, Walt 1991; Morgan 1992; Garnett 1996). Even when understood in narrowly military terms, security is not simply the concern or preserve of states.

A second pressure that further reinforces the case for an expanded conceptualization of security arises from the epistemological and political arguments that I have already put forward in this book for an emancipation-oriented approach to the study of the social world. As I argue in Chapter 4, security and emancipation are dialectically interrelated. Security in the sense of the absence of the threat of (involuntary) pain, fear, hunger, and poverty is an essential element in the struggle for emancipation. And security is both a means and an end. The achievement of enhanced security can be emancipatory in itself in a context characterized by chronic insecurity. Bearing in mind that emancipation is a process rather than an end point, however, security is also a vital precursor to the fuller development of human potential. If this viewpoint is accepted, then it is clear that the conceptualization of security will expand to include all those threats to human well-being and development.

This argument in favor of an expanded conceptualization of security—a concept that is both broadened and extended—does generate at least two potential problems for those attempting to develop critical security studies. There is the question of whether by expanding the conceptualization of security, its study becomes the study of everything, and hence, effectively, nothing; and there is also the issue of whether an expanded conceptualization of security inevitably leads analysts to pay less attention to military issues.

Does the expanded notion of security lying at the heart of critical security studies lead to a research project that lacks analytical rigor and bite? This does not seem to be a serious cause for concern. The case for an expanded conceptualization of security, and hence an expanded understanding of the scope of security studies, can be argued on two grounds, one negative and the other positive.

In a negative vein, as I argue at length in Chapter 4, the relatively focused nature of traditional security studies was based on a conceptualization of security that was far too narrow. The traditional state-centric, militarized, and largely apolitical understanding of security is theoretically and politically deficient. Although it may have suited the disciplinary purposes of traditional security studies in the battle for both academic and politico-military recognition, it has always been reifying, unhistorical, intellectual nonsense. So an expanded conceptualization of security is an improvement on the traditional version simply because it is more logically defensible. Whatever parsimoniousness was enjoyed by traditional security studies was purchased at the price of rigor and intellectual coherence.

A more positive response to the charge of "loss of focus" is that far from being a problem, an expanded conceptualization of security and a concomitant widening of focus actually facilitate the overcoming of the most damaging binary division afflicting the social sciences—that between the domestic (intrastate) and the international (interstate). In recent years this divide has been challenged from both sides. Those disciplines that have traditionally focused on the domestic—for example, sociology—have started to incorporate the international into their analysis (Giddens 1985 is an important landmark in this respect). In the field of international relations, events such as the oil shocks of the 1970s and the end of the Cold War have underlined the futility of attempting to analyze international politics without reference to domestic factors. This blurring of the distinction between what R. B. J. Walker has termed the "inside" and "outside" can be seen most clearly in the burgeoning contemporary literature on globalization. Although some of the globalization literature betrays a tendency toward faddism and hyperbole, taken as a whole, it does indicate a growing realization that the traditional distinctions between the domestic and the international, the political and the economic, and the natural (environment) and the social (society) are untenable.

The trend toward a more holistic approach—an attempt to understand the social totality—is in keeping with the spirit of critical theory (if not to the practice of its notoriously Eurocentric proponents). An expanded conceptualization of security provides an ideal means through which this more expansive perspective may be developed. The understanding of security developed in Chapter 4 links together consideration of military force with issues in political economy, environmental science, psychology, anthropology, ethics, and so on. This eclectic focus on linkages and interrelationships across arbitrary disciplinary boundaries is wholly in accord with the understanding of social science championed by Horkheimer in "Traditional and Critical Theory."

From a critical theory perspective, the obvious overlaps between the research agenda generated by an expanded understanding of security and the sociological analyses of the "risk society" pioneered by Ulrich Beck are not a cause for concern or intellectual demarcation disputes but rather an occasion for celebration. The two approaches have much to learn from each other. For example, those whose intellectual biography has led to their identification (and self-identification) as security specialists can profit from Beck's sophisticated treatment of environmental risk (see Beck 1995). Equally, Beck and his collaborators can benefit from the understanding of interstate dynamics, particularly security regimes and the international politics of risk management developed by international relations specialists. The point is that far from lacking rigor and bite, an expanded conceptualization of security actually facilitates studies relevant to the real world and invaluable intellectual cross-pollination.

A second concern that arises from the adoption of an expanded conceptualization of security is the possibility that the broader agenda that inevitably results from this expansion will somehow lead analysts to pay less attention to military issues. An associated assumption may be that even when analysts do give attention to the so-called military instrument, they will do so in a hopelessly idealistic manner. This concern would be valid if a broader notion of security implied an unwillingness or inability to think seriously about the military dimension of the theory and practice of world politics. But as I will seek to demonstrate in this chapter, this is not the case. Instead, I will argue that the outlook and assumptions outlined in the previous chapters actually generate a framework for the analysis of military force that is potentially richer and more sophisticated than that utilized by traditional security studies.

SECURITY AND STRATEGY

Buzan's work provides a useful starting point for attempts to think through the military dimension of world politics. Given the criticisms advanced against his work in Chapter 4, this may seem a somewhat surprising suggestion. Nevertheless, the fact remains that Buzan's broader conceptualization of security was a fundamental assault on the tendency of traditional security studies to conflate consideration of issues relating to military security with security per se. One result of this conflation was that Buzan had to consider how military force might be conceptualized when it is understood as a part—rather than the whole—of what has become known as the "security problematique." He first attempted to do so in his 1987 book *An Introduction to Strategic Studies: Military Technology and International Relations* (Buzan and Herring 1998 is its anointed successor). Therefore, despite objections to other basic assumptions underpinning Buzan's work—including, until very recently at least, his state-centrism and what may be termed, after Horkheimer, as his "traditional" epistemology—his conceptualization of the military dimension remains a useful point of departure.

In contrast to the tendency of analysts to use the terms "security studies" and "strategic studies" interchangeably, Buzan wishes to draw a strong distinction between the terms (Buzan 1987; also 1991: 270–291). Specifically, he attempts to reserve the latter term for the study of the role of military force in international relations; or, to use the terminology of *People,*

States and Fear, Buzan argues that strategic studies should concern itself with the "military sector" of the security problematique. Therefore, in disciplinary terms, Buzan regards strategic studies as a subset of what he terms "international security studies," which is in turn a subset of the study of international relations.

Turning to the specific consideration of strategy, Buzan argues that its subject matter "arises from two fundamental variables affecting the international system: its political structure, and the nature of the prevailing technologies available to the political actors within it" (Buzan 1987: 6). Given Buzan's neorealist inclinations, it is not surprising that he views the political structure as an epiphenomenon of global anarchy. As a result, he posits the following relationship between both variables:

> Anarchy creates the over-all need for strategy, and sets the conditions that determine the ends for which force is used. Technology is a major factor in determining the scope of military options, the character of military threats, and the consequences of resorting to the use of force. Technology, in other words, is [a] major variable affecting the instruments of force available to political actors. The nature of those instruments sets a basic condition of strategy, and one that is subject to continuous pressure of technological change. (Buzan 1987: 6–7)

Furthermore, because Buzan believes that "the raw fact of anarchy is in many ways a constant within the international system," he argues that strategists should focus on military technology (Buzan 1987: 9). Thus, according to this view, the correct conceptualization of strategy is as a focus on the impact of military technology on interstate relations.

The publication of *An Introduction to Strategic Studies* and a subsequent critical review by Lawrence Freedman in the journal *International Affairs* generated a lively debate among strategists, or at least among those working in the United Kingdom (Freedman 1988a). Unusually, this controversy was not confined to the pages of academic journals but also included a debate between the proponents of the various viewpoints conducted under the auspices of the Royal Institute of International Affairs (RIIA) (Segal 1989 provides an edited transcript). This debate provided a fascinating snapshot of the differing perceptions of the scope and purpose of strategy in the mid- to late 1980s.

The most frequent criticism of Buzan's conceptualization of strategy was that it was too narrow. This judgment represents a considerable irony given that the most common criticism of *People, States and Fear* was that it cast a conception of security that was unmanageably broad. Nevertheless, when Buzan attempted to conceptualize the place of strategy within this broader framework, the resulting definition was considered to be overly restrictive. Indeed, if those participating in the RIIA debate are representative, then the majority of strategists working in the United Kingdom seem to have regarded Buzan's understanding of strategy as a conceptual regression from the classical Clausewitzian focus on the interrelationship between political ends and military means. In this vein, Ken Booth, for example, argued that strategy should focus on "the relationship between the threat and use of force and politics. The title of Bernard Brodie's, *War and Politics,* should be regarded as synonymous with strategic studies" (Segal 1989: 18).

Booth's critique may be rephrased in terms of the critique of instrumental rationality that was advanced by Adorno and Horkheimer and reconstructed in Chapter 2. Buzan wants strategists to regard the ends pursued by the use of military force as a given (and in his schema they are given by the dynamics that are an inherent, and ultimately inescapable, feature of the international system) and concentrate wholly on the military means themselves. Although he recognizes that the ends pursued are the legitimate concern of international relations scholars—indeed, he posits a division of labor between international relations specialists and strategists on this score—Buzan's formulation of strategy as a subject that ignores ends provides what may be considered a paradigmatic example of instrumental rationality (Segal 1989: 3–6). This formulation, in critical theory terms, represents the atrophy of reason: a pathology, a moral blindness, the type of thinking that was exhibited in the mechanized slaughter at Auschwitz. In this context it is perhaps instructive to recall the title of Fred Kaplan's study of the architects of nuclear deterrence—*The Wizards of Armageddon* (1983).

To find such an explicit call as Buzan made for a conceptualization of strategy that ignores the ends—the human results—of military force is particularly disturbing given the destructiveness of the means under consideration. So, superficially at least, it might seem heartening that the overall tenor of the RIIA meeting was hostile to Buzan's formulation. For these participants, the concern with ends was a vital element of strategy. The following passage from one of Freedman's contributions is indicative of the general view:

> Strategic studies is an outcrop not of international relations, but of political theory, because the great political theorists were also preoccupied with this question of how it is that people relate ends and means. One is trying to understand how it is that people go about defining objectives and then obtaining them. That seems to me to be what strategic studies is about, and that is what I find so interesting. (Segal 1989: 2)

But despite Freedman's eminent position in the strategic studies communities of both Europe and North America, to conclude from this statement and the tenor of the RIIA debate that the study of strategy is not the preserve of instrumental rationality would be wrong.

Rather, as so many critics of strategic studies have pointed out, the subject has been dominated by an approach that disregards the ends for which military force is utilized and tends to ignore or gloss over the human and environmental consequences of its use (there are numerous critiques of the hegemonic view of strategy, including Rapoport 1960, 1964, 1970, 1978; Green 1966, 1973; Cohn 1987; Lawrence 1985, 1988; Klein 1994). Although the proponents of traditional security studies have invoked the Clausewitzian conceptualization of warfare, this invocation has been almost entirely ritualistic and lacking in any real substance. Strategy has tended to be the preserve of the bean counters and those whose parameters extend little further than a detailed knowledge of the capabilities of the latest weapons system. It is this narrowly instrumental focus of strategy that allows Buzan to defend his conceptualization of the subject on the ground that it "matches pretty much what the field actually does" (Segal 1989: 3). Though this hardly represents an overwhelming argument in favor of his position, it seems to me that Buzan's bald and concise conceptualization of strategy at least has the merit of laying bare the reality of contemporary strategic theory. I doubt very much that Clausewitz, with his speculative bent and his interest in Hegelian dialectics, would have ever made the grade in postwar traditional security studies.

How, then, can one develop an approach to strategy that is congruent within the overall set of assumptions that frame critical security studies? One obvious point of departure would be to subject traditional security understandings of strategy to an immanent critique that compares the field's self-image, which in Europe, at least, regards a concern with ends and consequences as an inherent part of the enterprise, with the instrumental, means-fetishism of so much strategy. If such a critique could be successfully coupled with a move to critique the actual ends pursued—the privileging of the state, for example—then it would certainly be a notable improvement on the current situation.

But the critical theory argument reconstructed in the first three chapters of this book is not that proponents of traditional theory are all conservative, although some may be, or that they are moral inadequates, although doubtless some are, but rather that the epistemological assumptions underlying their work leads to analysis that is pro–status quo and amoral. According to this perspective, strategy cannot be redeemed or reconstructed simply by attaching a concern with ends onto the actual practice of contemporary strategic thought. The atrophy of strategy—the tendency to concentrate solely on means—is a result of the assumptions made by strategists about what constitutes knowledge: most important, the relationship between fact and value and subject and object. Thus to transform strategy in a direction more attuned to the approach of critical security studies requires a fundamental transformation of the epistemological basis of the enterprise (see Bonß's critique of Horkheimer in Chapter 2).

Parenthetically, I submit that concern with epistemology points to the difference between critical security studies and much of peace research, two approaches that seem to have much in common. According to a critical theory–informed perspective, the attempt to utilize traditional methodology within a broader normative, peace-oriented framework—an approach that is prevalent in peace research—simply generates a contradictory intellectual project that must eventually succumb to conformism if the methodological logic is allowed to dominate or will collapse into pure idealism if the normative program is not supported by a different mode of analysis.

What is required, therefore, is a mode of analysis that recognizes two points: that it is not enough to combine traditional modes of analysis with a commitment to emancipation, and that ends and means are not somehow casually related but are mutually implicated. As a result of such recognition, analysis will focus on the actually-existing possibilities for change arising from a hardheaded, historically grounded reading of the present. I argue that a particularly useful model for such an approach in the field of strategy is provided by Andrew Feenberg's critical theory of technology (see Chapter 3).

TECHNOLOGY AND STRATEGY

Feenberg's conceptualization of technology is relevant in at least two ways. First, few would doubt that the implications of various military technologies are, quite legitimately, a central concern of strategists. True, in the context of the RIIA debate referred to earlier, Freedman did attempt to pour scorn on Buzan's emphasis on military technology:

> I cannot see why . . . military technology itself stands out as being the key variable. I can see a case for a focus upon military aspects of power. But the study of military technology is not going to explain an awful lot about, for example, the Iran-Iraq war. . . . There is a regular source of new thinking derived from new technologies, but that is not the same as saying that, in the end, the basic calculations with which people go to war have been changed that much simply by technology. (Segal 1989: 10)

However, the fact that Freedman's major work *The Evolution of Nuclear Strategy* (1987) deals with some of the implications of nuclear weapons technology in terms of force structures, doctrines, and the rest tends to suggest that this comment is more polemical than seriously meant.

Despite the fact that strategists have focused on military technology, their theoretical understanding of technology qua technology has been deficient. Despite the obvious parallels and overlaps, strategists have paid almost no heed to work in the fields of the history and sociology of technology (a point central to the argument in Flank 1993–1994). Buzan's *An Introduction to Strategic Studies* is an excellent example of the unwillingness of a strategist to take technology seriously. This may seem a somewhat paradoxical claim given that Buzan defines strategy in terms of the study of the effect of military technology on interstate relations. Yet in *An Introduction to Strategic Studies* he does not refer to any of the standard works on technology (see Buzan 1987: 302–319). So, despite making technology the key variable in his conceptualization of strategy, Buzan does not attempt to use the extensive social science literature on the subject. Even his most recent (joint) work on strategy makes no serious attempt to engage with this literature; a fact made all the more disappointing because of the avowed intention of the authors to place more emphasis on "the interaction of choice, politics and values with technology" (Buzan and Herring 1998).

Buzan is not alone in ignoring the work that has been carried out in other social science disciplines—the same is also true of the overwhelming majority of strategists (another good example is Garnett 1987b). This inattention would perhaps be excusable if strategists had developed their own sophisticated conceptualization of technology. But they have failed to do so: Their understanding of technology has been confused, crude, and unreflective. Thus one benefit of adopting Feenberg's critical approach to technology is that it is based on a detailed—and, to my mind, persuasive—reading of the voluminous literature on technology. As such, it brings a welcome broadness and sophistication to a field where these qualities have been absent.

A second feature of Feenberg's work that renders it particularly instructive in the attempt to reconceptualize strategy is his view of technology as the realm of ambivalent processes and possibilities. By stressing ambivalence, Feenberg's approach serves as a salutary reminder of the role of human agency in decisions relating to military technology. By focusing on human beings, and more specifically human subjectivity, in relation to the military realm, analysts are encouraged to recognize that ethical concerns and considerations are not extrinsic to the business of strategy but are a central part of strategic practice. This in turn invites strategic theory to scrutinize and evaluate those concerns and considerations not as additions or optional extras to real strategic analysis but as necessary conditions for such analysis. As I argue in Chapter 4, a critical theory perspective suggests that this scrutiny and evaluation should take place from the perspective of emancipation, for which individuals are the ultimate referent.

Indeed, Feenberg's work gives concrete indications of how a concern with emancipation can become part of the analysis of military technology. As already discussed, Feenberg analyzes technology in terms of processes embodying ambivalent possibilities and attempts to highlight the most progressive among them. Obviously, military technology, geared as it is toward the generation of slaughter and suffering, hardly lends itself to a progressive reading. Nevertheless, as I will demonstrate in the final section of this chapter, when viewed through the lenses of a critical theory of technology, even military technologies reveal an ambivalence that can be directed in ways that form a potentially useful part of a wider emancipatory project.

NUCLEAR WEAPONS AS TECHNOLOGY

By focusing on nuclear weapons in this section, I will seek to demonstrate the utility of Feenberg's critical theory of technology for the reconceptualization of strategy. Nuclear weapons are a good case for consideration because they are a hard case, for two reasons. First, they have been a central focus—often the only focus—of postwar strategists. Nuclear deterrence theory was the central achievement of strategy, and as such, basing, procurement, force postures, declaratory policies, and the rest became its basic bread-and-butter issues. If a critical theory–influenced approach can say something new and meaningful about nuclear weapons—or, perhaps more realistically, if it can make new sense of some of the things that have already been said—then this new understanding may constitute at least a prima facie case for using this approach.

A second reason for concentrating on nuclear weapons is the widespread perception that they represent a major change, indeed a revolution, not only in warfare but also in the relationship between "men and machines." Even after the first successful testing of a nuclear weapon, but before their deployment against human beings, Winston Churchill reportedly exclaimed: "What was gunpowder? Trivial. What was electricity? Meaningless. This Atomic Bomb is the Second Coming in Wrath" (Freedman 1987: 16). Since their use against Hiroshima on August 6, 1945, which resulted in the instantaneous slaughter of at least 68,000 civilians (Glasstone and Dolan 1977: 541–574), such biblical imagery has been a recurring feature of attempts to make sense of the awesome destructive power unleashed on that unsuspecting Japanese city.

According to the Book of Revelations, the Second Coming is to be accompanied by a final battle at Armageddon on Judgment Day. This will be the battle to end all battles, in which, according to the apocalyptic vision, the world will be shaken by "flashes of lightning and peals of thunder, and a violent earthquake, like none before in human history, so violent it was" (*The New English Bible with the Apocrypha* 1970: 330). The use of this type of imagery in relation to nuclear weapons is extremely suggestive. It indicates a belief that the attempt to harness the tremendous energy unlocked during nuclear fission, the physical process initiated by the detonation of an atomic bomb, and the even greater amounts of energy unleashed during nuclear fusion, utilized in hydrogen bombs, have released a kind of technological genie that is beyond human comprehension. Furthermore, such imagery suggests that the development of nuclear weapons represents a fundamental shift in the relationship of the human species with technology per se. Raymond Aron laments that as a result of the development of nuclear weapons, humanity now inhabits an age of "virile weapons and impotent men" (Herken 1985: 343). Again, this serves to make nuclear weapons a particularly challenging case for a critical approach to technology.

As I discussed in Chapter 3, Feenberg differentiates between three conceptualizations of the relationship between technology and society: the instrumental, the substantive, and the critical. To reprise them, the instrumental view posits that technology is a neutral medium or means; the substantive view argues that, far from being neutral, technology inexorably determines social relations in a particular way; the critical view holds that technology is an ambivalent process that contains a number of possibilities and that the decision over which of these possibilities is realized depends on a complex of (contestable) power relations.

Given the tendency to view nuclear weapons in apocalyptic terms, it would be reasonable to expect that most of the strategic literature on the implications of nuclear weapons would view them in substantive or critical terms. After all, these are the approaches that view technology as non-neutral, and the apocalyptic rhetoric strongly suggests that something fundamental changed with the advent of nuclear weapons. Surprisingly, therefore, as the following brief survey of the literature demonstrates, despite this rhetoric, many of those writing and thinking about nuclear weapons have perceived them in instrumental terms. Further, most of the writing on nuclear weapons adopts either the instrumental or substantive conceptualization of technology, with relatively few adopting the critical approach.

Instrumental Approaches to Nuclear Weapons

The instrumental approach argues that technology does not affect the social, political, and cultural fundamentals in either domestic or international politics. This "deep assumption" is held with regard to nuclear weapons technology by a rather unlikely group of people. For example, it seems that Colin Gray, the arch proponent of a "nuclear war–fighting" strategy, John Mueller, the proclaimer of the "essential irrelevance" of nuclear weapons, and Mao Tse-tung all share the same broad assumptions about the implications of nuclear weapons technology. Although they would all hold highly dissimilar views on the nature and trajectory of global social and political relationships, they would all agree that nuclear weapons do not significantly alter those relationships.

Gray and the nuclear war fighters have viewed nuclear weapons in what may be termed the "National Rifle Association perspective" (see Chapter 3). To paraphrase this view, "It's not the nuke, it's the person (state) holding the nuke." That is, in the hands of the free, civilized, and democratic Western powers, nuclear weapons could be deployed in such a way as to deter a potential aggressor, or if deterrence was unsuccessful, to defeat an adversary. However, those very same weapons in the hands of the aggressive, expansionist, even evil Soviets are inevitably dangerous and provocative. Thus nuclear weapons did not alter what were seen as the fundamental traits of Soviet behavior nor the goals of the Soviet Union; rather, nuclear weapons merely gave the Soviets a new (potentially very dangerous) means of pursuing those goals. Gray contemptuously dismisses those who argue "that all weapons are created equal and have equivalent consequences according to their technical qualities but regardless of their political ownership" (Gray 1993: 155).

For Gray and the other war fighters close to the Reagan administration in the early 1980s, the possibility that the Soviets might acquire a first-strike capability was intensely worrisome, but such a capability in the hands of the United States could be viewed benignly. Similarly, the development and deployment of the Soviet SS18 missile was regarded as a highly dangerous development, whereas the technically similar U.S. MX was dubbed the "peacemaker" (the significance of the language deployed in relation to the theory and practice of security is discussed further in Chapter 6). Thus "It isn't the gun, it's the person holding the gun" or, as Gray titled one of his works, *Weapons Don't Make War* (1993).

John Mueller's view of the nature of the Soviet Union and the essence of the East-West relationship since 1945, as advanced in his article "The Essential Irrelevance of Nuclear Weapons," differs fundamentally from that of Gray and the war fighters (Mueller 1988; see also 1990). He argues that a "general stability" existed in East-West relations, a stability created by a complex of sociopolitical and economic factors and a stability upon which nuclear weapons had no effect. Thus, despite their different interpretations of the nature of the Soviet Union, Gray and Mueller share the same conception of the role of technology in the superpower relationship. Both reject "the fallacious idea that weapons or technologies move history along" (Gray 1993: 155). According to Mueller, "nuclear weapons have changed little except our way of talking, gesturing, and spending money" (Mueller 1988: 68).

Mao Tse-tung was another proponent of the instrumental approach to technology in relation to nuclear weapons. His oft-stated belief was that no weapons system, no matter how sophisticated the technology incorporated within it, could alter the fundamental political and economic "correlation of forces." Thus Mao argued:

> The atom bomb is a paper tiger which the US reactionaries use to scare people. It looks terrible but in fact it isn't. Of course, the atom bomb is a weapon of mass slaughter, but the outcome of a war is decided by the people, not by one or two new types of weapon. (Mao 1968: 8)

Mao was convinced that the correlation of forces favored the socialist bloc and was concerned that those ensconced in the Kremlin would squander the historic opportunity offered by such apparently propitious circumstances because of their fear of these paper tigers. Indeed, he seemed convinced that not even a nuclear war could derail the global advance of Marxism-Leninism. In a discussion titled "We Must Not Fear Nuclear War," Mao remarked, "If the worse came to the worst and half of mankind died, the other half would remain while imperialism would be razed to the ground and the whole world would become socialist" (Mao 1968: 409; see also 1977: 152–153). Again, Mao's argument was that technology, even nuclear technology, could not affect the fundamental patterns of political and social relations, which Mao believed were heralding the inevitable triumph of socialism.

Examining nuclear technology from the perspective of underlying assumptions about that technology, we find that those who rang alarm bells about windows of opportunity seem to have shared the same deep assumptions as those who were sanguine about the intentions of the Soviet leadership. Similarly, we find an avowed defender of U.S. values like Colin Gray in the same camp as the author of the famous little red book.

Substantive Approaches to Nuclear Weapons

The substantive approach argues that technology has an autonomous logic of its own that determines a particular form of social organization. As was the case with proponents of the instrumental approach, when those who share a substantive approach to nuclear technology are gathered together, an unlikely combination emerges: in this case, McGeorge Bundy, the exponent of "existential deterrence," Kenneth Waltz, a supporter of (gradual) nuclear proliferation, and E. P. Thompson, one of the most indefatigable antinuclear campaigners.

According to Bundy and other proponents of existential deterrence, the very fact that a state possesses nuclear weapons is enough to ensure that other states will be deterred from threatening its vital interests no matter how hostile their political relationship. The existentialists believe that numbers, force postures, and targeting—in short, all those issues that have exercised generations of strategists and policymakers—are irrelevant. Mere possession of nuclear weapons is sufficient: or, in the words of an article by Freedman, "I Exist; Therefore I Deter" (Freedman 1988b). Bundy argues that nuclear weapons are so destructive that their mere presence will moderate state behavior because of the fear and uncertainty they introduce into any crisis situation:

> A decision that would bring even one hydrogen bomb on one city of one's country would be recognised in advance as a catastrophic blunder; ten bombs on ten cities would be a disaster beyond history; and a hundred bombs on a hundred cities are unthinkable. (Bundy 1969: 10; see also 1984)

Quite simply, existentialists believe that nuclear weapons technology is so lethally potent that its potential effects override all other political, social, and cultural considerations in the calculations of decisionmakers.

Kenneth Waltz's well-known argument in favor of gradual nuclear proliferation is based on the same kind of assumptions as those underlying the existential deterrence position; he merely pushes the argument to its logical conclusion. Like Bundy, Waltz believes that the presence of nuclear weapons inevitably moderates the behavior of states: "The probability of major war among states having nuclear weapons approaches zero" (Waltz 1990: 740). He underlines that this benefit accrues whatever the political hue of the states in question: "One need not become preoccupied with the characteristics of the state that is to be deterred or scrutinize its leaders" (Waltz 1990: 737–738).

Waltz argues that because of the technologically determined, pacifying nature of nuclear weapons, their benefits should be spread throughout the international system by gradual proliferation. In a paper subtitled "More May Be Better," he summarily dismisses the "ethnocentric views" of those wary of allowing nuclear weapons to fall into the hands of the leaders of unstable Southern states: "Many Westerners who write fearfully about a future in which third-world countries have nuclear weapons seem to view their people in the once familiar imperial manner as 'lesser breeds without the law'" (Waltz 1981: 11). Clearly, Waltz views nuclear technology as an autonomous force that determines a particular pattern of state behavior, thereby overriding all other social and political factors.

Both the arguments put forward by the proponents of existential deterrence and Waltz's arguments for proliferation suggest that the autonomous logic of nuclear weapons technology is benign. However, others who share a substantive understanding of the nature of nuclear technology have developed an analysis that is diametrically opposed to these arguments. In particular, many in the peace movement have argued that, to use Frank Barnaby's words, "we are being driven toward nuclear world war by the sheer momentum of military technology" (Barnaby 1982: 35).

Arguably the most eloquent exponent of this view was E. P. Thompson. In "Sources of Exterminism," an essay first published in the *New Left Review* in 1980 and subsequently reproduced as the centerpiece of a collection titled *Exterminism and Cold War* (E. Thompson 1982b), Thompson argued that the nuclear arms race had an autonomous, exterminist logic that would lead to the extermination of the human race. He regarded nuclear weapons in a deterministic fashion, claiming, for example, that the weapons "and their attendant support-systems, seem to grow of their own accord, as if possessed by an independent will" (E. Thompson 1982b: 5). Although Thompson called for and was a prominent participant in a movement of concerned citizens dedicated to checking exterminism, such is the autonomous power that he ascribes to nuclear weapons that it is hard to see how their deadly logic could be checked. His antinuclear activism seems to have been based on a Gramscian "pessimism of intellect and optimism of will."

Despite the very different conclusions arrived at in their work, the common thread in the thinking of Bundy, Waltz, and Thompson is a similar, substantive approach to the relationship between human beings and nuclear technology. They all see that technology as an autonomous force shaping social relations and as a universal destiny that overrides cultural particularity.

Critical Approaches to Nuclear Weapons

There can be little doubt that most contributions to the vast literature on the implications of nuclear weapons have been based on either instrumental or substantive conceptualizations of technology. For example, the recurrent debate in the United States between nuclear-use theorists and proponents of mutually assured destruction is essentially an argument between instrumentalist and substantivist positions, respectively (M. Williams 1992b). However, I would argue that those studies that have utilized a critical approach to technology—whether knowingly or not—offer the most insights into the actual behavior of nuclear-armed states.

The critical approach stresses the ambivalent nature of technology: Technology opens up a range of options or choices for society, and the options chosen depend in part on the configuration of power relations within that society and almost invariably serve to reinforce the position of the hegemonic group. Some of the studies of nuclear weapons that have adopted this type of approach fall into the broad category of "arms race literature." These studies have placed issues like procurement decisions in the context of domestic political disputes. By doing so, they have exposed the way that these decisions often reflect bureaucratic and political power struggles rather than any rational enemy threat (a particularly sophisticated treatment of the U.S.-Soviet nuclear arms race is provided by Evangelista 1988). This theme is given a further twist by those scholars who have analyzed the role played by nuclear weapons in the construction and legitimation of the national security states on both sides of the Cold War divide (see, for example, M. Cox 1984, 1986, 1990). Such work undermines both instrumental and substantive understandings of nuclear technology and simultaneously draws out the relationship between military technology and political and socioeconomic power.

Bruce Blair's comparative study of U.S. and Soviet nuclear forces provides further powerful support for proponents of a critical approach to technology (Blair 1993). Blair demonstrates the technological constraints within which both states had to operate. Developments in rocket technology reduced both the time needed to prepare missiles for firing and their flight time en route to their targets. These developments forced both countries to develop command and control systems that could react rapidly in times of crisis. However, the force structures developed by both sides to deal with this problem were very different and reflected their wider strategic and political cultures. The USSR, skeptical about the possibility of fighting a nuclear war and suspicious of military Bonapartism, was obsessed with retaining full political control over nuclear weapons and thus adopted a highly centralized command and control system. The United States, for its part, was deeply concerned both with the possibility of not being able to retaliate in the case of a Soviet first strike because of paralysis in decision-making structures and ensuring that its forces could destroy the wide range of targets allotted to them under the single integrated war plan. Thus U.S. politicians and planners adopted a highly decentralized command and control system in which the authority to launch nuclear weapons in a time of crisis was predelegated down the chain of command.

These force structures led to the development of a highly unstable system in which both sides' configuration of hardware and doctrine seem to have been almost custom-designed to inflame the other side's worst fears. The Soviets' highly centralized system was difficult for the Americans to analyze, whereas U.S. efforts toward predelegation were certain to fuel Soviet fears that a U.S. surprise strike was in the offing. Blair's analysis strongly suggests that the human race was extremely fortunate not to see the whole system break down disastrously.

The compatibility of Blair's study with the critical approach to technology lies in the fact that both the United States and the USSR were faced with technologically constrained choices and chose particular solutions that reflected the values and interests of the ruling elites in both states. The fact that some of the most detailed and sophisticated empirical studies of nuclear weapons, including Blair's, provide such a good fit with the critical approach to technology has broad theoretical implications for the conceptualization of strategic behavior. It also suggests a number of important political possibilities.

THEORETICAL IMPLICATIONS
AND POLITICAL POSSIBILITIES

Superficially, the critical approach to technology, with its emphasis on the importance of culture and politics, seems to be compatible with the literature on strategic culture (for an overview, see Booth and Macmillan 1998). If the insights of the critical approach are to be fully accommodated by students of strategic culture, however, then this accommodation will require the rethinking of the notion of strategic culture itself. Once this is accomplished, a revised understanding of strategic culture can take its place at the center of the conceptualization of strategy.

In his original formulation, Jack Snyder defined strategic culture as the outcome of a "socialisation process" through which "a set of general beliefs, attitudes and behavioural patterns" achieve "a state of semipermanence that places them on the level of 'culture' rather than mere 'policy'" (Snyder 1977: v). The concept has since been utilized to provide useful insights into different national styles in war and peace. Thus far, the implicit assumption about technology underlying the strategic culture literature has been instrumental. That is, analysts have concentrated their attention on the ways in which similar weapons are utilized differently by different states, reflecting different ways of warfare.

The critical approach to technology also focuses on the ways in which the usage of technology reflects different values in society, but it goes a stage further. The critical approach stresses the ways in which technology affects and shapes society. So, in the case of strategy, the critical argument is that analysts need to focus not only on the ways in which strategic culture influences decisions pertaining to the utilization of technology but also on the ways in which technological developments affect strategic culture and, furthermore, the ways in which particular technologies can actually embody social (cultural) values and power configurations. In short, the concept of strategic culture needs to be recast to include the dialectical interaction of culture and technology.

Definitionally, such a recasting is relatively unproblematic. Indeed, some current definitions of strategic culture can be read in a way that incorporates a focus on technology in the manner suggested here. Take, for example, Ken Booth's definition:

> The concept of strategic culture refers to a nation's traditions, values, attitudes, patterns of behaviour, habits, symbols, achievements and particular ways of adapting to the environment and solving problems with respect to the threat or use of force. (Booth 1990: 121)

It does not require a leap of imagination to incorporate a critical concern with technology into this formulation: Technological possibilities can be seen as part of the environment to which the nation is reacting; particular ways of developing, configuring, and deploying technology can be seen as part of the nation's patterns of behavior. One might conclude, therefore, that no major intellectual reorientation is necessary. But this conclusion would be mistaken. Booth hints at the difficulties that exist in such a reorientation:

> A strategic culture defines a set of patterns of and for a nation's behaviour on war and peace issues. It helps shape but does not determine how a nation interacts with others in the security field. Other explanations (e.g. technological push) play a greater or lesser role in particular circumstances. (Booth 1990: 121)

The reference to a "technological push" indicates the way in which the notion of strategic culture has developed as a response to, and partly as a rejection of, technological explanations. Thus, a move to a conceptualization that recognizes the mutual implication of technology and culture—a conceptualization that recognizes their dialectical interdependence rather than collapses one into the other or draws strict dividing lines between them—requires a major shift. Though the definitional implications may be limited, the change in intellectual horizons required is substantial.

The benefits that can accrue from such a transformation are significant. If the critical approach to technology is integrated into a broader conception of strategic culture, this integration will allow connections to be made between some of the most sophisticated empirical accounts of the development of particular weapons (for example, Blair 1993; Evangelista 1988) and the most sophisticated studies of strategic behavior. Furthermore, it should encourage long overdue cross-pollination between the study of military technology with the more general literature on the relationship between technology and society (among the few studies to make this link are Flank 1993–1994 and De Landa 1991)

As should be evident from Part 1, a critical theory perspective must be concerned with more than methodological sophistication; such sophistication is viewed as a necessary prerequisite for its ultimate purpose, emancipation. Another advantage of using a critical approach to technology as part of a reconceptualization of strategy is that it can aid in the highlighting of emancipatory possibilities.

By refusing to reify technology and instead viewing it as a process with ambivalent possibilities, the critical approach encourages analysts to look for alternative outcomes and to problematize the stability of the process itself. This point is illustrated by Steven Flank's discussion of the proliferation of nuclear weapons technology (Flank 1993–1994). Reflecting upon the examples of India and South Africa in particular, Flank stresses that the "difficult task of assembling nuclear weapons requires constructing large and stable networks," and that the "list of allies promoting that construction extends beyond security threats and foreign assistance" (Flank 1993–1994: 277). Thus the infrastructure necessary to underpin the development of nuclear weapons is not merely physical; the political, cultural, and economic underpinnings are equally important. In other words, nuclear weapons technology is a process embodying all these elements.

The political implications of this conclusion are highly significant. As Flank points out, if these elements are not reproduced, then "large technological systems" that make nuclear weapons possible "disintegrate" (Flank 1993–1994: 277). This puts the commonsense argument against disarmament on the grounds that nuclear weapons cannot be disinvented into a new light. As Donald MacKenzie points out, in a passage quoted approvingly by Flank:

> Outside of the human, intellectual, and material networks that give them life and force, technologies cease to exist. We cannot reverse the invention of the motor car, perhaps, but imagine a world in which there were no car factories, no gasoline, no roads, where no one alive had ever driven, and where there was satisfaction with whatever alternative form of transportation existed. The libraries might still contain pictures of automobiles and texts on motor mechanics, but there would be a sense in which that was a world in which the motor car had been uninvented. (MacKenzie 1990: 426)

Nuclear weapons could also become a historical curiosity with a similar lack of real-world relevance—but with inferior aesthetic qualities—as intricate medieval suits of armor. But this is less likely to occur if those analysts concerned with their study continue to treat nuclear weapons as immutable givens rather than as what they are in reality: the result of a rather fragile "interplay of professional, technical, economic, and political factors" (Bijker and Law 1992: 3) and the product of a coalition of interests and alliances that will disintegrate if not constantly reproduced.

Examined through the lenses of the critical approach to technology, nuclear weapons do not become less dangerous. But if the fetishism of nuclear weapons is rejected and they are conceived as a product of human endeavor that can be unconceived, then it becomes apparent that technology is not destiny; the specter of nuclear weapons can be removed from world politics. Furthermore, proponents of critical security studies have a potentially useful role to play in "denaturalizing" nuclear weapons and military technologies. Flank makes this point well in relation to his own work:

> Ultimately, this analysis should not stop at deconstruction. What might be called "reconstruction" is a purposive, positive undertaking, in contrast to the sometimes nihilistic dismantling of deconstruction. Instead of being left with scraps of the story in a chaotic pile on the cutting room floor, I want to put them back together in a new way, in the form of a story that can be *used* for something, namely, actively changing the world. When reconstructing weapons of mass destruction, I want to reassemble their histories in order to help us disassemble the weapons themselves. (Flank 1993–1994: 281)

By denaturalizing and exposing the processes (the interplay of interests, institutions, and technical possibilities) from which nuclear and other weapons emerge, critical intellectuals can play an important role in the struggle for emancipation. It is this role that will form the central theme of the next chapter.

6

Emancipation: Reconceptualizing Practice

The relationship between theory and practice is a central concern for critical theorists. Epistemologically, it is the orientation toward emancipatory practice that gives the critical theory tradition its distinctiveness. All critical theorists from Horkheimer to Habermas take seriously Marx's deceptively simple injunction that "philosophers have only interpreted the world, in various ways; the point is to change it" (Marx 1976b: 5). Logically, they are also committed to Fraser's injunction that "it is in the crucible of political practice that critical theories meet the ultimate test of vitality" (Fraser 1989: 2).

But despite this orientation toward practice, there have been no particularly convincing answers by the members of the Frankfurt tradition of critical theory to the question of how their theorizing can become a force for change in contemporary society. As outlined in Chapters 1 and 2, their experience of the rise of totalitarianism in both East and West, leavened no doubt by a certain elitist disdain for ordinary people, led Horkheimer and Adorno to despair at the possibility of having any positive influence on the world. The role that they posited for critical theorists was to bear witness to the "truth," which Horkheimer argued had "sought refuge among them" (Horkheimer 1972: 237–238), against all the prevailing tendencies in the world. Both critical theorists saw themselves, in the words of the main ceremonials at the National *Eisteddfod* in Wales, as upholding "the truth against the world." The critical theory of the 1930s and 1940s was a declaration of faith in the possibility of a better world—in the possibility of humanity triumphing over inhumanity, civilization over barbarity—despite the surrounding evidence of hatred, intolerance, and suffering. Understandably, perhaps, this became the end in itself.

Adorno viewed critical theory as a message in a bottle to be cast on the waters of history with the hope, but certainly not the guarantee, that it might be picked up at some point in the future by persons unknown. Even if this were to happen, Adorno did not expect his theory to influence practice. Rather, his hope was, in the words of Edward Said, "not that he will have an effect on the world, but that someday, somewhere, someone will read what he wrote exactly as he wrote it" (Said 1994: 42).

Given Habermas's belief in the power of dialogue and argumentation, a belief upheld not only in his theoretical work but also in his willingness to intervene in so many debates in Germany's public sphere, it is clear that he has more ambitious expectations for his work than his former tutor admitted for his own. Nevertheless, as I discussed in Chapter 3, Habermas's own account of the relationship between theory and practice is less than compelling. Specifically, he has yet to give an adequate account of the particular role that intellectuals play both in the legitimization of the prevailing order and in the conceptualization and articulation of alternative possibilities. Furthermore, his account of politics is too consensual. As a result, Habermas does not seem to grasp—or at least grasp the implications of—the way that politics (including emancipatory politics) revolves around the interplay of interests and ideas.

If this analysis of the conceptualization of the theory-practice nexus in the work of critical theorists is correct, then it is clear that this aspect of their work can be of little relevance to proponents of critical security studies. And yet these proponents are faced with the issue of the nature of the relationship between critical theory and emancipatory politics in a particularly acute way. The provision of national security is still the primary raison d'être of the sovereign state, and as such, it remains the state's most jealously guarded preserve. As a result, any attempt to create an alternative discourse in the field of security—and in particular any attempt to problematize the role of the state as the provider of security—is likely to be strongly resisted. This resistance was clearly seen in the United Kingdom in the early 1980s when the state made determined efforts to combat the peace movement and marginalize those who were perceived as its supporters in academia. Witness, for example, the Thatcher-inspired demonization of peace studies at the University of Bradford, an unedifying but instructive episode that has been discussed by the former head of the department, James O'Connell (*The Guardian,* October 16, 1993; *The Times,* October 25, 1993).

Two further problems arise from the mutual implication of traditional security discourse and statism. First, as Simon Dalby points out, security as it is traditionally conceived "is inherently politically conservative precisely because it emphasizes permanence, control, and predictability" (Dalby 1992: 98). This means that any alternative account that arises from within the discipline (or, more correctly, subdiscipline) must challenge disciplinary norms—its common sense—in a most profound way. As Carol Cohn illustrates, even the language of traditional security studies militates against any attempt to present alternative accounts of reality or alternative possibilities for the future (Cohn 1987).

Voices from beyond the discipline's boundaries are even further disadvantaged because they lack the basic legitimacy required in the contemporary culture of experts. This point is underlined by the disproportionate impact made by the numerous "conversions on retirement" undergone by those previously prominent in the security field (among the strategic confessionals to make an impact in the 1980s were Carver 1982; Bundy et al. 1982; Generals for Peace and Disarmament 1984; McNamara 1986; for a more recent manifestation of this phenomenon in the context of demands for the total elimination of nuclear weapons, see Sauer [forthcoming]). When those people who have had, for example, a role in the development, deployment, or justification of nuclear weapons subsequently declare themselves to be dissatisfied with their efficacy or morality, these declarations are given far greater weight than the arguments of so-called nonexperts even when the substance of those arguments are identical.

The innate conservatism of traditional security discourse is further reinforced by the way in which so many intellectuals (journalists and academics) active in the security field have been co-opted by the security establishments in many states (a standard study is Horowitz 1963). Such is the extent of the ties between security intellectuals and the security sector of both governments and the economy that it may be valid to posit the existence of what has been called the "military-industrial-academic complex." Even if this characterization is exaggerated, there is considerable prima facie evidence to suggest that many benefits accrue to those who refrain from rocking the boat. Conversely, those who insist on challenging the hegemonic ideas not only have to contend with a very deeply entrenched orthodoxy but are also unlikely to share some of the material and professional benefits enjoyed by their less radical colleagues (see, for example, Booth 1997a: 96–97).

In the face of such pressures, the scope for academic critical security studies to play a role in emancipatory political practice is particularly problematic. In this chapter I will explore this issue and conceptualize a possible orientation toward practice for critical security studies. I will develop the argument by first reconstructing the attitudes toward the theory-practice nexus that have prevailed in international relations, paying particular attention to traditional security studies. I will follow this with a brief account of the ways in which proponents of critical international theory have thought about the theory-practice nexus.

As an alternative to the deeply conservative implications of the traditional security studies approach and the inadequacy of the critical international theory account, I then outline a conceptualization of the theory-practice relationship, based on the ideas of Antonio Gramsci. Specifically, I argue that Gramsci's revolutionary strategy of a "war of position" provides important insights into the role of theory in supporting progressive social change. However, Gramsci's faith in the revolutionary potential of the working class and the guiding role of the "modern prince"—the Communist Party—is rejected as not only anachronistic but fundamentally misplaced. I argue that the experience of the so-called new or critical social movements suggests possible agents for change and thus addressees for critical security studies.

INTERNATIONAL RELATIONS THEORY
AND THE PRACTICES OF GLOBAL POLITICS

International relations specialists on the whole have been remarkably unre-flective on the relationship between their work—their theories—and political practice. Indeed, the literature on the issue is strikingly sparse, especial-ly given the proliferation of studies on a myriad of other, arguably less central topics (among the main studies are Tanter and Ullman 1972; Bell 1982; A. J. R. Groom 1984; Hill and Beshoff 1994; Girard, Eberwein, and Webb 1994; Wallace 1996; Smith 1997; Booth 1997b). Furthermore, it is fair to say that none of these works are considered classics in the field. Considerations of the theory-practice nexus in international relations are distinguished by neither quality nor quantity. Even a cursory survey of the discipline's relatively short history reveals that a number of very different attitudes to the relationship between theory and practice have been adopted by the various approaches that have characterized the subject.

During the pioneer years of the 1920s and 1930s, the fledgling disci-pline reflected its origins in Welsh liberal internationalism and peace activism by concerning itself explicitly with political practice (Jones 1969 provides a flavor of the activism of which the foundation of the world's first chair in international relations at the University of Wales, Aberystwyth, formed only a part). Indeed, it is clear that David Davies, who endowed the first chair, hoped that the discipline would become the academic arm of the League of Nations, providing the world body with both intellectual support and practical advice. In effect, he regarded theory and practice as inextricably linked, with the whole point of the former being to inform and improve the latter (Porter 1989).

After World War II, as the center of gravity of the discipline shifted across the Atlantic to the United States, the ruling realist orthodoxy in international relations gradually adopted an explicitly positivist approach to the subject that has attempted to disentangle theory from practice by claiming to distinguish sharply between questions of fact and value (on international relations as a U.S.-dominated discipline, see S. Hoffman 1977; Krippendorf 1987). In paradigmatically traditional theory fashion, questions of fact are viewed as those that pertain to the nature of political reality and are regarded as the only valid subject for scientific enquiry. Furthermore, the knowledge accrued through such study has been claimed to be value-neutral, that is, containing no implicit worldview or, indeed, policy prescriptions. Policy prescription has always been relegated to the realm of value and thus seen as falling beyond the purview of objective social theory. Although theorists may have their own views regarding correct or desirable political practice, the dominant forms of realism—currently neorealism—have tended to disregard these views as mere reflections of subjective personal opinion that may well be theoretically informed but are extrinsic to the theoretical activity itself.

Of course, proponents of positivist international relations theory have almost invariably provided a willing ear to what Christopher Hill refers to as "the siren call of policy relevance" and have thus often pursued research agendas that reflect the preoccupations of policymakers (Hill 1994: 16–19). The point is that this concern with policy—with political practice—has been seen by postwar realists as an optional extra. Furthermore, when these scholars have attempted to try to feed their ideas into the political process, they have limited themselves almost exclusively to addressing policymakers and elite opinion formers. The aim has been to gain the ear of the powerful rather than engage with those who are presently powerless (the exchange between Wallace [1996] and Booth [1997b] is instructive).

The quest for influence has met with varying degrees of success, reflecting the differing political cultures of the states where academic international relations has developed. In the United States, for example, there has been a close, symbiotic relationship between academia and government. In contrast, in the United Kingdom it is usually argued that relations have remained more distant. However, appearances, in the British case at least, may be deceptive. Commenting on the apparent lack of contact between academics and what he terms "practitioners," A. J. R. Groom claims that

> little communication between them was necessary since their paradigmatic unity [by which he means allegiance to the realist model of power politics] was so strong that they could go their separate ways safe in the knowledge that their work was compatible. (Groom 1984: 194)

From this comment we can infer that, in the main, British international relations specialists—in effect, if not always in intention—have provided "objective" academic support and justification for the main thrust of British foreign policy.

Groom's argument resonates with the critical theory critique of traditional theory, which charges that the distinction between fact and value, and between "is" and "ought," is spurious, that "all theory is *for* someone and *for* some purpose" (R. Cox 1981: 128). From this perspective, whatever the aims of its proponents, far from providing an objective view of political reality, the effect of mainstream realist tradition in international relations theory has been to aid in the production, reproduction, and legitimation of global realpolitik.

Considering the somewhat mealy-mouthed attitude of so much international relations literature, it is refreshing to see a more candid attitude among some of those working within traditional security studies. Whereas John Garnett claims to be pursuing the grail of "academic objectivity" (Garnett 1987a: 22–23), Edward N. Luttwak is quite willing to abandon all such pretense. For Luttwak "strategy is not a neutral pursuit and its only purpose is to strengthen one's own side in the contention of nations" (Luttwak 1985: xiii). Luttwak, however, still upholds the distinction between fact and value. He still wishes to gather facts as objectively as possible; the point at issue is to what ends this information should be applied. Whereas Garnett, betraying an uncertain grasp of the history of Western thought, claims that "strategic analysis, like philosophy, leaves the world as it is" (Garnett 1987a: 13), Luttwak makes no apology for wanting his analysis "to strengthen one's own side." So, although the distinction between both positions is interesting, it does not significantly affect the contents of their analyses.

The saving grace for Luttwak's position is its honesty. Other proponents of traditional security studies have been more than willing to undertake consultancy or recruitment work for defense ministries, to supervise theses that depend on secret documentation with all the attendant restrictions on access and so on, to accept generous remuneration for attending supervised propaganda ("information") visits to military establishments and still claim that their work has been unaffected by such activities. Luttwak at least has the integrity to proudly embrace the logic and implications of his structural position. His work is a frank, unashamed, and, above all, credible account of the relationship between the more orthodox approaches to the study of international relations and the practice of global politics. The problem from a critical theory perspective is that Luttwak's aim is not to encourage emancipation, at least in any sense that critical theorists can accept. Rather, his aim is to strengthen the prevailing order, or at least one element of it—his own side's power. In other words, he is explicit about wanting to do what his less forthright colleagues actually do behind a veil of spurious "Victorian" strategic respectability.

CRITICAL INTERNATIONAL THEORY
AND EMANCIPATORY POLITICS

Because emancipatory political practice is central to the claims of critical theory, one might expect that proponents of a critical approach to the study of international relations would be reflexive about the relationship between theory and practice. Yet their thinking on this issue thus far does not seem to have progressed much beyond grandiose statements of intent. There have been no systematic considerations of how critical international theory can help generate, support, or sustain emancipatory politics beyond the seminar room or conference hotel.

Robert Cox, for example, has described the task of critical theorists as providing "a guide to strategic action for bringing about an alternative order" (R. Cox 1981: 130). Although he has also gone on to identify possible agents for change and has outlined the nature and structure of some feasible alternative orders, he has not explicitly indicated whom he regards as the addressee of critical theory (i.e., who is being guided) and thus how the theory can hope to become a part of the political process (see R. Cox 1981, 1983, 1996).

Similarly, Andrew Linklater has argued that "a critical theory of international relations must regard the practical project of extending community beyond the nation-state as its most important problem" (Linklater 1990b: 171). However, he has little to say about the role of theory in the realization of this "practical project." Indeed, his main point is to suggest that the role of critical theory "is not to offer instructions on how to act but to reveal the existence of unrealised possibilities" (Linklater 1990b: 172). But the question still remains, reveal to whom? Is the audience enlightened politicians? Particular social classes? Particular social movements? Or particular (and presumably particularized) communities? In light of Linklater's primary concern with emancipation, one might expect more guidance as to whom he believes might do the emancipating and how critical theory can impinge upon the emancipatory process.

There is, likewise, little enlightenment to be gleaned from Mark Hoffman's otherwise important contribution. He argues that critical international theory

> seeks not simply to reproduce society via description, but to understand society and change it. It is both descriptive and constructive in its theoretical intent: it is both an intellectual and a social act. It is not merely an expression of the concrete realities of the historical situation, but also a force for change within those conditions. (M. Hoffman 1987: 233)

Despite this very ambitious declaration, once again, Hoffman gives no suggestion as to how this "force for change" should be operationalized and what concrete role critical theorizing might play in changing society.

Thus, although the critical international theorists' critique of the role that more conventional approaches to the study of world politics play in reproducing the contemporary world order may be persuasive, their account of the relationship between their own work and emancipatory political practice is unconvincing. Given the centrality of practice to the claims of critical theory, this is a very significant weakness. Without some plausible account of the mechanisms by which they hope to aid in the achievement of their emancipatory goals, proponents of critical international theory are hardly in a position to justify the assertion that "it represents the next stage in the development of International Relations theory" (M. Hoffman 1987: 244). Indeed, without a more convincing conceptualization of the theory-practice nexus, one can argue that critical international theory, by its own terms, has no way of redeeming some of its central epistemological and methodological claims and thus that it is a fatally flawed enterprise.

The provision of such an account is therefore necessary for all critical theorists working on the study of world politics, including, of course, those engaged in the development of critical security studies. However, it is a task made more difficult not only by the unconvincing accounts of the theory-practice nexus offered by the leading lights in the Frankfurt School tradition but also by the breadth of the issues raised when the theory-practice question is broached. To trace the relationship between theory and practice is to address the nature and social role of intellectuals and intellectual activity. It is also to question the role that intellectuals play in supporting and promoting social change. In turn, this raises the thorny issue of the audience to which critical intellectuals are addressing their ideas. Ultimately, of course, all of this leads inexorably to one of the central, perennial issues of social theory: the relationship between agents and structures.

Although recent discussions of the agent-structure debate in international relations have tended to concentrate on the perhaps rarefied issues of "levels of analysis" and ontology, any discussion of the social role of critical theory also has to consider the problematic relationship between agents and structure at the micro level of academic life. Quite simply, how are critical theorists working within the university system to pursue what must inevitably be their twin goals of academic respectability and political relevance? How much autonomy does the agent—in this case the critical theorist—enjoy within the often hostile structures of Western academe? Can the chasm ever be bridged between, on the one hand, the ghettoizing nature of academic language itself, as well as the professional constraints created by tenure requirements, research selectivity exercises, and the like, and, on the other hand, the desire to make critical theorizing accessible and relevant to particular political struggles? Jürgen Habermas frames these issues well when he ruefully wonders

> how theories that have wrapped themselves up in their own problems, and have retreated so far into the scientific system under the pull of the social division of labor—how such autistic undertakings are at all able to place themselves in relation to praxis and to develop a force for the direction of action. (Habermas 1994: 116)

How much more pertinent are these questions to the area of security studies, where the pressures for conformism are so much greater than in other fields of social study?

In the remainder of this chapter, I will attempt to conceptualize how critical security studies can orient toward political practice in a manner that encourages and supports emancipatory transformation. However, as should by now be apparent, the relevance of this reconceptualization of the theory-practice nexus is not confined to critical security studies. Rather, if it is persuasive, then it has important implications for the whole enterprise of critical international theory.

GRAMSCI ON THE ROLE OF INTELLECTUALS

Critical international theory has drawn on two main intellectual strands. Writers like Robert Cox and Stephen Gill have been heavily influenced by the work of Antonio Gramsci in their attempt to develop critical approaches to international political economy (see Gill 1993). Other theorists, most notably Linklater and Mark Hoffman, have drawn on the Frankfurt School tradition. Although there are many broad similarities between the thinking of Gramsci and the Frankfurt School, there are also important differences (Renate Holub 1992: 3–30). One difference relates to the role of intellectuals.

Of all the thinkers in the Western Marxist tradition, Gramsci devoted perhaps the most thought to the role of intellectuals and ideas in general in society. This is hardly surprising given his consistent focus on eschewing the abstract in order to concentrate on the concrete, that is, on theorizing with a practical and revolutionary intent. In his *Prison Notebooks,* he referred to his reading of Marxism as "the philosophy of praxis" (Gramsci 1971). Many scholars claim that this was done in order to confuse the prison censors. If this is true, then, as Robert Cox points out, the censors "must have been particularly slow-witted" (R. Cox 1983: 175ff.). The English translators of the *Notebooks* provide a more plausible explanation in their introduction:

> "Philosophy of praxis" is both a euphemism for Marxism and an autonomous term used by Gramsci to define what he saw to be the central characteristic of the philosophy of Marxism, the inescapable link it establishes between theory and practice, thought and action. (Gramsci 1971: xiii)

It is in this light that Gramsci developed his theorizing on the role of intellectuals.

As is almost invariably the case with Gramsci, his theory of intellectuals and the role of intellectual activity is presented in a series of fragmentary notes scattered throughout the *Prison Notebooks* (particularly relevant is Gramsci 1971: 5–23, 323–377). Obviously, Gramsci can hardly be blamed for their fragmentary nature, considering the appalling privations he was forced to endure during their writing (Fiori 1990: 220–291). However, his theory has to be reconstructed from these fragments, and they are not without their contradictions. What follows is, I believe, a plausible and coherent reading.

Gramsci's first move is to broaden the concept of intellectuals by arguing that "all men are intellectuals . . . but not all men have in society the function of intellectuals" (Gramsci 1971: 9). He argues that those with the social function of intellectuals fall into two groups. One group he refers to as "traditional intellectuals." This concept represents the way in which most intellectuals view their own role in society. Traditional intellectuals, according to their self-image, have a relatively autonomous social role that lifts them above the class cleavages of society to the Mannheimian realm of universal, "free-floating" thinkers (Mannheim 1976: 137–143). For Gramsci, this independence is a chimera. He ultimately regards traditional intellectuals as playing a vital, if subconscious, role in producing and reproducing the hegemony that provides an indispensable buttress to the prevailing patterns of domination within society. Here the parallels with Horkheimer's critique of the role of traditional theory are clear and striking.

Gramsci contrasts traditional intellectuals with "organic intellectuals." Organic intellectuals play a crucial and far more self-conscious role in articulating and organizing the interests and aspirations of a particular social class. Each class has its own organic intellectuals—although the intellectuals of the ruling strata often see themselves in a different, traditional light. This point may be illustrated by referring to two proponents of traditional security studies. In Gramsci's terminology, John Garnett is a traditional intellectual and Edward Luttwak is an organic intellectual. Both in effect support the status quo, but Luttwak does this self-consciously and explicitly.

Gramsci points out that in contrast to that of the ruling class, the structural position of the working class means that it has fewer intellectual resources at its disposal. He therefore stresses the need for that class to develop its own organic intellectuals and argues that they have a crucial role to play in advancing proletarian and thus for him human emancipation. Discussing their role, Gramsci argues:

> The mode of being of the new intellectuals can no longer consist in eloquence, which is an exterior and momentary mover of feelings and passions, but in active participation in practical life, as constructor, organizer, "permanent persuader" and not just a simple orator. (Gramsci 1971: 10)

The central political task of the intellectuals is to aid in the construction of a counterhegemony and thus undermine the prevailing patterns of discourse and interaction that make up the currently dominant hegemony. This task is accomplished through educational activity, because, as Gramsci argues, "every relationship of 'hegemony' is necessarily a pedagogic relationship" (Gramsci 1971: 350).

Discussing the relationship of the "philosophy of praxis" to political practice, Gramsci claims:

> It [the theory] does not tend to leave the "simple" in their primitive philosophy of common sense, but rather to lead them to a higher conception of life. If it affirms the need for contact between intellectuals and "simple" it is not in order to restrict scientific activity and preserve unity at the low level of the masses, but precisely in order to construct an intellectual-moral bloc which can make politically possible the intellectual progress of the mass and not only of small intellectual groups. (Gramsci 1971: 332–333)

According to Gramsci, this attempt to construct an alternative "intellectual-moral bloc" should take place under the auspices of the Communist Party—a body he described as the "modern prince." Just as Niccolò Machiavelli hoped to see a prince unite Italy, rid the country of foreign barbarians, and create a *virtù*-ous state, Gramsci believed that the modern prince could lead the working class on its journey toward its revolutionary destiny of an emancipated society (Gramsci 1971: 125–205).

Gramsci's relative optimism about the possibility of progressive theorists playing a constructive role in emancipatory political practice was predicated on his belief in the existence of a universal class (a class whose emancipation would inevitably presage the emancipation of humanity itself) with revolutionary potential. It was a gradual loss of faith in this axiom that led Horkheimer and Adorno to their extremely pessimistic prognosis about the possibilities of progressive social change. But does a loss of faith in the revolutionary vocation of the proletariat necessarily lead to the kind of quietism ultimately embraced by the first generation of the Frankfurt School? The conflict that erupted in the 1960s between them and their more radical students suggests not. Indeed, contemporary critical theorists claim that the deprivileging of the role of the proletariat in the struggle for emancipation is actually a positive move.

Class remains a very important axis of domination in society, but it is not the only such axis (Fraser 1995). Nor is it valid to reduce all other forms of domination—for example, in the case of gender—to class relations, as orthodox Marxists tend to do. To recognize these points is not only a first step toward the development of an analysis of forms of exploitation and exclusion within society that is more attuned to social reality; it is also a realization that there are other forms of emancipatory politics than those associated with class conflict.[1] This in turn suggests new possibilities and problems for emancipatory theory.

Furthermore, the abandonment of faith in revolutionary parties is also a positive development. The history of the European left during the twentieth century provides myriad examples of the ways in which the fetishization of party organizations has led to bureaucratic immobility and the confusion of means with ends (see, for example, Salvadori 1990). The failure of the Bolshevik experiment illustrates how disciplined, vanguard parties are an ideal vehicle for totalitarian domination (Serge 1984). Faith in the "infallible party" has obviously been the source of strength and comfort to many in this period and, as the experience of the southern Wales coalfield demonstrates, has inspired brave and progressive behavior (see, for example, the account of support for the Spanish Republic in Francis 1984). But such parties have so often been the enemies of emancipation that they should be treated with the utmost caution. Parties are necessary, but their fetishization is potentially disastrous.

History furnishes examples of progressive developments that have been positively influenced by organic intellectuals operating outside the bounds of a particular party structure (G. Williams 1984). Some of these developments have occurred in the particularly intractable realm of security. These examples may be considered as "resources of hope" for critical security studies (R. Williams 1989). They illustrate that ideas are important or, more correctly, that change is the product of the dialectical interaction of ideas and material reality.

One clear security-related example of the role of critical thinking and critical thinkers in aiding and abetting progressive social change is the experience of the peace movement of the 1980s. At that time the ideas of dissident defense intellectuals (the "alternative defense" school) encouraged and drew strength from peace activism. Together they had an effect not only on short-term policy but on the dominant discourses of strategy and security, a far more important result in the long run. The synergy between critical security intellectuals and critical social movements and the potential influence of both working in tandem can be witnessed particularly clearly in the fate of common security.

As Thomas Risse-Kappen points out, the term "common security" originated in the contribution of peace researchers to the German security debate of the 1970s (Risse-Kappen 1994: 186ff.); it was subsequently popularized by the Palme Commission report (Independent Commission on Disarmament and Security Issues 1982). Initially, mainstream defense intellectuals dismissed the concept as hopelessly idealistic; it certainly had no place in their allegedly hardheaded and realist view of the world. However, notions of common security were taken up by a number of different intellectual communities, including the liberal arms control community in the United States, Western European peace researchers, security specialists in the center-left political parties of Western Europe, and Soviet "institutchiks"—members of the influential policy institutes in the Soviet Union such as the United States of America and Canada Institute (Landau 1996: 52–54; Risse-Kappen 1994: 196–200; Kaldor 1995; Spencer 1995).

These communities were subsequently able to take advantage of public pressure exerted through social movements in order to gain broader acceptance for common security. In Germany, for example, "in response to social movement pressure, German social organizations such as churches and trade unions quickly supported the ideas promoted by peace researchers and the SPD" (Risse-Kappen 1994: 207). Similar pressures even had an effect on the Reagan administration. As Risse-Kappen notes:

> When the Reagan administration brought hard-liners into power, the US arms control community was removed from policy influence. It was the American peace movement and what became known as the "freeze campaign" that revived the arms control process together with pressure from the European allies. (Risse-Kappen 1994: 205; also Cortright 1993: 90–110)

Although it would be difficult to sustain a claim that the combination of critical movements and intellectuals persuaded the Reagan government to adopt the rhetoric and substance of common security in its entirety, it is clear that it did at least have a substantial impact on ameliorating U.S. behavior.

The most dramatic and certainly the most unexpected impact of alternative defense ideas was felt in the Soviet Union. Through various East-West links, which included arms control institutions, Pugwash conferences, interparty contacts, and even direct personal links, a coterie of Soviet policy analysts and advisers were drawn toward common security and such attendant notions as "nonoffensive defense" (these links are detailed in Evangelista 1995; Kaldor 1995; Checkel 1993; Risse-Kappen 1994;

Landau 1996 and Spencer 1995 concentrate on the role of the Pugwash conferences). This group, including Palme Commission member Georgii Arbatov, Pugwash attendee Andrei Kokoshin, and Sergei Karaganov, a senior adviser who was in regular contact with the Western peace researchers Anders Boserup and Lutz Unterseher (Risse-Kappen 1994: 203), then influenced Soviet leader Mikhail Gorbachev.

Gorbachev's subsequent championing of common security may be attributed to several factors. It is clear, for example, that new Soviet leadership had a strong interest in alleviating tensions in East-West relations in order to facilitate much-needed domestic reforms ("the interaction of ideas and material reality"). But what is significant is that the Soviets' commitment to common security led to significant changes in force sizes and postures. These in turn aided in the winding down of the Cold War, the end of Soviet domination over Eastern Europe, and even the collapse of Russian control over much of the territory of the former Soviet Union.

At the present time, in marked contrast to the situation in the early 1980s, common security is part of the common sense of security discourse. As MccGwire points out, the North Atlantic Treaty Organization (NATO) (a common defense pact) is using the rhetoric of common security in order to justify its expansion into Eastern Europe (MccGwire 1997). This points to an interesting and potentially important aspect of the impact of ideas on politics. As concepts such as common security, and collective security before it (Claude 1984: 223–260), are adopted by governments and military services, they inevitably become somewhat debased. The hope is that enough of the residual meaning can survive to shift the parameters of the debate in a potentially progressive direction. Moreover, the adoption of the concept of common security by official circles provides critics with a useful tool for (immanently) critiquing aspects of security policy (as MccGwire 1997 demonstrates in relation to NATO expansion).

The example of common security is highly instructive. First, it indicates that critical intellectuals can be politically engaged and play a role—a significant one at that—in making the world a better and safer place. Second, it points to potential future addressees for critical international theory in general, and critical security studies in particular. Third, it also underlines the role of ideas in the evolution of society.

CRITICAL SECURITY STUDIES
AND THE THEORY-PRACTICE NEXUS

Although most proponents of critical security studies reject aspects of Gramsci's theory of organic intellectuals, in particular his exclusive concentration on class and his emphasis on the guiding role of the party, the desire for engagement and relevance must remain at the heart of their project. The example of the peace movement suggests that critical theorists can still play the role of organic intellectuals and that this organic relationship need not confine itself to a single class; it can involve alignment with different coalitions of social movements that campaign on an issue or a series of issues pertinent to the struggle for emancipation (Shaw 1994b; R. Walker 1994). Edward Said captures this broader orientation when he suggests that critical intellectuals "are always tied to and ought to remain an organic part of an ongoing experience in society: of the poor, the disadvantaged, the voiceless, the unrepresented, the powerless" (Said 1994: 84). In the specific case of critical security studies, this means placing the experience of those men and women and communities for whom the present world order is a cause of insecurity rather than security at the center of the agenda and making suffering humanity rather than raison d'état the prism through which problems are viewed. Here the project stands full-square within the critical theory tradition. If "all theory is *for* someone and *for* some purpose," then critical security studies is for "the voiceless, the unrepresented, the powerless," and its purpose is their emancipation.

The theoretical implications of this orientation have already been discussed in the previous chapters. They involve a fundamental reconceptualization of security with a shift in referent object and a broadening of the range of issues considered as a legitimate part of the discourse. They also involve a reconceptualization of strategy within this expanded notion of security. But the question remains at the conceptual level of how these alternative types of theorizing—even if they are self-consciously aligned to the practices of critical or new social movements, such as peace activism, the struggle for human rights, and the survival of minority cultures—can become "a force for the direction of action."

Again, Gramsci's work is insightful. In the *Prison Notebooks,* Gramsci advances a sophisticated analysis of how dominant discourses play a vital role in upholding particular political and economic orders, or, in Gramsci's terminology, "historic blocs" (Gramsci 1971: 323–377). Gramsci adopted Machiavelli's view of power as a centaur, half man, half beast: a mixture of consent and coercion. Consent is produced and reproduced by a ruling hegemony that holds sway through civil society and through which ruling or dominant ideas become widely dispersed.[2] In particular, Gramsci describes how ideology becomes sedimented in society and takes on the status of common sense; it becomes subconsciously accepted and even regarded as beyond question. Obviously, for Gramsci, there is nothing immutable about the values that permeate society; they can and do change. In the social realm, ideas and institutions that were once seen as natural and beyond question (i.e., commonsensical) in the West, such as feudalism and slavery, are now seen as anachronistic, unjust, and unacceptable. In Marx's well-worn phrase, "All that is solid melts into the air."

Gramsci's intention is to harness this potential for change and ensure that it moves in the direction of emancipation. To do this he suggests a strategy of a "war of position" (Gramsci 1971: 229–239). Gramsci argues that in states with developed civil societies, such as those in Western liberal democracies, any successful attempt at progressive social change requires a slow, incremental, even molecular, struggle to break down the prevailing hegemony and construct an alternative counterhegemony to take its place. Organic intellectuals have a crucial role to play in this process by helping to undermine the "natural," "commonsense," internalized nature of the status quo. This in turn helps create political space within which alternative conceptions of politics can be developed and new historic blocs created. I contend that Gramsci's strategy of a war of position suggests an appropriate model for proponents of critical security studies to adopt in relating their theorizing to political practice.

THE TASKS OF CRITICAL SECURITY STUDIES

If the project of critical security studies is conceived in terms of a war of position, then the main task of those intellectuals who align themselves with the enterprise is to attempt to undermine the prevailing hegemonic security discourse. This may be accomplished by utilizing specialist information and expertise to engage in an immanent critique of the prevailing security regimes, that is, comparing the justifications of those regimes with actual outcomes. When this is attempted in the security field, the prevailing structures and regimes are found to fail grievously on their own terms. Such an approach also involves challenging the pronouncements of those intellectuals, traditional or organic, whose views serve to legitimate, and hence reproduce, the prevailing world order. This challenge entails teasing out the often subconscious and certainly unexamined assumptions that underlie their arguments while drawing attention to the normative viewpoints that are smuggled into mainstream thinking about security behind its positivist facade. In this sense, proponents of critical security studies approximate to Foucault's notion of "specific intellectuals" who use their expert knowledge to challenge the prevailing "regime of truth" (Foucault 1980: 132). However, critical theorists might wish to reformulate this sentiment along more familiar Quaker lines of "speaking truth to power" (this sentiment is also central to Said 1994) or even along the *eisteddfod* lines of speaking "truth against the world."

Of course, traditional strategists can, and indeed do, sometimes claim a similar role. Colin S. Gray, for example, states that "strategists must be prepared to 'speak truth to power'" (Gray 1982a: 193). But the difference between Gray and proponents of critical security studies is that, whereas the former seeks to influence policymakers in particular directions without questioning the basis of their power, the latter aim at a thoroughgoing critique of all that traditional security studies has taken for granted. Furthermore, critical theorists base their critique on the presupposition, elegantly stated by Adorno, that "the need to lend suffering a voice is the precondition of all truth" (cited in Jameson 1990: 66).

The aim of critical security studies in attempting to undermine the prevailing orthodoxy is ultimately educational. As Gramsci notes, "Every relationship of 'hegemony' is necessarily a pedagogic relationship" (Gramsci 1971: 350; see also the discussion of critical pedagogy in Neufeld 1995: 116–121). Thus, by criticizing the hegemonic discourse and advancing alternative conceptions of security based on different understandings of human potentialities, the approach is simultaneously playing a part in eroding the legitimacy of the ruling historic bloc and contributing to the development of a counterhegemonic position.

There are a number of avenues open to critical security specialists in pursuing this educational strategy. As teachers, they can try to foster and encourage skepticism toward accepted wisdom and open minds to other possibilities. They can also take advantage of the seemingly unquenchable thirst of the media for instant punditry to forward alternative views onto a broader stage. Nancy Fraser argues: "As teachers, we try to foster an emergent pedagogical counterculture. . . . As critical public intellectuals we try to inject our perspectives into whatever cultural or political public spheres we have access to" (Fraser 1989: 11).

Perhaps significantly, support for this type of emancipatory strategy can even be found in the work of the ultrapessimistic Adorno, who argues:

> In the history of civilization there have been not a few instances when delusions were healed not by focused propaganda, but, in the final analysis, because scholars, with their unobtrusive yet insistent work habits, studied what lay at the root of the delusion. (cited in Kellner 1992: vii)

Such "unobtrusive yet insistent work" does not in itself create the social change to which Adorno alludes. The conceptual and the practical dangers of collapsing practice into theory must be guarded against. Rather, through their educational activities, proponents of critical security studies should aim to provide support for those social movements that promote emancipatory social change. By providing a critique of the prevailing order and legitimating alternative views, critical theorists can perform a valuable role in supporting the struggles of social movements.

That said, the role of theorists is not to direct and instruct those movements with which they are aligned; instead, the relationship is reciprocal. The experience of the European, North American, and Antipodean peace movements of the 1980s shows how influential social movements can become when their efforts are harnessed to the intellectual and educational activity of critical thinkers. For example, in his account of New Zealand's antinuclear stance in the 1980s, Michael C. Pugh cites the importance of the visits of critical intellectuals such as Helen Caldicott and Richard Falk in changing the country's political climate and encouraging the growth of the antinuclear movement (Pugh 1989: 108; see also Cortright 1993: 5–13). In the 1980s peace movements and critical intellectuals interested in issues of security and strategy drew strength and succor from each other's efforts.

If such critical social movements do not exist, then this creates obvious difficulties for the critical theorist. But even under these circumstances, the theorist need not abandon all hope of an eventual orientation toward practice. Once again, the peace movement of the 1980s provides evidence of the possibilities. At that time, the movement benefited from the intellectual work undertaken in the lean years of the peace movement in the late 1970s. Some of the theories and concepts developed then, such as common security and nonoffensive defense, were eventually taken up even in the Kremlin and played a significant role in defusing the second Cold War. Those ideas developed in the 1970s can be seen in Adornian terms of a "message in a bottle," but in this case, contra Adorno's expectations, they were picked up and used to support a program of emancipatory political practice.

Obviously, one would be naive to understate the difficulties facing those attempting to develop alternative critical approaches within academia. Some of these problems have been alluded to already and involve the structural constraints of academic life itself. Said argues that many problems are caused by what he describes as the growing "professionalisation" of academic life (Said 1994: 49–62). Academics are now so constrained by the requirements of job security and marketability that they are extremely risk-averse. It pays—in all senses—to stick with the crowd and avoid the exposed limb by following the prevalent disciplinary preoccupations, publish in certain prescribed journals, and so on. The result is the navel gazing so prevalent in the study of international relations and the seeming inability of security specialists to deal with the changes brought about by the end of the Cold War (Kristensen 1997 highlights the search of U.S. nuclear planners for "new targets for old weapons"). And, of course, the pressures for conformism are heightened in the field of security studies when governments have a very real interest in marginalizing dissent.

Nevertheless, opportunities for critical thinking do exist, and this thinking can connect with the practices of social movements and become a "force for the direction of action." The experience of the 1980s, when, in the depths of the second Cold War, critical thinkers risked demonization and in some countries far worse in order to challenge received wisdom, thus arguably playing a crucial role in the very survival of the human race, should act as both an inspiration and a challenge to critical security studies.

NOTES

1. This should not be read as a denial of the continuing existence or importance of class struggle. Rather I am merely suggesting that other axes of domination and subordination are also important. Nor do I deny that class conflict and other forms of domination are often mutually reinforcing.

2. Civil society is the network of institutions and practices within society through which "groups in society in general represent themselves—both to each other and to the state" (Shaw 1994b: 647). Jean Cohen and Andrew Arato, in what remains the most illuminating discussion of the concept, relate it closely to Habermas's notion of the "lifeworld" (Cohen and Arato 1992).

Epilogue

In Part 1 of this book I attempted to delineate and evaluate some of the central ideas in the work of the Frankfurt School of critical theory, at least as they are relevant to the study of global politics and, particularly of course, security. I did this by tracing the thinking of Horkheimer, Adorno, and the second generation of critical theorists in relation to the three key themes of theory, technology, and emancipation. I used these ideas in Part 2 both to criticize the prevailing orthodoxy of traditional security studies and to lay the conceptual foundations for an alternative critical security studies: to deconstruct and to reconstruct. The following brief remarks will recapitulate and summarize the main lines of argument, focusing in turn on conceptualizations of security, strategy, and the relationship between theory and practice.

RECONCEPTUALIZING SECURITY

It has been argued that the conceptualization of security underlying traditional security studies

- Tends to reify the prevailing status quo because of its scientific-objectivist epistemology (and, indeed, is a paradigmatic example of Horkheimer's "traditional theory")
- Is ahistorical and deeply resistant to notions of contingency and change because of its state-centric ontology
- Is blind to the way in which notions of security are dependent on deeper assumptions concerning the nature of politics
- Focuses exclusively on a narrowly military understanding of security
- Is tied to the state in a way that privileges the state's ethical position

165

above all others and is also unable to capture the way that the power of security as a speech act is utilized by many other actors and other forms of political community than the state

In place of this traditional conception of security, the case has been made for an alternative, critical conception of security that is

- Deeper, in that it understands that security is a derivative concept; that is, security reflects deeper assumptions about the nature of politics and the role of conflict in political life
- Broader, in that it recognizes that military force is not the only potential threat to security and that other threats are equally important and equally worthy of consideration in security studies
- Extended to include referent objects other than the state; individual human beings, however, are regarded as the ultimate referents
- Focused, crucially, on emancipation as the prism through which both the theory and the practice of security should be viewed

Reconceptualized in this way, the concept of security can take its place at the center of a new critical security studies capable not only of mapping out the contours of the present but of plotting a course for the future.

RECONCEPTUALIZING STRATEGY

It has further been argued that a critical theory–influenced approach to security—critical security studies—not only encourages the development of a more analytically useful conceptualization of security but also generates a more sophisticated framework for the analysis of military force (strategy) than that utilized by traditional security studies.

The conceptualization of strategy used in traditional security studies has been characterized by

- A tendency to ignore ends—and (human) consequences—and to become concerned with a calculus of means, a tendency generated by, and inherent in, a reifying traditional mode of analysis
- An erroneous, undialectical, and ahistorical understanding of technology and particularly the interaction of military technology and strategic culture

In place of this traditional understanding, I have argued for a critical reconceptualization that

- Utilizes modes of analysis in which normative concerns are regarded as intrinsic rather than as an optional extra
- Deploys, in the case of military technology, a critical understanding of technology to denaturalize and challenge the processes from which weapons emerge

RECONCEPTUALIZING PRACTICE

The central issue of how these reconceptualized understandings of security and strategy might aid in the transformation of the real-world practices in these areas has also been addressed. Traditional understandings of the relationship between theory and practice were criticized on the grounds that they have

- Tended to regard the addressees for its theorizing as state leaders and their servants
- Served to legitimate the status quo by naturalizing the practices of global (in)security and reinforcing "commonsense" assumptions about what constitutes security and who should provide it
- Attempted to delegitimate and silence alternative approaches to security

An alternative conceptualization of the theory-practice nexus was developed based on a reading of the work of Antonio Gramsci, a reading reinforced by the historical experience of the 1980s peace movement. This suggested that critical security studies should

- Focus on the delegitimation of the prevailing hegemonic ideas and promote realizable alternatives to it
- View those within civil society who are challenging this hegemony as its addressees
- Become the organic intellectuals of critical social movements when they exist, or encourage the creation of the political space necessary for their emergence if they do not

In these ways proponents of critical security studies can not only interpret the world but also play a role in changing it.

Although I do not wish to underestimate the difficulties of achieving such emancipatory change, I also believe that critical security studies is an idea whose time has come. The contemporary world order exhibits all the morbid symptoms of a period of interregnum foreseen by Gramsci "when the old is dying and the new cannot be born" (Gramsci 1971: 276; this quotation is used by Booth 1991c: 1). Aspects of the old are certainly withering: Not only has the Warsaw Pact disintegrated following the collapse of the Soviet empire, but far more fundamentally, some important voices believe that the Westphalian system itself is losing its legitimacy (see the discussions in Rosenau 1990; Linklater 1998a). The main reason for what may be termed—after Habermas (1976)—as the "legitimation crisis" is that those political structures whose primary justification rests on their ability to provide security—namely, sovereign states—are patently failing in their task. When security is considered in its widest sense, incorporating ecological concerns, economic questions, human rights—both individual and communal—as well as military issues, those proffering traditional statist solutions to contemporary problems are engaging in a Canute-like attempt to resist the irresistible rising tide of change.

Even so, the character of the new still remains to be seen. And new does not necessarily mean better. Morbid symptoms abound, and barbarism is one possibility. Barbarism will become more of a probability if those engaged in the study of security continue to think in ways that have the effect of legitimating and supporting the failing status quo. Another possibility is the development of a peaceful and rational world order, what Adorno foresaw, in a typically beguiling turn of phrase, as a "landscape of benignly interacting particularities" (cited in Jay 1984: 20). Such a development will undoubtedly be aided if those intellectuals concerned with issues of security attempt to emulate Habermas in seeking out "traces of reason that unites without effacing separation, that binds without unaming [*sic*] difference, that points out the common and the shared among strangers, without depriving the other of otherness" (Habermas 1994: 119–120).

Ultimately, only political practice can bring about the development of a peaceful, secure, and just world order. Critical security studies can assist those political practices that aim at expanding human security through expanding processes of emancipation, but it cannot be a substitute for them. Critical theorists cannot hope to emulate those Australian aboriginal people so memorably portrayed by Bruce Chatwin in his book *The Songlines* (1987), who, during their "dream-time," sang their world into existence. Critical security studies cannot sing a more secure world into existence, but it can become an important voice informing and legitimating those political practices that might turn the dream of a "landscape of benignly interacting particularities" into a reality.

Bibliography

Adorno, Theodor W. (1973), *Negative Dialectics,* translated by E. B. Ashton. London: Routledge and Kegan Paul.

——— (1974), *Minima Moralia: Reflections from Damaged Life,* translated by E. F. N. Jephcott. London: Verso.

——— (1991), *Notes to Literature,* Vol. 1, translated by Shierry Weber Nicholsen. New York: Columbia University Press.

——— (1994), *The Stars Down to Earth and Other Essays on the Irrational in Culture,* edited with an introduction by Stephen Crook. London: Routledge.

——— (1997), *Aesthetic Theory,* translated and edited by Robert Hullot-Kentor. Minneapolis: University of Minnesota Press.

Adorno, Theodor W., and Max Horkheimer (1979), *Dialectic of Enlightenment,* translated by John Cumming. London: Verso.

Amis, Martin (1988), *Einstein's Monsters.* Harmondsworth, U.K.: Penguin.

Anderson, Perry (1976), *Considerations on Western Marxism.* London: New Left Books.

Arato, Andrew, and Eike Gebhardt (1982), *The Essential Frankfurt School Reader.* New York: Continuum.

Ashley, Richard K. (1981), "Political Realism and Human Interests," *International Studies Quarterly* Vol. 25, No. 2, pp. 204–236.

Augelli, Enrico, and Craig Murphy (1988), *America's Quest for Supremacy and the Third World.* London: Pinter.

Baldwin, David A. (1997), "The Concept of Security," *Review of International Studies* Vol. 23, No. 1, pp. 5–26.

Barnaby, Frank (1982), "Nuclear Conflict: A Global Prospect?" in Frank Barnaby and Geoffrey Thomas (eds.), *The Nuclear Arms Race—Control or Catastrophe?* London: Frances Pinter, pp. 7–47.

Beck, Ulrich (1992a), *Risk Society: Towards a New Modernity,* translated by Mark Ritter. London: Sage Publications.

——— (1992b), "From Industrial Society to the Risk Society: Questions of Survival, Social Structure and Ecological Enlightenment," translated by Mark Ritter, *Theory, Culture and Society* Vol. 9, No. 1, pp. 97–123.

——— (1995), *Ecological Politics in an Age of Risk,* translated by Amos Weisz. Cambridge: Polity Press.

Bell, Coral (ed.) (1982), *Academic Studies and International Politics.* Canberra: Department of International Relations, Australian National University.

Benhabib, Seyla (1986), *Critique, Norm and Utopia: A Study of the Foundations of Critical Theory.* New York: Columbia University Press.

Benhabib, Seyla, and Maurizio Passerin d'Entrèves (eds.) (1996), *Habermas and the Unfinished Project of Modernity.* Cambridge: Polity Press.

Benhabib, Seyla, Wolfgang Bonß, and John McCole (eds.) (1993), *On Max Horkheimer: New Perspectives.* Cambridge: MIT Press.

Berghahn, Volker R. (1981), *Militarism: The History of an International Debate, 1861–1979.* Cambridge: Cambridge University Press.

Bernstein, Jay M. (1994), *Recovering Ethical Life: Jürgen Habermas and the Future of Critical Theory.* London: Routledge.

Bijker, Wiebe, and John Law (1992), "General Introduction," in Wiebe Bijker and John Law (eds.), *Shaping Technology/Building Society: Studies in Sociotechnical Change.* Cambridge: MIT Press.

Bilgin, Pinar, Ken Booth, and Richard Wyn Jones (1998), "Security Studies: The Next Stage?" *Nação e Defensa* (Lisbon) No. 84 (Winter), pp. 131–157.

Blair, Bruce G. (1993), *The Logic of Accidental Nuclear War.* Washington D.C.: Brookings Institution.

Bonß, Wolfgang (1993), "The Program of Interdisciplinary Materialism and the Beginnings of Critical Theory," in Seyla Benhabib, Wolfgang Bonß, and John McCole (eds.), *On Max Horkheimer: New Perspectives.* Cambridge: MIT Press, pp. 99–125.

Booth, Ken (1979), *Strategy and Ethnocentrism.* London: Croom Helm.

——— (1987), "Nuclear Deterrence and 'World War III': How Will History Judge?" in Roman Kolkowicz (ed.), *The Logic of Nuclear Terror.* Winchester, Mass.: Allen and Unwin, pp. 251–282.

——— (1990), "The Concept of Strategic Culture Affirmed," in Carl G. Jacobsen (ed.), *Strategic Power: USA/USSR.* London: Macmillan, pp. 121–128.

——— (1991a), "Security and Emancipation," *Review of International Studies* Vol. 17, No. 4, pp. 313–326.

——— (1991b), "Security in Anarchy: Utopian Realism in Theory and Practice," *International Affairs* Vol. 63, No. 3, pp. 527–545.

——— (1991c), "The Interregnum: World Politics in Transition," in Ken Booth (ed.), *New Thinking About Strategy and International Security.* London: HarperCollins, pp. 1–28.

——— (1994), "A Security Regime in Southern Africa: Theoretical Consideration," *South African Perspectives* No. 30 (February), Centre for Southern African Studies, University of the Western Cape.

——— (1995), "Human Wrongs and International Relations," *International Affairs* Vol. 71, No. 1, pp. 103–126.

——— (1997a), "Security and Self: Reflections of a Fallen Realist," in Keith Krause and Michael C. Williams (eds.), *Critical Security Studies: Concepts and Cases.* Minneapolis: University of Minnesota Press, pp. 83–119.

——— (1997b), "A Reply to Wallace," *Review of International Studies* Vol. 23, No. 3, pp. 371–377.

——— (1999), "Three Tyrannies," in Timothy Dunne and Nicholas Wheeler (eds.), *Human Rights in Global Politics.* Cambridge: Cambridge University Press.

Booth, Ken, and John Baylis (1989), *Britain, NATO and Nuclear Weapons: Alternative Defence Versus Alliance Reform.* London: Macmillan.

Booth, Ken, and Eric Herring (1994), *Keyguide to Information in Strategic Studies.* London: Mansell.

Booth, Ken, and Alan Macmillan (1998), "Strategic Culture: Concept and Development," in Ken Booth and Russell Trood (eds.), *Strategic Cultures in the Asia-Pacific.* London: Macmillan.

Booth, Ken, and Russell Trood (eds.) (1998), *Strategic Cultures in the Asia-Pacific.* London: Macmillan.

Booth, Ken, and Peter Vale (1997), "Critical Security Studies and Regional Insecurity: The Case of Southern Africa," in Keith Krause and Michael C. Williams (eds.), *Critical Security Studies.* Minneapolis: University of Minnesota Press, pp. 329–358.

Booth, Ken, and Nicholas Wheeler (1992), "Contending Philosophies About Security in Europe," in Colin McInnes (ed.), *Security and Strategy in Europe.* London: Routledge, pp. 3–36.

Bottomore, Tom (1984), *The Frankfurt School.* London: Ellis Horwood and Tavistock.

Brodersen, Momme (1996), *Walter Benjamin: A Biography,* translated by Malcolm R. Green and Ingrida Ligers, edited by Martina Dervis. London: Verso.

Bronner, Stephen Eric (1994), *Of Critical Theory and Its Theorists.* Oxford: Blackwell.

Brown, Chris (1994), "'Turtles All the Way Down': Anti-Foundationalism, Critical Theory and International Relations," *Millennium: Journal of International Studies* Vol. 23, No. 2, pp. 213–236.

Brown, Michael E., Sean M. Lynn-Jones, and Steven E. Miller (eds.) (1995), *The Perils of Anarchy: Contemporary Realism and International Security,* Cambridge: MIT Press.

Brown, Michael E., Owen R. Coté Jr., Sean M. Lynn-Jones, and Steven E. Miller (eds.) (1997), *Nationalism and Ethnic Conflict.* Cambridge: MIT Press.

Brunkhorst, Hauke (1993), "Dialectical Positivism of Happiness: Horkheimer's Materialist Deconstruction of Philosophy," in Seyla Benhabib, Wolfgang Bonß and John McCole (eds.), *On Max Horkheimer: New Perspectives.* Cambridge: MIT Press, pp. 67–98.

—— (forthcoming), "Critique Instead of Theory: Adorno's Idea of Experimental Freedom."

Buck-Morss, Susan (1977), *The Origins of Negative Dialectics: Theodor W. Adorno, Walter Benjamin, and the Frankfurt Institute.* New York: Free Press.

Bundy, McGeorge (1969), "To Cap the Volcano," *Foreign Affairs* Vol. 48, No. 1, pp. 1–20.

—— (1984), "Existential Deterrence and Its Consequences," in Douglas McClean (ed.), *The Security Gamble: Deterrence Dilemmas in the Nuclear Age.* Totowa, N.J.: Rowman and Allenheld, pp. 3–13.

Bundy, McGeorge, George F. Kennan, Robert S. McNamara, and Gerald Smith (1982), "Nuclear Weapons and the Atlantic Alliance," *Foreign Affairs* Vol. 60, No. 4, pp. 753–768.

Buzan, Barry (1987), *An Introduction to Strategic Studies: Military Technology and International Relations.* London: Macmillan.

—— (1991), *People, States and Fear: An Agenda for International Security Studies in the Post–Cold War Era,* 2nd ed. (1st ed. published in 1983). London: Harvester Wheatsheaf; Boulder: Lynne Rienner.

Buzan, Barry, and Eric Herring (1998), *The Arms Dynamic in World Politics.* Boulder: Lynne Rienner.

Buzan, Barry, and Ole Wæver (1997), "Slippery? Contradictory? Sociologically

Untenable? The Copenhagen School Replies," *Review of International Studies* Vol. 23, No. 2, pp. 241–250.

Buzan, Barry, Ole Wæver, and Jaap de Wilde (1998), *Security: A New Framework for Analysis.* Boulder: Lynne Rienner.

Calhoun, Craig (1995), *Critical Social Theory: Culture, History and the Challenge of Difference.* Oxford: Blackwell.

Campbell, David (1992), *Writing Security: United States Foreign Policy and the Politics of Identity.* Manchester, U.K.: Manchester University Press.

Carver, Field-Marshall Lord (1982), *A Policy for Peace.* London: Faber & Faber.

Chaloupka, William (1992), *Knowing Nukes: The Politics and Culture of the Atom.* Minneapolis: University of Minnesota Press.

Charter of the United Nations and Statute of the International Court of Justice (1987). New York: Department of Public Information, United Nations.

Chatwin, Bruce (1987), *The Songlines.* London: Jonathan Cape.

Checkel, Jeff (1993), "Ideas, Institutions, and the Gorbachev Foreign Policy," *World Politics* Vol. 45, No. 2, pp. 271–300.

Claude, Jr., Inis L. (1984), *Swords into Ploughshares: The Problems and Progress of International Organization,* London: University of London Press, pp. 223–260.

Claudin, Fernando (1975), *The Communist Movement: From Comintern to Cominform,* translated by Brian Price and Francis MacDonagh. Harmondsworth, U.K.: Penguin.

Clausewitz, Carl von (1968), *On War,* edited with an introduction by Anatol Rapoport. Harmondsworth, U.K.: Penguin.

Cohen, Jean L., and Andrew Arato (1992), *Civil Society and Political Theory.* Cambridge: MIT Press.

Cohn, Carol (1987), "Sex and Death in the Rational World of Defense Intellectuals," *Signs: Journal of Women in Culture and Society* Vol. 12, No. 4, pp. 687–718.

Colás, Alejandro (1994), "Putting Cosmopolitanism into Practice: The Case of Socialist Internationalism," *Millennium: Journal of International Studies* Vol. 23, No. 3, pp. 513–534.

Commission on Global Governance (1995), *Our Global Neighbourhood. The Report of the Commission on Global Governance.* Oxford: Oxford University Press.

Commission on International Development Issues (1980), *North-South: A Programme for Survival. The Report of the Commission on International Development Issues Under the Chairmanship of Willy Brandt.* London: Pan Books.

Connolly, William E. (1988), *Political Theory and Modernity.* Oxford: Blackwell.

Cooke, Maeve (1994), *Language and Reason: A Study of Habermas's Pragmatics.* Cambridge: MIT Press.

Cortright, David (1993), *Peace Works: The Citizen's Role in Ending the Cold War.* Boulder: Westview.

Cox, Michael (1984), "Western Capitalism and the Cold War System," in Martin Shaw (ed.), *War, State and Society.* London: Macmillan, pp. 136–194.

———— (1986), "The Cold War as a System," *Critique* No. 17, pp. 17–82.

———— (1990), "From the Truman Doctrine to the Second Superpower Detente: The Rise and Fall of the Cold War," *Journal of Peace Research* Vol. 27, No. 1, pp. 25–41.

Cox, Robert W. (1981), "Social Forces, States and World Orders: Beyond International Relations Theory," *Millennium: Journal of International Studies* Vol. 10, No. 2, pp. 126–155.

———— (1983), "Gramsci, Hegemony and International Relations: An Essay in Method," *Millennium: Journal of International Studies* Vol. 12, No. 2, pp. 162–175.

———— (1987), *Production, Power and World Order.* New York: Columbia University Press.

———— (1996), with Timothy J. Sinclair, *Approaches to World Politics.* Cambridge, U.K.: Cambridge University Press.

Crawford, Neta C. (1991), "Once and Future Security Studies," *Security Studies* Vol. 1, No. 2, pp. 283–316.

Dalby, Simon (1992), "Security, Modernity, Ecology: The Dilemmas of Post–Cold War Security Discourse," *Alternatives* Vol. 17, No. 1, pp. 95–134.

De Landa, Manuel (1991), *War in the Age of Intelligent Machines.* New York: Zone Books.

Deudney, Daniel (1990), "The Case Against Linking Environmental Degradation and National Security," *Millennium: Journal of International Studies* Vol. 19, No. 3, pp. 461–476.

Dews, Peter (1995), *The Limits of Disenchantment: Essays on Contemporary European Philosophy.* London: Verso.

Dibblin, Jane (1988), *The Day of Two Suns: U.S. Nuclear Testing and the Pacific Islanders.* London: Virago.

Dubiel, Helmut (1983), "Farewell to Critical Theory?" *Praxis International* Vol. 3, No. 2, pp. 121–137.

———— (1985), *Theory and Politics: Studies in the Development of Critical Theory,* translated by Benjamin Gregg. Cambridge: MIT Press.

Eckersley, Robyn (1992), *Enviromentalism and Political Theory: Toward an Ecocentric Approach.* London: UCL Press.

Ellul, Jacques (1964), *The Technological Society,* translated by J. Wilikinson. New York: Vintage.

Ettinger, Elzbieta (1987), *Rosa Luxemburg: A Life.* London: Harrap.

Evangelista, Matthew (1988), *Innovation and the Arms Race: How the United States and the Soviet Union Develop New Military Technologies.* Ithaca, N.Y.: Cornell University Press.

———— (1995), "Transnational Relations, Domestic Structures, and Security Policy in the U.S.S.R. and Russia," in Thomas Risse-Kappen (ed.), *Bringing Transnational Relations Back In.* Cambridge, U.K.: Cambridge University Press, pp. 146–188.

Falk, Richard, and Stephen Jay Lifton (1982), *Indefensible Weapons: The Political and Psychological Case Against Nuclearism.* New York: Basic Books.

Feenberg, Andrew (1991), *Critical Theory of Technology.* Oxford: Oxford University Press.

Finkelstein, Norman G. (1997), "Daniel Jonah Goldhagen's 'Crazy' Thesis: A Critique of *Hitler's Willing Executioners*," *New Left Review* No. 224 (July/August), pp. 39–87.

Fiori, Giuseppe (1990), *Antonio Gramsci: Life of a Revolutionary,* translated by Tom Nairn. London: Verso.

Flank, Steven (1993–1994), "Exploding the Black Box: The Historical Sociology of Nuclear Proliferation," *Security Studies* Vol. 3, No. 2, pp. 259–294.

Foucault, Michel (1980), *Power/Knowledge: Selected Interviews and Other Writings, 1972–1977,* edited by Colin Gordon, translated by Colin Gordon, Leo Marshall, John Mepham, and Kate Soper. Brighton, U.K.: Harvester.

Francis, Hywel (1984), *Miners Against Fascism: Wales and the Spanish Civil War.* London: Lawrence and Wishart.

Fraser, Nancy (1989), *Unruly Practices: Power, Discourse and Gender in Contemporary Social Theory.* Cambridge: Polity.

——— (1995), "From Redistribution to Recognition? Dilemmas of Justice in a 'Post-Socialist' Age," *New Left Review* No. 212 (July/August), pp. 68–93.

Freedman, Lawrence (1987), *The Evolution of Nuclear Strategy.* London: Macmillan.

——— (1988a), Review of Barry Buzan, *An Introduction to Strategic Studies: Military Technology and International Relations* (1987), *International Affairs* Vol. 64, No. 3 (Summer), p. 476.

——— (1988b), "I Exist; Therefore I Deter," *International Security* Vol. 13, No. 1, pp. 177–195.

Gaddis, John Lewis (1992–1993), "International Relations Theory and the End of the Cold War," *International Security* Vol. 17, No. 3, pp. 5–58.

Garnett, John (1987a), "Strategic Studies and Its Assumptions," in John Baylis, Ken Booth, John Garnett, and Phil Williams, *Contemporary Strategy.* Vol. 1: *Theories and Concepts,* 2nd ed. London: Croom Helm, pp. 3–29.

——— (1987b), "Technology and Strategy," in John Baylis, Ken Booth, John Garnett, and Phil Williams, *Contemporary Strategy.* Vol. 1: *Theories and Concepts,* 2nd ed. London: Croom Helm, pp. 91–109.

——— (1996) "European Security After the Cold War," in M. Jane Davis (ed.), *Security Issues in the Post–Cold War World.* Cheltenham, U.K.: Edward Elgar, pp. 12–39.

Gat, Azar (1989), *The Origins of Military Thought: From the Enlightenment to Clausewitz.* Oxford: Clarendon Press.

Generals for Peace and Disarmament (1984), *The Arms Race to Armageddon: A Challenge to U.S./NATO Strategy,* Leamington Spa, U.K.: Berg Publishers.

Geras, Norman (1983), *Marx and Human Nature: Refutation of a Legend.* London: Verso.

Giddens, Anthony (1985), *The Nation-State and Violence: Volume Two of A Contemporary Critique of Historical Materialism.* Cambridge: Polity.

——— (1990), "Jürgen Habermas," in Quentin Skinner (ed.), *The Return of Grand Theory in the Human Sciences.* Cambridge: Canto, pp. 121–139.

Gill, Stephen (1993), "Epistemology, Ontology, and the 'Italian School,'" in Stephen Gill (ed.), *Gramsci, Historical Materialism and International Relations.* Cambridge: Cambridge University Press, pp. 21–48.

Girard, Michel, Wolf-Dieter Eberwein, and Keith Webb (eds.) (1994), *Theory and Practice in Foreign Policy-making: National Perspectives on Academics and Professionals in International Relations.* London: Pinter.

Glasstone, Samuel, and Philip J. Dolan (eds.) (1977), *The Effects of Nuclear Weapons,* 3rd ed. Washington, D.C.: U.S. Department of Defense, pp. 541–574.

Goldhagen, Daniel Jonah (1997), *Hitler's Willing Executioners: Ordinary Germans and the Holocaust.* London: Abacus.

Gorz, André (1994), *Capitalism, Socialism, Ecology,* translated by Chris Turner. London: Verso.

Gramsci, Antonio (1971), *Selections from the Prison Notebooks,* edited and translated by Quintin Hoare and Geoffrey Nowell Smith. London: Lawrence and Wishart.

Gray, Colin S. (1979), "Nuclear Strategy: The Case for a Theory of Victory," *International Security* Vol. 1, No. 4, pp. 14–27.

—— (1982a), *Strategic Studies and Public Policy: The American Experience.* Lexington: University Press of Kentucky.

—— (1982b), *Strategic Studies: A Critical Assessment.* Westport, Conn.: Greenwood Press.

—— (1992), "New Directions for Strategic Studies? How Can Theory Help Practice?" *Security Studies* Vol. 1, No. 4, pp. 610–635.

—— (1993), *Weapons Don't Make War: Politics, Strategy, and Military Technology.* Lawrence: University of Kansas Press.

Green, Philip (1966), *Deadly Logic: The Theory of Nuclear Deterrence.* Columbus: Ohio State University Press.

—— (1973), "Strategy, Politics, and Social Scientists," in Morton A. Kaplan (ed.), *Strategic Thinking and Its Moral Implications.* Chicago: Center for Policy Study, University of Chicago, pp. 39–68.

Groom, A. J. R. (1984), "Practitioners and Academics: Towards a Happier Relationship?" in Michael Banks (ed.), *Conflict in World Society: A New Perspective on International Relations.* New York: St Martin's Press, pp. 192–208.

Haacke, Jürgen (1996), "Theory and Praxis in International Relations: Habermas, Self-Reflection, Rational Argumentation," *Millennium: Journal of International Studies* Vol. 25, No. 2, pp. 255–289.

Habermas, Jürgen (1970), *Towards a Rational Society: Student Protest, Science and Politics,* translated by Jeremy J. Shapiro. Boston: Beacon Press.

—— (1976), *Legitimation Crisis,* translated by Thomas McCarthy. London: Heinemann.

—— (1979), *Communication and the Evolution of Society,* translated by Thomas McCarthy. London: Heinemann.

—— (1980), "The Inimitable *Zeitschrift für Socialforschung*: How Horkheimer Took Advantage of a Historically Oppressive Hour," translated by David J. Parent, *Telos* Vol. 45 (Fall), pp. 114–121.

—— (1981), "Modernity Versus Postmodernity," *New German Critique* Vol. 22, pp. 3–14.

—— (1984), *The Theory of Communicative Action.* Vol. 1: *Reason and the Rationalization of Society,* translated by Thomas McCarthy. London: Heinemann.

—— (1986a), *Theory and Practice,* translated by John Viertel. Cambridge: Polity.

—— (1986b), *Knowledge and Human Interests,* translated by Jeremy J. Shapiro. Cambridge: Polity.

—— (1987), *The Theory of Communicative Action.* Vol. 2: *Lifeworld and System: A Critique of Functionalist Reason,* translated by Thomas McCarthy. Cambridge: Polity.

—— (1991), *The Philosophical Discourse of Modernity,* translated by Frederick G. Lawrence. Cambridge: MIT Press.

—— (1992a), "A Ggeneration Apart from Adorno," interview with J. Früchtl translated by James Swindal, *Philosophy and Social Criticism* Vol. 18, No. 2, pp. 119–124.

—— (1992b), *Autonomy and Solidarity: Interviews with Jürgen Habermas,* edited and introduced by Peter Dews. London: Verso.

———— (1993a), "Notes on the Developmental History of Horkheimer's Work," *Theory, Culture and Society* Vol. 10, pp. 61–77.

———— (1993b), "The Second Life-Fiction of the Federal Republic: We Have Become 'Normal' Again," *New Left Review* No. 197 (January–February), pp. 58–66.

———— (1994), *The Past as Future,* interview by Michael Haller, translated and edited by Max Pensky. Cambridge: Polity.

———— (1996), *Between Facts and Norms: Contributions to a Discourse Theory of Law and Democracy,* translated by William Rehg. Cambridge: Polity.

Heidegger, Martin (1977), *The Question Concerning Technology,* translated by W. Lovitt. New York: Harper and Row.

Held David (1980), *Introduction to Critical Theory: Horkheimer to Habermas.* Cambridge: Polity.

———— (1982), "Critical Theory and Political Transformation," *Media, Culture and Society* Vol. 4, pp. 153–160.

Herbst, Jeffrey (1996–1997), "Responding to State Failure in Africa," *International Security* Vol. 21, No. 3, pp. 120–144.

Herf, Jeffrey (1977), "Science and Class or Philosophy and Revolution: Perry Anderson on Western Marxism," *Socialist Review* Vol. 7, pp. 129–144.

———— (1984), *Reactionary Modernism: Technology, Culture, and Politics in Weimar and the Third Reich.* Cambridge: Cambridge University Press.

Herken, Gregg (1985), *Counsels of War.* New York: Alfred A. Knopf.

Hill, Christopher (1994), "Academic International Relations: The Siren Song of Policy Relevance," in Christopher Hill and Pamela Beshoff (eds.), *Two Worlds of International Relations: Academics, Practitioners and the Trade in Ideas.* London: Routledge, pp. 3–25.

Hill, Christopher, and Pamela Beshoff (eds.) (1994), *Two Worlds of International Relations: Academics, Practitioners and the Trade in Ideas.* London: Routledge.

Hobden, Steve, and Richard Wyn Jones (1997), "World-System Theory," in John Baylis and Steve Smith (eds.), *The Globalisation of World Politics.* Oxford: Oxford University Press, pp. 125–145.

Hoffman, Mark (1987), "Critical Theory and the Inter-Paradigm Debate," *Millennium: Journal of International Studies* Vol. 16, No. 2, pp. 232–249.

———— (1989), "Critical Theory and the Inter-Paradigm Debate," in Hugh C. Dyer and Leon Mangasarian (eds.), *The Study of International Relations: The State of the Art.* London: Macmillan, pp. 60–86.

———— (1991), "Restructuring, Reconstruction, Reinscription, Rearticulation: Four Voices in Critical International Relations Theory," *Millennium: Journal of International Studies* Vol. 20, No. 2, pp. 169–185.

———— (1992), "Third-Party Mediation and Conflict-Resolution in the Post–Cold War World," in John Baylis and Nick Rengger (eds.), *Dilemmas of World Politics: International Issues in a Changing World.* Oxford: Clarendon Press, pp. 261–286.

———— (1993), "Agency, Identity and Intervention," in Ian Forbes and Mark Hoffman (eds.), *Political Theory, International Relations and the Ethics of Intervention.* London: Macmillan, pp. 194–211.

Hoffman, Stanley (1977), "An American Social Science: International Relations," *Daedalus* Vol. 106, No. 3, pp. 41–60.

Hohendahl, Peter Uwe (1991), *Reappraisals: Shifting Alignments in Postwar Critical Theory.* Ithaca, N.Y.: Cornell University Press.

———— (1992a), "Adorno Criticism Today," *New German Critique* No. 56 (Spring–Summer), pp. 3–15.

———— (1992b), "The Displaced Intellectual? Adorno's American Years Revisited," *New German Critique* No. 56 (Spring–Summer), pp. 76–100.

———— (1995), *Prismatic Thought: Theodor W. Adorno.* Lincoln: University of Nebraska Press.

Holloway, David (1983), *The Soviet Union and the Arms Race.* London: Yale University Press.

Holub, Renate (1992), *Antonio Gramsci: Beyond Marxism and Postmodernism.* London: Routledge.

Holub, Robert C. (1991), *Jürgen Habermas: Critic in the Public Sphere.* London: Routledge.

Honig, Jan Willem (1994), "Interpreting Clausewitz," *Security Studies* Vol. 3, No. 3, pp. 571–580.

Honneth, Axel (1982), "Work and Instrumental Action," *New German Critique* No. 25, pp. 31–54.

———— (1993), "Max Horkheimer and the Sociological Deficit of Critical Theory," translated by Kenneth Baynes, in Seyla Benhabib, Wolfgang Bonß, and John McCole (eds.) (1993), *On Max Horkheimer: New Perspectives.* Cambridge: MIT Press, pp. 187–214.

———— (1994), "The Social Dynamics of Disrespect: On the Location of Critical Theory Today," translated by John Farrell, *Constellations* Vol. 1, No. 2 (October), pp. 255–269.

———— (1995), *The Struggle for Recognition: The Moral Grammar of Social Conflicts,* translated by Joel Anderson. Cambridge: Polity.

Honneth, Axel, and Hans Joas (1991), *Communicative Action: Essays on Jürgen Habermas's* The Theory of Communicative Action, translated by Jeremy Gaines and Doris L. Jones. Cambridge: Polity.

Horkheimer, Max (1972), *Critical Theory: Selected Essays,* translated by Matthew J. O'Connell and others. New York: Seabury Press.

———— (1974), *Eclipse of Reason.* New York: Continuum.

———— (1978), *Dawn and Decline: Notes 1926–1931 and 1950–1969,* translated by Michael Shaw. New York: Seabury Press.

———— (1993), *Between Philosophy and Social Science: Selected Early Writings,* translated by G. Frederick Hunter, Matthew S. Kramer, and John Torpey. Cambridge: MIT Press.

Horowitz, Irving L. (1963), *The War Game: Studies on the New Civilian Militarists.* New York: Paine-Whitman.

Howard, Michael (1983), *The Causes of Wars, and Other Essays.* London: Unwin, pp. 133–150.

Howe, Herbert (1996–1997), "Lessons of Liberia: ECOMOG and Regional Peacekeeping," *International Security* Vol. 21, No. 3, pp. 145–176.

Hunter, Jerry, and Richard Wyn Jones (1995), "O'r Chwith: Pa Mor Feirniadol yw Beirniadaeth Ôl-fodernaidd?" [How Critical Is Postmodern Criticism?], *Taliesin* Vol. 92, pp. 9–32.

Huntington, Samuel (1993), "The Clash of Civilizations," *Foreign Affairs* Vol. 72, No. 3, pp. 22–49

Huysmans, Jef (1995), "Migrants as a Security Problem: Dangers of 'Securitizing' Societal Issues," in Roberth Miles and Dietrich Thänhardt (eds.), *Migration and European Integration: The Dynamics of Inclusion and Exclusion.* London: Pinter.

Independent Commission on Disarmament and Security Issues (1982), *Common Security: A Programme for Disarmament. The Report of the Independent Commission on Disarmament and Security Issues Under the Chairmanship of Olof Palme.* London: Pan.

Jameson, Frederic (1971), *Marxism and Form: Twentieth Century Dialectical Theories of Literature.* Princeton, N.J.: Princeton University Press.

—— (1990), *Late Marxism: Adorno, or, the Persistence of the Dialectic.* London: Verso.

Jay, Martin (1973), *The Dialectical Imagination: A History of the Frankfurt School and the Institute of Social Research, 1923–1950.* Boston: Little, Brown and Company.

—— (1982), "Misrepresentations of the Frankfurt School," *Survey 26* Vol. 2 (Summer), pp. 131–141.

—— (1984), *Adorno.* London: Fontana.

Jervis, Robert (1989), *The Meaning of the Nuclear Revolution: Statecraft and the Prospect of Armageddon,* Ithaca, N.Y.: Cornell University Press.

Joll, James (1977), *Gramsci.* London: Fontana.

Jones, Goronwy J. (1969), *Wales and the Quest for Peace.* Cardiff: University of Wales Press.

Joyce, James (1990), *The Essential James Joyce,* with an introduction and notes by Harry Levin. London: Grafton.

Jungk, Robert (1979), *The Nuclear State,* translated by Eric Mosbacher. London: Calder.

Kaldor, Mary (ed.) (1991), *Europe from Below: An East-West Dialogue.* London: Verso.

—— (1995), "Who Killed the Cold War," *Bulletin of the Atomic Scientists* Vol. 51, No. 4 (July–August), pp. 57–60.

Kaplan, Fred (1983), *The Wizards of Armageddon.* New York: Simon and Schuster.

Kato, Masahide (1993), "Nuclear Globalism: Traversing Rockets, Satellites, and Nuclear War," *Alternatives* Vol. 18, No. 3, pp. 339–360.

Kellner, Douglas (1984), *Herbert Marcuse and the Crisis of Marxism.* London: Macmillan.

—— (1989), *Critical Theory, Marxism and Modernity.* Cambridge: Polity.

—— (1992), *The Persian Gulf TV War.* Boulder: Westview.

—— (1993), "Critical Theory Today: Revisiting the Classics," *Theory, Culture and Society* Vol. 10, No. 2, pp. 43–60.

Kellner, Douglas, and Rick Roderick (1981), "Recent Literature on Critical Theory," *New German Critique* Vol. 23, pp. 141–170.

Keohane, Robert O. (1986), *Neorealism and Its Critics,* New York: Columbia University Press.

Klein, Bradley S. (1994), *Strategic Studies and World Order: The Global Politics of Deterrence.* Cambridge: Cambridge University Press.

—— (1997), "Conclusion: Every Month Is 'Security Awareness Month,'" in Keith Krause and Michael C. Williams (eds.), *Critical Security Studies: Cases and Concepts.* Minneapolis: University of Minnesota Press, pp. 359–368.

"Known Nuclear Tests Worldwide, 1945–1993" (1994), *The Bulletin of the Atomic Scientists* (May–June), pp. 62–63.

Krause, Keith (1998), "Critical Theory and Security Studies: The Research Programme of 'Critical Security Studies,'" *Cooperation and Conflict: Nordic Journal of International Studies* Vol. 33, No. 3, pp. 298–333.

Krause, Keith, and Michael C. Williams (1997), "From Strategy to Security:

Foundations of Critical Security Studies," in Keith Krause and Michael C. Williams, *Critical Security Studies: Cases and Concepts.* Minneapolis: University of Minnesota Press, pp. 33–59.

Krippendorf, Ekkehart (1987), "The Dominance of American Approaches in International Relations," *Millennium: Journal of International Studies* Vol. 16, No. 2, pp. 207–214.

Kristensen, Hans (1997), "Targets of Opportunity," *The Bulletin of the Atomic Scientists* Vol. 53, No. 5 (September–October), pp. 22–28.

Laclau, Ernesto (1996), *Emancipation(s).* London: Verso.

Landau, Susan (1996), "Joseph Rotblat: The Road Less Traveled," *The Bulletin of the Atomic Scientists,* Vol. 52, No. 1 (January–February), pp. 46–54.

Lawrence, Philip K. (1985), "Nuclear Strategy and Politcal Theory: A Critical Assessment," *Review of International Studies* Vol. 11, No. 2, pp. 105–121.

——— (1988), *Preparing for Armageddon: A Critique of Western Strategy.* Brighton, U.K.: Wheatsheaf.

Lebow, Richard Ned (1994), "The Long Peace, the End of the Cold War, and the Failure of Realism," *International Organization* Vol. 48, No. 2, pp. 249–277.

Linklater, Andrew (1990a), *Men and Citizens in the Theory of International Relations,* 2nd ed. London: Macmillan.

——— (1990b), *Beyond Realism and Marxism: Critical Theory and International Relations.* London: Macmillan.

——— (1992), "The Question of the Next Stage in International Relations Theory: A Critical-Theoretical Point of View," *Millennium: Journal of International Studies* Vol. 21, No. 1, pp. 77–98.

——— (1995), "Neo-Realism in Theory and Practice," in Ken Booth and Steve Smith (eds.), *International Relations Theory Today.* Cambridge: Polity, pp. 241–262.

——— (1996a), "Citizenship and Sovereignty in the Post-Westphalian State," *European Journal of International Relations* Vol. 2, No. 1, pp. 77–103.

——— (1996b), "The Achievements of Critical Theory," in Steve Smith, Ken Booth, and Marysia Zalewski, *International Theory: Positivism and Beyond.* Cambridge: Cambridge University Press, pp. 279–298.

——— (1998a), *The Transformation of Political Community: Ethical Foundations of the Post-Westphalian Era.* Cambridge: Polity.

——— (1998b), "Cosmopolitan Citizenship," *Citizenship Studies* Vol. 2, No. 1, pp. 23–41.

Lipschutz, Ronnie D. (ed.) (1995), *On Security.* New York: Columbia University Press.

Lukács, Georg (1971), *The Theory of the Novel: A Historico-Philosophical Essay on the Forms of Great Epic Literature,* translated by Anna Bostock. Cambridge: MIT Press.

Luttwak, Edward N. (1985), *Strategy and History: Collected Essays,* Vol. 2. New Brunswick, N.J.: Transaction Books.

Lynn-Jones, Sean M., and Steven E. Miller (1995), *Global Dangers: Changing Dimensions of International Security.* Cambridge: MIT Press.

Lyotard, Jean-Francois (1986), *Postmodern Condition,* translated by Geoff Bennington and Brian Massumi. Manchester, U.K.: Manchester University Press.

Macey, David (1994), *The Lives of Michel Foucault.* London: Vintage.

Maclean, John (1981a), "Marxist Epistemology, Explanations of 'Change' and the Study of International Relations," in Barry Buzan and R. J. Barry Jones (eds.),

Change and the Study of International Relations: The Evaded Dimension. London: Pinter, pp. 46–67.

―――― (1981b), "Political Theory, International Theory, and Problems of Ideology," *Millennium: Journal of International Studies* Vol. 10, No. 2, pp. 102–125.

MacKenzie, Donald (1989), "Technology and the Arms Race," *International Security* Vol. 14, No. 1, pp. 161–175.

―――― (1990), *Inventing Accuracy: A Historical Sociology of Nuclear Missile Guidance.* Cambridge: MIT Press.

Makhijani, Arjun (1994), "Energy Enters Guilty Plea," *The Bulletin of the Atomic Scientists* (March–April), pp. 18–28.

Mannheim, Karl (1976), *Ideology and Utopia.* London: Routledge and Kegan Paul.

Mao Tse-tung (1968), *Talk with American Correspondent Anna Louise Strong.* Peking: Foreign Languages Press.

―――― (1977), "The Chinese People Cannot Be Cowed by the Atom Bomb," *Selected Works of Mao Tse-Tung,* Vol. 5. Peking: Foreign Languages Press.

Marcuse, Herbert (1978–1979), "Theory and Politics: A Discussion with Herbert Marcuse, Jürgen Habermas, Heinz Lubasz and Telman Spenger," translated by Leslie Adelson, Susan Hegger, Betty Sun, and Herbert Weinryb. *Telos* Vol. 38 (Winter), pp. 124–153.

―――― (1988), *Negations: Essays in Critical Theory,* translated by Jeremy J. Shapiro. London: Free Association Books.

Marx, Karl (1976a), *Capital: A Critique of Political Economy,* Vol. 1, introduced by Ernest Mandel and translated by Ben Foulkes. Harmondsworth, U.K.: Penguin in association with New Left Review.

―――― (1976b), "Thesis on Feuerbach," in Karl Marx and Friedrich Engels, *Collected Works, Vol. 5 (1845–47).* London: Lawrence and Wishart.

Marx, Karl, and Friedrich Engels (1948), *Y Maniffesto Gomiwnyddol,* translated by W. J. Rees. Cardiff: Pwyllgor Cymreig y Blaid Gomiwnyddol.

Matthews, Jessica Tuchman (1989), "Redefining Security," *Foreign Affairs* Vol. 68, No. 2, pp. 162–177.

McCarthy, Thomas (1993), "The Idea of a Critical Theory and Its Relation to Philosophy," in Seyla Benhabib, Wolfgang Bonß, and John McCole (eds.), *On Max Horkheimer: New Perspectives.* Cambridge: MIT Press, pp. 127–151.

MccGwire, Michael (1997), "A Policy Error of Historic Importance," unpublished paper, August 1997.

McLellan, David (1995), *The Thought of Karl Marx: An Introduction,* 3rd ed. London: Papermac.

McNamara, Robert S. (1986), *Blundering into Disaster: Surviving the First Century of the Nuclear Age.* New York: Pantheon.

McSweeney, Bill (1996a), "Security, Identity and the Peace Process in Northern Ireland," *Security Dialogue* Vol. 27, No. 2, pp. 167–178.

―――― (1996b), "Identity and Security: Buzan and the Copenhagen School," *Review of International Studies* Vol. 22, No. 1, pp. 85–97.

Mearsheimer, John J. (1995), "Back to the Future: Instability in Europe After the Cold War," in Michael E. Brown, Sean M. Lynn-Jones, and Steven E. Miller (eds.), *The Perils of Anarchy: Contemporary Realism and International Security.* Cambridge: MIT Press.

Morgan, Patrick M. (1992), "Safeguarding Security Studies," *Arms Control* Vol. 13, No. 3, pp. 464–479.

Mueller, John (1988), "The Essential Irrelevance of Nuclear Weapons: Stability in the Postwar World," *International Security* Vol. 13, No. 2, pp. 55–79.

────── (1990), *Retreat from Doomsday: The Obsolescence of Major War.* New York: Basic Books.

────── (1995), *Quiet Cataclysm: Reflections on the Recent Transformation of World Politics.* New York: HarperCollins College.

Negt, Oskar, and Alexander Kluge (1993), *Public Sphere and Experience: Towards an Analysis of the Bourgeois and Proletarian Public Sphere,* translated by Peter Labanyi, Jamie Owen Daniel, and Assenka Oksiloff. Minneapolis: University of Minnesota Press.

Neufeld, Mark (1995), *The Restructuring of International Relations Theory.* Cambridge: Cambridge University Press.

The New English Bible with the Apocrypha (1970), translated by the Joint Comittee on the New Translation of the Bible. London: Oxford University Press.

Newhouse, John (1989), *The Nuclear Age: From Hiroshima to Star Wars.* London: Joseph.

Noel Baker, P. J. (1926), *Disarmament.* London: Hogarth Press.

Norris, Christopher (1992), *Uncritical Theory: Postmodernism, Intellectuals and the Gulf War.* London: Lawrence and Wishart.

Nye, Joseph (1987), "The Long-Term Future of Deterrence," in Roman Kolkowicz (ed.), *The Logic of Nuclear Terror.* Boston: Allen and Unwin, pp. 233–250.

Nye, Joseph S., and Sean M. Lynn-Jones (1988), "International Security Studies: A Report of a Conference on the State of the Field," *International Security* Vol. 12, No. 4, pp. 5–27.

Osborne, Peter (1992), "A Marxism for the Postmodern? Jameson's Adorno," *New German Critique* No. 56 (Spring–Summer), pp. 171–192.

────── (1996), "A Paradigm Too Far?" *Radical Philosophy* No. 80 (November–December), pp. 34–37.

Osgood, Robert E., and Robert W. Tucker (1967), *Force, Order, and Justice.* Baltimore: Johns Hopkins University Press.

Outhwaite, William (1994), *Habermas: A Critical Introduction.* Stanford, Calif.: Stanford University Press.

────── (ed.) (1996), *The Habermas Reader.* Cambridge: Polity.

Parker, Geoffrey (1996), *The Military Revolution: Military Innovation and the Rise of the West 1500–1800,* 2nd ed. Cambridge: Cambridge University Press.

Pasha, Mustapha Kamal (1996), "Security as Hegemony," *Alternatives* Vol. 21, No. 3, pp. 283–302.

Pick, Daniel (1993), *War Machine: The Rationalisation of Slaughter in the Modern Age.* London: Yale University Press.

Porter, Brian (1989), "David Davies: A Hunter After Peace," *Review of International Studies* Vol. 15, No. 1, pp. 27–36.

Postone, Moishe (1993), *Time, Labor, and Social Domination: A Reinterpretation of Marx's Critical Theory.* Cambridge: Cambridge Universtity Press.

Postone, Moishe, and Barbara Brick (1993), "Critical Theory and Political Economy," in Seyla Benhabib, Wolfgang Bonß, and John McCole (eds.), *On Max Horkheimer: New Perspectives.* Cambridge: MIT Press, pp. 215–256.

Pugh, Michael C. (1989), *The ANZUS Crisis, Nuclear Visiting and Deterrence.* Cambridge: Cambridge University Press.

Rapoport, Anatol (1960), *Fights, Games and Debates.* Ann Arbor: University of Michigan Press.

────── (1964), *Strategy and Conscience.* New York: Harper and Row.

—— (1970), "Critique of Strategic Thinking," in Naomi Rosenbaum (ed.), *Readings on the International Political System.* Englewood Cliffs, N.J.: Prentice-Hall, pp. 201–227.

—— (1978), "Changing Conceptions of War in the United States," in Ken Booth and Moorhead Wright (eds.), *American Thinking About Peace and War.* Hassocks, U.K.: Harvester Press, pp. 59–82.

Ray, Larry J. (1993), *Rethinking Critical Theory: Emancipation in the Age of Global Social Movements.* London: Sage.

Rengger, Nicholas J. (1988), "Going Critical? A Response to Hoffman," *Millennium: Journal of International Studies* Vol. 17, No. 1, pp. 81–89.

Reus-Smit, Christian (1992), "Realist and Resistance Utopias: Community, Security and Political Action in the New Europe," *Millennium: Journal of International Studies* Vol. 21, No. 1, pp. 1–28.

Rhodes, Edward (1995), "Constructing Peace and War: An Analysis of the Power of Ideas to Shape American Military Power," *Millennium: Journal of International Studies* Vol. 24, No. 1, pp. 53–85.

Rhodes, Richard (1988), *The Making of the Atomic Bomb.* Harmondsworth, U.K.: Penguin.

Risse-Kappen, Thomas (1994), "Ideas Do Not Float Freely: Transnational Coalitions, Domestic Structures, and the End of the Cold War," *International Organisation* Vol. 48, No. 2, pp. 185–214.

Rorty, Richard (1993), "Human Rights, Rationality, and Sensibility," in Stephen Schute and Susan Hurley (eds.), *On Human Rights.* New York: Basic Books, pp. 111–134.

Rose, Gillian (1978), *The Melancholy Science: An Introduction to the Thought of Theodor W. Adorno.* London: Macmillan.

Rosen, Stephen Peter (1995), "Military Effectiveness: Why Society Matters," *International Security* Vol. 19, No. 4, pp. 5–31.

Rosenau, James R. (1990), *Turbulence in World Politics: A Theory of Change and Continuity.* Princeton, N.J.: Princeton University Press.

Rubenstein, William (1997), "The Myth of Rescue," *Prospect* (July), pp. 20–24.

Sagan, Scott D. (1994), "The Perils of Proliferation: Organization Theory, Deterrence Theory, and the Spread of Nuclear Weapons," *International Security* Vol. 18, No. 4, pp. 66–107.

—— (1996–1997), "Why Do States Build Nuclear Weapons? Three Models in Search of a Bomb," *International Security* Vol. 21, No. 3, pp. 54–86.

Said, Edward W. (1994), *Representations of the Intellectual.* London: Vintage.

Salvadori, Massimo (1990), *Karl Kautsky and the Socialist Revolution, 1880–1938,* London: Verso.

Sauer, Tom (forthcoming), *Nuclear Weapons Unplugged: Nuclear Arms Control and Proliferation Beyond the 1995 NPT Conference.* London: Macmillan.

Schmidt, Alfred (1993), "Max Horkheimer's Intellectual Physiognomy," in Seyla Benhabib, Wolfgang Bonß, and John McCole (eds.) (1993), *On Max Horkheimer: New Perspectives.* Cambridge: MIT Press, pp. 25–47.

Schram, Stuart R. (1969), *The Political Thought of Mao Tse Tung.* London: Praeger.

Segal, Gerald (ed.) (1989), "New Directions in Strategic Studies: A Chatham House Debate," *Royal Institute of International Affairs Discussion Papers,* No. 17. London: The Royal Institute of International Affairs.

Serge, Victor (1984), *Memoirs of a Revolutionary,* edited and translated by Peter Sedgwick. London: Writers and Readers.

Shaw, Martin (1994a), *Global Society and International Relations*. Cambridge: Polity.

────── (1994b), "Civil Society and Global Politics: Beyond a Social Movements Approach," *Millennium: Journal of International Studies* Vol. 23, No. 3, pp. 647–667.

Smith, Steve (1991), "Mature Anarchy, Strong States and Security," *Arms Control* Vol. 12, No. 2, pp. 325–339.

────── (1992), "The Forty Years Detour: The Resurgence of Normative Theory in International Relations," *Millennium: Journal of International Relations* Vol. 21, No. 3, pp. 489–506.

────── (1997), "Power and Truth: A Reply to William Wallace," *Review of International Studies* Vol. 23, No. 4, pp. 507–516.

Smith, Steve, Ken Booth, and Marysia Zalewski (1996), *International Theory: Positivism and Beyond*. Cambridge: Cambridge University Press.

Snyder, Jack (1977), *The Soviet Strategic Culture: Implications for Limited Nuclear Operations*. Santa Monica, Calif.: RAND Report R-2154-AF.

Spencer, Metta (1995), "'Political' Scientists," *Bulletin of the Atomic Scientists* Vol. 51, No. 4 (July–August), pp. 62–68.

Stirk, Peter M. R. (1992), *Max Horkheimer: A New Interpretation*. Hemel Hempstead, U.K.: Harvester Wheatsheaf.

Tanter, Raymond, and Richard H. Ullman (eds.) (1972), *Theory and Policy in International Relations*. Princeton, N.J.: Princeton University Press.

Tar, Zoltán (1985), *The Frankfurt School: The Critical Theories of Max Horkheimer and Theodor W. Adorno*. New York: Schocken Books.

Therborn, Göran (1970), "The Frankfurt School," *New Left Review* No. 63, pp. 66–96.

Thomas, D. R. (1984), *Fromm*. Dinbych, Wales: Gwasg Gee.

Thompson, Edward P. (1980), "Sources of Exterminism: The Last Stage of Civilization," *New Left Review* No. 121, pp. 3–31.

────── (1982a), *Beyond the Cold War*. London: Merlin.

────── (1982b), "Notes on Exterminism, the Last Stage of Civilization," in Edward P. Thompson and others, *Exterminism and Cold War*. London: Verso, pp. 1–33.

Thompson, John B. (1983), "Rationality and Social Rationalization: An Assessment of Habermas's Theory of Communicative Action," *Sociology* Vol. 17, No. 2, pp. 278–294.

Thompson, John B., and David Held (eds.) (1982), *Habermas: Critical Debates*. London: Macmillan.

Tickner, J. Ann (1995), "Re-visioning Security," in Ken Booth and Steve Smith (eds.), *International Relations Theory Today*. Cambridge: Polity, pp. 175–197.

Ullman, Richard H. (1983), "Redefining Security," *International Security* Vol. 8, No. 1, pp. 129–153.

Vale, Peter (1986), "Regional Security in Southern Africa," *Alternatives* Vol. 21, No. 3, pp. 363–391.

Wæver, Ole (1994), "Insecurity and Identity Unlimited," Working Paper 14. Copenhagen: Centre for Peace and Conflict Research.

────── (1995), "Securitization and Desecuritization," in Ronnie D. Lipschutz (ed.), *On Security*. New York: Columbia University Press, pp. 46–86.

Wæver, Ole, Barry Buzan, Morten Kelstrup, and Pierre Lemaitre (1993), *Indentity, Migration and the New Security Agenda in Europe*. London: Pinter.

Walker, J. Samuel (1990), "The Decision to Use the Bomb: A Historiographical Update," *Diplomatic History* Vol. 14, No. 1, pp. 97–114.

Walker, R. B. J. (1990), "Security, Sovereignty, and the Challenge of World Politics," *Alternatives* Vol. 15, No. 1, pp. 3–27.

—— (1993), *Inside/Outside: International Relations as Political Theory.* Cambridge: Cambridge University Press.

—— (1994), "Social Movements/World Politics," *Millennium: Journal of International Studies* Vol. 23, No. 3, pp. 669–700.

—— (1997), "The Subject of Security," in Keith Krause and Michael C. Williams (eds.), *Critical Security Studies: Cases and Concepts.* Minneapolis: University of Minnesota Press, pp. 33–59.

Wallace, William (1996), "Truth and Power, Monks and Technocrats: Theory and Practice in International Relations," *Review of International Studies* Vol. 22, No. 3, pp. 301–321.

Walt, Stephen M. (1991), "The Renaissance of Security Studies," *International Studies Quarterly* Vol. 35, No. 2, pp. 211–239.

Waltz, Kenneth N. (1979), *Theory of International Politics.* New York: Random House.

—— (1981), "The Spread of Nuclear Weapons: More May Be Better," Adelphi Paper No. 171. London: International Institute of Strategic Studies.

—— (1990), "Nuclear Myths and Political Realities," *American Political Science Review* Vol. 84, No. 3, pp. 731–745.

—— (1995), "The Emerging Structure of International Politics," in Michael E. Brown, Sean M. Lynn-Jones, and Steven E. Miller (eds.), *The Perils of Anarchy: Contemporary Realism and International Security.* Cambridge: MIT Press, pp. 42–77.

Wellmer, Albrecht (1983), "Reason, Utopia, and the Dialectic of Enlightenment," *Praxis International* Vol. 3, No. 2, pp. 83–107.

Wheeler, Nicholas J. (1993), Untitled book review of Barry Buzan, Charles Jones, and Richard Little's *The Logic of Anarchy: Neorealism to Structural Realism* in *International Affairs* Vol. 69, No. 4, pp. 743–744.

—— (1996), "Guardian Angel or Global Gangster: A Review of the Ethical Claims of International Society," *Political Studies* Vol. 44, No. 1, pp. 123–135.

White, Stephen (1988), *The Recent Work of Jürgen Habermas: Reason, Justice and Modernity.* Cambridge: Cambridge University Press.

—— (ed.) (1995), *The Cambridge Companion to Habermas.* Cambridge: Cambridge University Press.

Wiggershaus, Rolf (1994), *The Frankfurt School: Its History, Theories and Political Significance,* translated by Michael Robertson. Cambridge: Polity.

Williams, Gwyn A. (1984), "Marcsydd o Sardiniwr ac Argyfwng Cymru," *Efrydiau Athronyddol* Vol. 47, pp. 16–27.

—— (1985), *When Was Wales?* Harmondsworth, U.K.: Penguin.

Williams, Michael C. (1992a), "Rethinking the 'Logic' of Deterrence," *Alternatives* Vol. 17, No. 1, pp. 67–93.

—— (1992b), "Apocalyptic Knowledge: Theory and Practice in the Evolution of Nuclear Strategy," unpublished Ph.D. thesis, York University, Toronto, Canada.

Williams, Raymond (1982), "The Politics of Nuclear Deterrence," in Edward P. Thompson and others, *Exterminism and Cold War.* London: Verso, pp. 65–85.

—— (1989), *Resources of Hope,* edited by Robin Gable. London: Verso.

Winkler, Alan M. (1993), *Life Under a Cloud: American Anxiety About the Atom.* Oxford: Oxford University Press.

Wohlforth, William C. (1995), "Realism and the End of the Cold War," in Michael E. Brown, Sean M. Lynn-Jones, and Steven E. Miller (eds.), *The Perils of Anarchy: Contemporary Realism and International Security.* Cambridge: MIT Press, pp. 3–41.

Wyn Jones, Richard (1995), "Care of the Community: Contemporary Welsh Political Thought," *Planet: The Welsh Internationalist* No. 109 (February–March), pp. 16–25.

——— (1996a), "Gwleidyddiaeth Ryddfreiniol ar ôl Auschwitz: Athroniaeth Wleidyddol Theodor Weisengrund Adorno," *Efrydiau Athronyddol* Vol. 59, pp. 84–96.

——— (1996b), "From 'Community Socialism' to Quango Wales: The Amazing Odyssey of Dafydd Elis Thomas," translated by Meg Elis and Richard Wyn Jones, *Planet: The Welsh Internationalist* No. 119 (August–September), pp. 59–70.

Zuidervaart, Lambert (1991), *Adorno's Aesthetic Theory: The Redemption of Illusion.* Cambridge: MIT Press.

Index

187

About the Book

Laying out the conceptual foundations of critical security studies, Richard Wyn Jones uses the ideas of the Frankfurt School to advance critical thought about security, strategy, and the relationship between the theory and practice of security.

Wyn Jones provides an accessible overview of the ideas of the Frankfurt School's main thinkers—Horkheimer, Adorno, Habermas, Honneth, and Beck—and applies their insights to the study of security. His analysis challenges many of the assumptions underlying both the traditional and some alternative approaches to security studies.

Richard Wyn Jones is a lecturer in the Department of International Politics at the University of Wales, Aberystwyth. He is editor of *Critical Theory and World Politics*.